Essays on Employer Engagement in Education

Building on new theories about the meaning of employability in the twenty-first century and the power of social and cultural capital in enabling access to economic opportunities, *Essays on Employer Engagement in Education* considers how employer engagement is delivered and explores the employment and attainment outcomes linked to participation.

Introducing international policy, research and conceptual approaches, contributors to the volume illustrate the role of employer engagement within schooling and the life courses of young people. The book considers employer engagement within economic and educational contexts and its delivery and impact from a global perspective. The work explores strategic approaches to the engagement of employers in education and concludes with a discussion of the implications for policy, practice and future research.

Essays on Employer Engagement in Education will be of great interest to academics, researchers and postgraduate students engaged in the study of careers guidance, work-related learning, teacher professional development, the sociology of education, educational policy and human resource management. It will also be essential reading for policymakers and practitioners working for organisations engaging employers in education.

Anthony Mann is Senior Policy Advisor (Vocational Education and Training) at the Organisation for Economic Co-operation and Development.

Prue Huddleston is Emeritus Professor in the Centre for Education Studies, University of Warwick, UK

Elnaz Kashefpakdel is Head of Research at the Education and Employers, a UK education charity.

Essays on Employer Engagement in Education

Edited by Anthony Mann,
Prue Huddleston and
Elnaz Kashefpakdel

Routledge
Taylor & Francis Group

LONDON AND NEW YORK

First published 2019 by Routledge

2 Park Square, Milton Park, Abingdon, Oxfordshire OX14 4RN
52 Vanderbilt Avenue, New York, NY 10017

Routledge is an imprint of the Taylor & Francis Group, an informa business

First issued in paperback 2019

British Library Cataloguing-in-Publication Data
A catalogue record for this book is available from the British Library

Library of Congress Cataloging-in-Publication Data
A catalog record has been requested for this book

ISBN: 978-1-138-50104-1 (hbk)
ISBN: 978-0-367-23214-6 (pbk)

Typeset in Bembo
by Apex CoVantage, LLC

Contents

Figures

Tables

Contributors

Fatima Abdulghani is currently working as a Projects Leader at the Office of First Deputy Prime Minister, Kingdom of Bahrain. Fatima comes from a background in economics, education and research. The findings of this research have been utilised in her current employment which involves supporting the implementation of a series of projects and initiatives, which focus on delivering sustainable development to meet the needs of the kingdom.

Louise Archer is the Karl Mannheim Professor of Sociology of Education at UCL Institute of Education. She is co-director of the Centre for Sociology of Education and Equity, and her research focuses on educational identities and inequalities, particularly in relation to gender, ethnicity, social class and young people's engagement with science.

Heidi Ashton is a senior lecturer and former dancer/choreographer. Her research interests include the training, transitions and work experiences of creative workers, particularly freelance dancers. She also examines the nature and organisation of freelance work more generally in relation to skills, work intensity and policy.

Jonathan Boys is Senior Researcher at The Careers & Enterprise Company. While in this role he has worked on a project to allocate a £12 million fund for employer mentoring. He has held various other research roles in the Education and Higher Education sectors often focusing on labour markets and pay.

Simon Field is an expert on the comparative analysis of vocational education and training (VET) systems. Over the last 18 months, as an independent consultant, he has been working with OECD, UNESCO, the World Bank and other bodies. Previously, as leader of the OECD's flagship programme of work on VET for over a decade, he led and delivered reviews of policy in more than 30 countries throughout the world and was the lead author of the OECD's two main publications on VET policy (Skills beyond School and Learning for Jobs), as well as many individual country reviews. He was also the lead author of the OECD's report on equity: No More Failures: ten steps to equity in education. He holds a Ph.D in philosophy and social policy from the University of Cambridge and an M.Sc in Economics from Birkbeck College London.

Lynn Gambin is Assistant Professor in the Department of Economics at Memorial University of Newfoundland (Canada) interested in labour market issues and policy, including the operation of education and training systems. She has conducted extensive research on apprenticeships, vocational education and training and employers in the U.K. and Europe.

Mary Gatta is Associate Professor of Sociology at City University of New York: Guttman Community College; her research focuses on workforce development, economic security and the experiences of women in the workplace. She has published extensively in the area. She has worked previously at Rutgers University and Wider Opportunities for Women in Washington, DC.

Nancy Hoffman is Senior Advisor at Jobs for the Future, a national NGO, and co-founder of the Pathways to Prosperity Network which seeks to ensure that U.S. youth attain a postsecondary credential with currency in the labour market and launch careers. Her most recent book is Learning for Careers, Harvard Education Press, 2017.

Terence Hogarth is Senior Adviser at Fondazione Giacomo Brodolini (FGB), a not-for-profit European research foundation, where he leads a programme of research on vocational education and training with a particular emphasis on apprenticeships.

Tristram Hooley is Director of Research at The Careers & Enterprise Company, Professor of Career Education at the University of Derby and Professor II at the Inland Norway University of Applied Sciences. He is a writer, researcher and teacher specialising in career and career guidance. He writes the Adventures in Career Development blog at https://adventuresincareerdevelopment.wordpress.com/.

John Hope is Associate Dean International Programmes in the Faculty of Education, University of Auckland, New Zealand. John's research foci are educational leadership and internationalisation. He has been an educational leader in schools for 20 years and latterly in teacher education for 20 years.

Prue Huddleston is Emeritus Professor and formerly Director of the Centre for Education and Industry, University of Warwick; her research focuses on vocational education, vocational qualifications and work-related learning. She worked previously within the further education sector and on community and outreach programmes; she has published extensively on the sector and been involved in teacher training for over 20 years.

Steven Jones is a Senior Lecturer at the Manchester Institute of Education. In 2014, he created the University of Manchester's PGCert in Higher

Education, and he is currently Director of Postgraduate Research for his School. Steven conducts research into policy and practice in post-compulsory education. He has co-authored reports for the Sutton Trust, the Higher Education Academy and the Joseph Rowntree Foundation that explore how socially disadvantaged young people conceptualise, engage with and perform at university. He was named as one of JISC's top 50 social media influencers in HIM and currently sits on HEFCE's Expert Group for Learning Gain.

Elnaz Kashefpakdel is Head of Research at Education and Employers. She is responsible for providing on-going evidence towards the importance of employer engagement in education and training. She is a trained quantitative analyst and co-authored several works on employer engagement in education and school-to-work transitions. Elnaz has a Ph.D from University of Bath in the area of higher education policy evaluation.

Andrea Laczik works as a Research and Policy manager at the Edge Foundation and teaches at the University of Oxford. Andrea has 20 years of research experience. Her research interests include VET, apprenticeships, employer engagement and alternative programmes to support disadvantaged young people. She is also interested in comparative and international education, especially in VET developments in East European countries.

Kerry Lee's research is focused on innovation in education. She has been involved in the development of and research into enterprise and entrepreneurship education, partnerships, technology education and digital literacy. Kerry is an Associate Dean in the Faculty of Education at the University of Auckland, New Zealand. Prior to becoming a researcher and tertiary lecturer, Kerry taught in low socio-economic primary schools.

Anthony Mann leads the team responsible for Vocational Education and Training and Adult Learning at the Organisation for Economic Co-operation and Development (OECD) in Paris. Anthony's contribution to this book is in a personal capacity and does not necessarily reflect the official views of the OECD or of its member countries. Formerly, he acted as a policy lead in the U.K. Department for Education and was Director of Policy and Research at London-based charity, Education and Employers.

Rachael McKeown has a background in Human Geography, gaining degrees at University College London (UCL) and the University of Amsterdam with a focus on issues of inequality and social mobility. She was a former Research Assistant at Education and Employers, where she took a keen interest in the role of social capital in education-to-work pathways. She is currently working in a health policy role at the Royal College of Paediatrics and Child Health, promoting reductions in health inequalities in the U.K.

Julie Moote is a post-doctoral Research Associate working on the ASPIRES 2 project at UCL Institute of Education. A science teacher by background, her research focuses on exploring how educational and occupational aspirations are formed among young students and how they change over time.

Christian Percy is a policy and strategy advisor, working primarily on education, labour market effectiveness and social change. His clients cover a range of organisations, from the World Bank and governments through to universities, charities and investors. He has a long-running research collaboration with Education and Employers.

Roy Priest is a Programme Leader and Director of Learning, Teaching and Employability at Birmingham City University. Prior to working in higher education, Roy worked in the music industry. Roy's teaching focuses on developing students' industrial awareness and his research explores the implementation of university strategies related to the enhancement of graduate employability.

Jordan Rehill is Research Assistant at the London-based charity Education and Employers. Prior to joining Education and Employers, he worked for the youth violence charity Redthread, where he assisted in research on trends in youth violence and gang-related violence in central London in conjunction with the Mayor's Office for Policing and Crime. He has co-authored a number of projects on employer engagement in education, including Drawing the Future (2018) and Contemporary Transitions (2017).

Andreas Schleicher is Director for Education and Skills and Special Advisor on Education Policy to the Secretary-General at the Organisation for Economic Co-operation and Development (OECD). As a key member of the OECD's Senior Management team, he supports the Secretary-General's strategy to produce analysis and policy advice that advances economic growth and social progress. In addition to policy and country reviews, he oversees the Programme for International Student Assessment (PISA), the OECD Survey of Adult Skills (PIAAC), the OECD Skills Strategy, the OECD Teaching and Learning International Survey (TALIS) and the development and analysis of benchmarks on the performance of education systems (INES).

Matteo Schleicher is an M.Sc student in Social Research Methods at the London School of Economics, focusing on qualitative and quantitative research methods, as well as meta-analysis of scientific research. He did his undergraduate degree at the University of Durham in Philosophy, Politics and Economics, and interned (in 2016/2017) at Education and Employers Taskforce in London, carrying out various research projects in comparative international education.

Michael Tomlinson is Associate Professor at the Southampton Education School, University of Southampton. His interests are in the sociology of education and work, with a particular focus on higher education and the labour market and critical analysis of HE policy. He has published widely in this field and is the author of two books: *Education, Work and Identity* (Bloomsbury, 2013) and *Graduate Employability in Context: theory, research and debate* (Palgrave, 2017).

Tobie Baker Wright is senior program manager for the Pathways to Prosperity Network based at the Jobs for the Future (JFF) NGO located in Boston, Massachusetts. Among her responsibilities is management of the Possible Futures, Possible Selves initiative which focuses on empowering young people through career exploration beginning in the middle grades. Prior to joining JFF, she taught science in US schools and at Oregon State University.

Preface

Andreas Schleicher

Education now needs to prepare students for more rapid change than ever before, to learn for jobs that have not been created, to tackle societal challenges that we can't yet imagine, and to use technologies that have not yet been invented. This is a tall order for educational institutions, but it can get so much easier and become so much more effective if educational institutions work hand in hand with employers who are at the centre of the economic transformations.

This collection of essays analyses how employers are uniquely placed to provide a distinctive and valuable contribution to the schooling of young people. Employers and their employees, indeed anyone who engages in the world of work, brings with them privileged information about the realities of modern employment and how the knowledge and skills cultivated in our schools are actually deployed in workplaces. Such information is critical to young people as they reflect on who they might become and how they might seek to achieve their emerging aspirations. Many in the economic community, moreover, can offer young people the opportunity to test out what they have learnt in the classroom in real workplaces. It is the authenticity of the workplace experience which underlies its influence. By exposing students to multiple, real-life situations and people, powerful new opportunities for learning emerge.

The Organisation for Economic Co-operation and Development (OECD) has long contended that employers have an essential role to play in careers guidance and work-based learning (OECD, 2010; Musset and Kurekova, 2018). It is gratifying to see in this collection chapters by Simon Field, who for so long led the OECD's work on vocational education and training (VET), and Nancy Hoffman, who played such a central role in the team which produced Learning for Jobs (2010). The thematic analysis, benefiting too from the work of Tony Watts, shows how effective career guidance should involve workplace experience. Essays in this collection go further. Collectively, while presenting new evidence of improved economic outcomes linked to teenage involvement with employers, they show why the positive benefits of employer engagement cannot be taken for granted. It is the responsibility of schools to be strategic about how they deploy the employer resource and be wary of its risks, as well as its opportunities. Effective employer engagement recognises the ways in which work itself is changing; for example, in the growth of self-employment. To be strategic means thinking beyond careers guidance and VET. Important evidence is presented from the OECD's PISA dataset, exploring relationships between workplace exposure and student engagement in learning. The collection also raises questions about the limits of employer involvement in education, notably problematizing its role in qualification design. There is no automaticity with respect to positive outcomes; that's why how engagement is delivered is so important. Quantity and quality clearly matter. The more young people are exposed to the working world and the more highly they value it, the greater the chance that they will encounter the new and useful information which will help them draw a better connection with adults whom they might become. Young people appear to be able to judge for themselves whether the employer engagement they received will be of value to them. Employer engagement, however, does not necessarily lead to more equitable outcomes. There is a risk that it supports patterns of social reproduction.

This is a timely collection. Policy makers are recognising the value of employer engagement as an educational tool. Over the last generation, considerable advancements have been made around the world in ensuring that more students than ever before stay in education beyond compulsory leaving ages. The current generation of young people entering the labour market is better educated than any predecessor, and yet in many countries even well qualified young people struggle to find their place in the labour market. Human capital accumulation is proving insufficient to ensure smooth transitions into work. The coexistence of unemployed graduates on the street, while employers say they cannot find the people with the skills they need, shows clearly that more education alone does not automatically translate into better jobs and better lives. We need to equip young people for their futures by going beyond narrow academic learning. The dynamic twenty-first century economy values people who are personally effective in mobilising and applying their cognitive, social and emotional capabilities in changing situations – and employer engagement presents a perfect vehicle through which schools can teach such an experiential approach to learning. In this, it is essential that it is teachers, informed by high quality research, who decide how, when and where employers are engaged – nobody is better placed to understand their students' needs and aspirations. Schools must have ownership over the process and be willing and confident to make requests of employers, trade unions and professional bodies. Governments can champion, encourage and enable engagement. We need to see them making it easy for employers to respond to requests from schools.

Many of the chapters in this collection were first presented at research conferences and seminars of Education and Employers, a London-based not-for-profit organisation which has undertaken remarkable work in both driving back our knowledge of what employer engagement can do and leading the way by harnessing technology to massively reduce the costs for schools to find the local employee volunteers they want at the time they need them. Under the leadership of CEO Nick Chambers, Education and Employers has built a community of interest embracing teacher unions and employer bodies, government departments and leading researchers, including the editors of this book. It reflects the culture of collaboration essential to making employer engagement work as a strategic tool for all young people.

References

Musset, Pauline and Lucia Mýtna Kureková. (2018). *Career guidance and employer engagement: A review of the evidence.* Paris: Organisation for Economic Co-operation and Development.

OECD. (2010). *Learning for jobs.* Paris: Organisation for Economic Co-operation and Development.

Introduction

Anthony Mann

This collection of essays is a companion piece to 2014's *Understanding Employer Engagement in Education* (Mann, Stanley and Archer, 2014). Both collections have drawn heavily on papers first given at the seminars and conferences of Education and Employers, a London-based charity which since 2009 has devoted energy and resources to better understanding of the potential impacts of employer engagement and how any positive outcomes can expect to be optimised. All the editors of the current collection have some recent or past connection with the charity.

Understanding Employer Engagement in Education was the first collection of research essays with a dedicated focus on the subject, and it represented a coming together of thinking which centred on the role of the employer (and employee, indeed any member of the economic community) as a means of making theoretical and practical sense of a range of activities which had long been undertaken in schools in the U.K. and overseas. It offered a definition of employer engagement in education, influential in the current collection, as "the process through which a young person engages with members of the economic community, under the auspices of their school, with the aim of influencing their educational achievement, engagement and/or progression out of education into ultimate employment" (Stanley, Mann and Archer, 2014, 1). The volume focused attention consequently on the employer/employee as offering something distinct within educational processes, highlighting notable activities such as enterprises competitions, mentoring, work placements, careers talks and job fairs. Through a series of essays, the collection recognised the long history of employer engagement in education in order to critically explore that distinctiveness. Disdaining a once dominant view that the primary purpose of employer engagement was to develop the technical and especially 'employability' skills of young people, essays drew on concepts of social and cultural capital to isolate and highlight the value in the authentic insights into the working world which employers were uniquely and authoritatively placed to offer. With such authentic insight conceived as a resource which is inherently inequitably distributed across society, employer engagement was positioned as a contested good – something which might be deployed to challenge social inequalities, but could also be expected to reinforce social reproduction – but also as a mechanism which might potentially be strategically delivered to address wider educational, economic and social policy objectives.

Since the publication of the 2014 volume, the idea of employer engagement in education has gained a stronger foothold within policy-making communities. Three recent documents are illustrative. It is centre stage, for example, in the careers strategy published by the English Department for Education in December 2017. The strategy stressed the "critical role of employers" in careers guidance and called on schools to ensure that every young person should be offered at least seven encounters with employers over the course of their secondary schooling with greater attention being devoted to students in more deprived areas. The document, which drew on the work of many of the authors in this collection, argued:

> Employers are integral to great careers advice. We need employers of all sizes, and from all sectors, to provide encounters that inspire people and give them the opportunity to learn about what work is like and what it takes to be successful in the workforce. These activities could include work experience or shadowing, workshops or talks run by employers, or other activities that develop the skills needed to deal with business challenges. They could include encounters with people who are self-employed and working for themselves, reflecting the growing number of freelancers in the workforce.
>
> (DfE, 2017, 10)

The publication in 2018 of two studies further reinforces the growing acceptance of employer engagement as a policy tool and situates it within an emerging research literature. *Employer Engagement in Education: Insights from the International Evidence for Effective Practice and Future Research* (Mann, Rehill and Kashefpakdel, 2018) was funded by the U.K. government-sponsored Education Endowment Foundation while *Career Guidance and Employer Engagement: A Review of the Evidence* (Musset and Kurekova, 2018) represents the first OECD study to dedicate so much attention to the subject. The former study drew on extensive policy and research literature to conceptualise employer engagement around four strategic outcomes for young people:

- enhancing understanding of jobs and careers;
- providing the knowledge and skills demanded by the contemporary labour market;
- providing the knowledge and skills demanded for successful school-to-work transitions; and
- enriching education and underpinning pupil attainment.

The approach allowed for a literature review structured by these practical outcomes and to consider the relative value of different forms of employer engagement as a means to achieve them. The review identified just 42 pieces of literature published in English across the OECD countries providing conclusions through use of social science methodologies. The review highlighted the ambiguity of employer engagement – while positive impacts related to educational and economic outcomes were often identified, this was not always the case. Benefits cannot be taken for granted and relate, it is argued, to the characteristics both of participating students and the qualities of provision. While notably improved since 2014, the research literature can still only be described as limited and incomplete. It has next to nothing to say about the value of employer engagement in primary education and little to say about how different types of young people engage in episodes of engagement. The review calls on the research community to dig deeper into the black box of causality to try and better understand why and how young people can be expected to respond to encounters with the economic community. This collection to some extent picks up that challenge, while acknowledging that much new research is still demanded if it is to catch up with policy and practice.

The OECD study looked more narrowly at the role of employer engagement within careers guidance and called on schools to best prepare young people to make informed educational decisions by encouraging "a first-hand understanding of the world of work from an early age" (p. 6). Yet, reviewing data from the organisation's Programme for International Student Assessment (PISA) on the extent of employer engagement within the educational experiences of 15-year-olds across the OECD countries, on average 37% had shadowed a worker at his or her job and fewer than 30% reported had participated in an internship programme or attended a job fair (p. 74). Across the averages, variations are significant with students in Denmark, Finland, Australia, New Zealand, Portugal and Latvia being much more likely to experience employer-led activities. Disproportionately, across the OECD, it is young people engaged on programmes of vocational education and training who can expect to have greater levels of engagement in such experiences.

In this collection, the editors have encouraged such an international perspective. Employer engagement has long formed part of different educational cultures, presenting opportunity to disentangle the universal from the particular in making sense of the employer role. The editors have also sought out contributions which shine light across the breadth of employer engagement's different forms, applying different methodological approaches to making sense of the phenomenon. In so doing, the intention is to add some muscle and definition to the existing skeletal literature.

The collection begins at the beginning. Huddleston and Laczik review a generation of U.K. government initiatives to put "employers in the driving seat" of qualification reform and ask what is reasonable to expect of such a heterogeneous group. Lee, Abdulghani and Hope explore patterns of engagement in schools by 40 New Zealand employers, investigating questions of motivation, and detecting variation by sector. The study considers how such engagement leads to student participation in activities, a question which is the focus of Moote and Archer's chapter who draw on a unique survey dataset of over 13,000 British teenagers to understand patterns of engagement in work experience placements. Once a ubiquitous aspect of British secondary education undertaken by the great majority of teenagers (Mann and Kashefpakdel, 2014), Moote and Archer find that only 45% of their 2013 sample had undertaken a placement. They find, moreover, that participation had become patterned by the social characteristics of students, raising significant questions about equity in access.

This snapshot of practice paves the way for two essays which consider episodes of employer engagement from a theoretical perspective. Tomlinson locates employer engagement in the literature of skills acquisition and student 'employability.' Drawing on a wide range of sources, he draws on the approaches related to competency and capability formation commonly found in studies of vocational education and training and the capitals approaches of sociology and psychology. Mann, Kashefpakdel and Percy focus more narrowly on the idea of social capital as a resource of potential value to individuals. Adopting an experimental analysis of longitudinal data, they ask whether employer engagement enabled by schools can ever compare with that encountered within family units. In these essays, it is the capacity of employer engagement to provide trusted, authentic insights into the labour market which is explored. Effective employer engagement reflects the breadth of the labour market, and the wider its scope, the greater the likelihood of individual students gaining information which is new and useful to them. By exploring the experiences of students and workers in relation to the creative industries, chapters by Huddleston and Ashton and by Priest offer worked examples of the distinctiveness of what it means to be employable in different occupational settings and the limitations of conventional careers guidance. Jones, Mann, Kashefpakdel and McKeown pick up the theme, looking specifically at the role of employer engagement in enabling student access to Medical Schools and highlighting an area where British schools have struggled to compensate for the strength of family ties.

The collection turns then to consider specific approaches to employer engagement. Hooley and Boys review the international literature on mentoring and provide an overview of the current practice in England. Hogarth and Gambin consider a programme of employer engagement interventions undertaken by English secondary schools and ask what impact they have on students within a labour market which has become increasingly hostile to young people. Hoffman with Wright and Gatta completes the triptych of studies, describing innovative practice found in Middle Schools and in an institution of Higher Education in the United States. Recalling the conceptual approaches laid out earlier in the volume, Hoffman and colleagues make a strong case for employer engagement as a means to enhance the intellectual engagement of young people with the labour market, encouraging the adoption of critical approaches to make sense of contemporary employment.

The collection moves towards its conclusion with a clutch of essays which draw on quantitative data to assess the prospective impacts of employer engagement on the lives of young people. In an important essay, Kashefpakdel, Rehill and Schleicher draw upon data from the OECD's Programme for International Student Assessment (PISA) in six countries to identify significant patterns in the relationships between the participation of 15-year-olds in career development activities which involve employers and student attitudes towards education and their performance on the PISA tests. Turning to the question of labour market outcomes, Kashefpakdel, Mann, McKeown, Rehill and Huddleston draw on data from a large survey of young British adults and find associations between teenage participation in school-mediated employer engagement activities and employment outcomes experienced between the ages of 19 and 24. In making sense of the outcomes, the authors identify patterns of quantity (volume of employer engagement activities experienced) and quality (respondent perception of the value of the activity) in relation to economic outcomes. Such insights for practice are also considered by Percy and Kashefpakdel who draw on data from the British Cohort Study to consider how wage premiums linked to participation in careers talks first identified by Kashefpakdel and Percy (2016) relate to the wider school culture of careers guidance.

The book draws to an end with reflections from Field on a decade working with OECD member countries to close the gap between the worlds of education and employment. Taking a view which is long in historical context and wide in national practice, Field calls for a reappraisal of the stubborn divide between the vocational and the academic. In a concluding chapter, the editors look across the essays to reflect the state of the emerging discipline of employer engagement in education and to set out insights for practice. Employer engagement is acknowledged as a complicated subject involving many different activities, delivered in different ways and in different settings to students from different backgrounds, abilities and aspirations. This work values collective insight into these questions. The editors are hugely grateful to all the authors allowing their work to feature in this volume and to Jordan Rehill and Trish Caswell who have worked so assiduously to help to bring it to press.

References

DfE. (2017). *Careers strategy: Making the most of everyone's skills and talents*. London: Department for Education.

Kashefpakdel, E. and Percy, C. (2016). Career education that works: An economic analysis using the British Cohort Study. *Journal of Education and Work* 30(3): 217–234.

Mann, A. and Kashefpakdel, E. (2014). The views of young Britons (aged 19–24) on their teenage experiences of school-mediated employer engagement. In Mann, A., Stanley, J. and Archer, L. (eds.). *Understanding employer engagement in education: Theories and evidence*. London: Routledge.

Mann, A., Rehill, J. and Kashefpakdel, E. (2018). *Employer engagement in education: Insights from the international evidence for effective practice and future research*. London: Education Endowment Foundation.

Mann, A., Stanley, J. and Archer, L. (eds.). (2014). *Understanding employer engagement in education: Theories and evidence*. London: Routledge.

Musset, P. and Kurekova, M. (2018). *Career guidance and employer engagement: A review of the evidence*. Paris: Organisation for Economic Co-operation and Development.

Stanley, J., Mann, A. and Archer, L. (2014). Introduction, in Mann, A., Stanley, J., and Archer, L. (eds.), *Understanding employer engagement in education: Theories and evidence*. London: Routledge.

Chapter 1

'Employers at the heart of the system?'

The role of employers in qualification development

Prue Huddleston and Andrea Laczik

Introduction

This chapter explores the longstanding exhortations from government for employers to engage with the education system within England, in particular the drive to encourage employers to become involved in the development of qualifications within the compulsory phase. We do not consider the role of employers in qualification development within the post-compulsory phase, nor within workplace training, where alignment between qualifications and the needs of the labour market may be considered more compelling (Panteia, 2017). Rather, in this chapter we chart the history and rationale for such an approach within the later stages of secondary education between the ages of 14 and 19 years.

In reviewing these developments, we draw upon research evidence and policy documents over the past thirty years. We also draw upon examples of qualifications, some already developed and some still under development, to identify common themes and recurring challenges. This is supplemented by interviews with those responsible for developing qualifications within awarding organisations (AOs) who are charged with the responsibility of engaging employers in their work.

We suggest that the recurring policy rhetoric has been couched in the same terms, with encouragement for employers to be "key partners from the outset" (DfES/DTI/HMT/DWP, 2005); to jump "in the driving seat" (DBIS/DfE, 2016); to "sit at the heart of the system" (DBIS/DfE, 2016). What emerges is that employers have been asked to engage with increasing degrees of intensity within the education system, but more recently within the development of qualifications. It is argued that this presents a number of challenges, not least that this engagement is on a voluntary basis (Keep, 2015a) and that there exists no regulatory framework for their engagement. A further challenge is the actual expertise and heterogeneity of the employer constituency: who are employers and what is their competence in qualification design? How far should their influence extend over what is taught and assessed in our schools and colleges?

What has been presented within these policy discourses is frequently a deficit image of school leavers, with whom employers are 'dissatisfied'; this line of argument has been traced back over a hundred years (Huddleston, 2012). The simplistic answer appears to be 'it's the qualifications', if we make them tougher, more suited to the needs of employers and, more recently, if we allow employers some input into their design, all will be well. However, Evans (2014) argues that reforming qualifications will make a limited contribution: "it is not the type or content of qualifications that primarily or in isolation make a difference." She presents evidence from other countries to suggest that stability, clear purpose and clear pathways that are supported by institutional structures (p. 7) make a real difference to student employment prospects. Changing or reforming qualifications is only a part of the picture: the curriculum should encompass far wider aims than simply ensuring students pass tests. As Billett (2014) suggests, the curriculum comprises that which is "intended", that which is "enacted" and that which is "experienced". This goes beyond the competence or capacity of employers and of what should reasonably be expected of them.

We conclude that while there may be a role for employers in qualification development, the nature and extent of this should be clearly articulated from the outset. It should be within the competence and capacity of those recruited and rewarded appropriately. This whole endeavour rests upon voluntary commitment, and unless such goodwill is recognised, the enterprise will founder. The most egregious outcome of which will be young people holding qualifications that are neither recognised, nor regarded, by employers because the next round of 'reform' has already begun.

Background

There is nothing new in the recent calls contained within the Sainsbury Review (DfE/BIS, 2016), the Skills Plan (DBIS/DfE, 2016) and in the exhortations framed within the revised specifications for technical qualifications, at all levels, for employers to be engaged in the education system. For over forty years, employers have been urged to engage with education in order to provide themselves with the recruits that industry requires and to address concerns about the assumed shortcomings of youth in terms of their 'employability' (however defined). This tendency has put the spotlight on education as a means of achieving economic ends within an increasingly competitive and global economy (Watts, 1985; Jamieson, 1991; Hodgson and Spours, 1997); Tomlinson, 2005). Hodgson and Spours (1999) however, suggest that such policies have gone beyond purely economic goals to include social control and social cohesion objectives as well. Other chapters within this volume also recognise possible implications for social mobility through employer engagement.

Driving the economy through employer engagement and qualifications development

The predominant narrative throughout the numerous education policy documents, Acts and White Papers over recent decades in England has been the perceived need to align the education system more closely to the needs of the economy and, by association, the needs of employers. As the government uses qualifications as proxies for skills (Stasz, 2011), the high volume of qualification reforms in the past thirty years targeting the 14–19 education phase comes as no surprise (Raffe, 2013; City and Guilds, 2014). Whatever the merits, or demerits, of using education as a driver for the economy (Dynes, 2012), employers have been urged to engage with the education system in a multiplicity of ways. Examples include the provision of work experience for school pupils; contributing to enterprise activities and challenges; mentoring; giving careers talks and interviews. In 1998, at least forty education-related activities, from primary to higher education, involving employers were identified (Huddleston, 2012).

Employers are now being asked to design and develop the content of technical qualifications, to give their imprimatur to every technical qualification before sign off, even to contribute to assessment. This is in addition to the request to provide extended work placements for every student following a T level qualification (see below). It could be argued that this is the most intense manifestation of employer engagement within the education system. However, this is not the first time that employers have been invited to contribute to the design and development of qualifications. The introduction of the short-lived 14–19 Diplomas between 2005 and 2010 specifically urged employers to become involved in the design and development of Diploma qualifications, as well as other aspects of their delivery (Huddleston and Laczik, 2012). The use of 'invited' and 'urged' is deliberate since there exists no regulatory framework or statutory requirement for employer engagement; the whole enterprise is predicated upon a voluntarist model. However, it is impossible to judge "how widespread and enthusiastic employer involvement has been" (Laczik and Mayhew, 2015). If potential recruits appear to lack the perceived knowledge, skills and attributes necessary to function in the modern labour market, then employers are expected to state what those knowledge, skills and attributes are. The simplistic answer is that it is the content of the qualification that requires remedy.

Every recent reform proposed within the education and training system for 14–19-year-olds, since 2000 at least, has been predicated on qualification reform. In effect, while qualification reform has been used as a proxy for curriculum reform, the two are not synonymous (Raffe, 2015). Simply juggling the content of the qualification, and its associated assessment strategy, will not necessarily lead to "oven ready and self-basting" labour market entrants (Atkins, 1999). Despite constant qualification reform, employers still bemoan young people's lack of preparedness for labour market entry. Yet, many employers do not directly recruit school or college leavers (Hogarth et al. 2009) and so are not in the best position to judge if the qualifications young people possess are fit for purpose.

Expectations of employers and from employers: qualification development 1984–2010

Reviewing the past thirty years of vocational qualification reform within the English context reveals continuous attempts to engage employers with varying degrees of intensity. 'Employer ownership' has become a buzzword (Laczik and Mayhew, 2015, 567). For example, the development in the 1980s of what became highly successful Business and Technology Education Council (BTEC) qualifications required, at least, that some consultation with employers had occurred during their development. This could amount to letters of endorsement, industry advisory panels and suggestion of possible employment outcomes for those gaining the qualification. This evidence was required when submitting a qualification for approval on the register of regulated qualifications. In addition, those responsible for drafting the content within AOs were expected to possess knowledge of the related economic sector.

But this represents employers operating at arm's length from the technicalities of writing qualification content. It is one thing to suggest in general what current requirements might be in terms of workplace knowledge, skills and attributes, but quite another to write content and to transform that content into viable and valid qualifications. This lesson could be learnt from the development of 14–19 Diplomas in the 2000s where employers reported feeling distant from the content of the qualifications at the final stage; they considered that the content, as devised by them, had been lost as the qualification went through the different technical development phases (Laczik and White, 2009, 403).

These experiences of employer engagement revealed a consistent challenge. Workplaces are so varied in their structure, organisation and composition and in the products and services provided, it is difficult to see how a panel of, allegedly representative, employers could adequately address this complexity. Employers present a heterogeneous group (Gleeson and Keep, 2004; Huddleston and Laczik, 2012) in terms of their size, the sectors they represent and the geographical area within which they operate. Whilst some sectors require employees to be innovative and self-directing, others require strict adherence to set procedures and manuals, where variation could be deemed as subversive. Even within the same sector there are likely to be differences; for example, a large retailer compared to a small, exclusive, independent shop.

A further layer of complexity is added when we enter the territory of 'soft skills', much lauded by employers as essential for workplace performance but very difficult to capture within qualification design (Barnett, 2004; Keep, 2015a, Keep, 2015b; Vaughan, 2017). What contribution can employers make here? Arguably the most important contribution is ensuring that their workplaces offer rich learning environments and opportunities (Fuller and Unwin, 2003). Writing a qualification specification that adequately describes and is able to assess 'soft skills' to meet the needs of employers is challenging, even for assessment experts (Ahmed, 2015). As long as the two main goals of qualifications are confused/conflated, that is, labour market currency and broader educational aims, then employers will always be disappointed. What appears to them is that qualifications simply do not do "what it says on the tin" (Huddleston, 2017).

General National Vocational Qualifications (GNVQs), 1992–2007, were broad-based vocational qualifications relevant to a wide range of occupational areas of work and designed to allow an alternative route for post-16 students not wishing to pursue an academic qualification. They built on previous work throughout the 1980s in developing BTEC qualifications and the Certificate of Pre-Vocational Education (CPVE). All these reforms were predicated on some form of employer engagement and involved employer organisations, where willing, to work with awarding organisations in developing the qualifications and to provide a source of advice and point of reference in terms of industry relevance.

However, the extent to which this could be achieved, or was even valued, varied over time and reflects the predispositions of civil servants and their political masters. It also reflects the primacy accorded to academic qualifications and to higher education at the expense of developing highly regarded technical routes into employment or further education or training. It seems that employers were expendable: "at one meeting totally unannounced we were informed by a very senior person from the Qualification Curriculum Authority that he felt such advisory groups served little or no purpose and were to be disbanded!" (Technical Education Matters, November, 2011).

Similarly, with the development of the 14–19 Diplomas (2005–2010), employers were invited to take a leading role in their design, development and indeed some aspects of their delivery. They were also expected to canvass support from other employers, to engage in promoting the qualifications, to design teaching support materials and to provide work experience placements – all this on a voluntary basis (Ertl et al. 2009; Huddleston and Laczik, 2012; Ertl and Stasz, 2010). Perhaps this was the most extensive manifestation of employer engagement in recent times. While there were clear achievements, the Diploma qualifications development faced challenges because of the heterogeneous character of employers, their vested interests and the lack of expertise exactly in their core responsibility – the development of the content of qualifications (Haynes, Wade and Lynch, 2013; Laczik and White, 2009). Given that employers were waved 'adieu' before the development of the full range of Diploma qualifications were completed (they were withdrawn in 2010 by the new Coalition government), it is surprising that any goodwill, or appetite, for further employer engagement in qualification development remains.

Qualifications and employer engagement: more recent examples

We now turn our attention to specific examples of attempts to involve employers in qualification development that have been introduced since 2015, and still continue. We consider the extent to which it is merely the reprise of an old refrain, or whether this time, to quote a former Skills Minister, "It is finally getting fixed."

Tech levels

Tech levels were introduced as part of the implementation of the recommendations set out in the Review of Vocational Education, widely known as the Wolf Review (DfE, 2011). Faced with the prospect of more young people remaining in education or training post-16, following the Raising of the Participation Age (RPA) to 17 in 2013 and to 18 in 2015, there was a need to provide an alternative route for those remaining in full-time education who did not wish to pursue an academic route. As we have shown above, this has been attempted since the last Raising of the School Leaving Age in 1972. It should be stressed that Apprenticeships and workplace training remain outside this provision and are covered by other on-going 'reforms'. Naturally, these also require substantial employer engagement.

The first group of qualifications resulting from this directive were the so-called Tech levels (level 3) and Tech certificates (level2) qualifications. According to Guidance issued by the DfE (DfE, 2015) to awarding organisations developing these qualifications, or attempting to shoehorn existing qualifications into the 'new look' design, Tech levels should be "rigorous advanced level qualifications on a par with A levels and recognised by employers" (p. 8). Similarly, Tech certificates should be "rigorous intermediate qualifications for students wishing to specialise in a specific industry, occupation or occupational group" (p. 8). They "provide post-16 students with the knowledge and skills they need for skilled employment or for further technical study" (DfE, 2017a).

So what is the role for employers here? This time the approach was to canvass employer support and engagement in two ways. Firstly, to insist that awarding bodies, in submitting qualifications for recognition on the register of regulated qualifications, should carry signed endorsements from at least eight employers. Secondly, the qualification content should be mapped against existing sector qualifications to identify overlap and compliance with 'licence to practice' criteria (where such exist). In addition, the qualification descriptors should indicate the type of job that someone achieving such a qualification might occupy, in itself something of a shot in the dark since qualifications at that time were in development and not live.

The process appears to involve concept testing a draft qualification with sector representative employers, or a professional body (examples given include the Chartered Institute of Marketing and the Royal Academy of Engineering), to consult them on the resulting qualification and to gain endorsement in terms of a letter of support to be appended to the qualification submission.

Another feature of the design includes the incorporation of 'industry focused assignments', but how these are to be developed remains unclear. What is the expectation on employers here? Are they to design the assignments, sign them off as sufficiently industry focused, and/or to provide work place experience in which students can complete such assignments? Even as these developments work their way through the system, yet another technical education reform for the 16–19 age group has been proposed and may indeed signal the demise of some of the Tech levels and certificates still under development, or they may be subsumed within the new proposals. It is to these latest proposals that we now turn.

T level programmes

One thing that may immediately surprise the reader is the title of this section. The previous section described a recent, and on-going, qualification reform; this one describes yet another on which the DfE at the time of writing is consulting and which is in the early stages of development (DfE, 2017b), yet the titles bear surprising similarity. Both seek employer engagement, the T levels in a much more intensive manner than the Tech levels, but the titling alone may lead to confusion about what this all means and what is being requested.

> T levels are new technical study programmes that will sit alongside Apprenticeships within a reformed skills training system. The reforms are at the heart of a skills partnership between government, business and education and training providers – a partnership that will create the skills revolution needed to meet the needs of our economy.
>
> (DfE, 2017b, 4)

T levels are intended as full-time programmes for 16–19 year olds to be studied either in a college or with a private training provider. In addition to studying for an approved technical qualification, students will be required to undertake an extended period of work placement, on average 50 working days. The placement should be with an employer within the sector being studied – for example, construction or childcare – and should involve a real job with appropriate occupational tasks. Students will also be required to complete English and maths qualifications at level 2, if not already achieved, or at a higher level if demanded by the technical qualification, plus digital skills. Other components designed to enhance "the knowledge, skills and behaviours necessary to enter skilled employment in their sector" will be included (DfE, 2017b, 8). Because T level is a composite qualification, the student must successfully achieve all components of the programme for a T level certificate to be awarded. If not, a transcript of achievement will be issued.

T levels are envisaged as one of three full-time routes for young people to pursue post 16: A levels (academic route), apprenticeships (full-time work-based route) and T levels. The high level design for T level programmes sets out a framework of fifteen occupational routes (as suggested by the Independent Panel on Technical Education, DfE/BIS, 2016).

> A route is a group of occupations which share some common knowledge, skills and behaviours. Within each route, there are a number of pathways which reflect different occupational specialisms. Four routes are expected to be delivered through apprenticeships only(transport and logistics; sales, marketing and procurement; social care; and protective services). The remaining eleven routes will be institution based with substantial work placement.
>
> (DfE, 2017b. 8)

All this is to be achieved by 2022.

Within this emerging plan, fifteen T level panels have been established to develop the outline content for each T level, based on the relevant standards. They will identify the content common across the route and pathway, as well as the specialist content required for each occupation listed on the relevant occupational map. Panels will advise on broader programme requirements, including the study of further qualifications where needed and the maths, English and digital requirements to secure skilled employment following completion of the T level (ibid, p. 13). Employers are expected to play a substantial role in this process. There are also suggestions that employers will advise on industry-designed assignments and even contribute to discussions on structuring, assessing and grading qualifications. They will also play a role in quality assuring the qualifications.

Although this bears considerable similarity to the ill-fated Diploma development process, what is being proposed here is an even more 'hands-on', intensive employer engagement. In summary, employers are being expected to identify the level and type of skill demand they have, contribute to the design of the standards, content and even the assessment processes involved. They will, it is hoped, provide thousands of work placements, again with an involvement in the design of the placement and its assessment – all this on a voluntary basis. As a small token, members of the 15 Technical Panels will receive some remuneration for attendance.

We now consider specialist institutions whose rationale from the outset was to engage employers in a fundamental way, not just in qualification design, but also in the wider aspects of the curriculum. Although small in number, we ask if lessons can be learnt.

University technical colleges (UTCs)

The first University Technical Colleges (UTCs) were established in 2011; there are, in early 2018, forty-nine UTCs across England. As UTCs are relatively new, little research has been conducted into them (Daniel et al. 2017). They are educational institutions catering for all ability 14–19-year-old young people in England. As their title suggests, they focus on technical areas, mainly science, technology, engineering and maths (STEM) subjects. UTCs are sponsored by a local university and by local employers who also contribute to curriculum development. The curriculum that UTCs offer is a combination of academic, practical and technical learning. At KS4 (14–16 years), 60% of the curriculum covers academic subjects and 40% a technical specialism; at post-16 these proportions are reversed. Technical specialisms at UTCs are linked to local skills gaps (Kettlewell et al. 2017).UTCs specifically focus on the development of employability skills and prepare young people for further learning, training and employment.

Recent research (McCrone et al. 2017) has focused on project-based learning and employer engagement in the development and delivery of the curriculum in UTCs. McCrone et al. (2017) conducted ten case studies of UTCs during the first year of their study. They refer to employer engagement at three levels: 'profound', 'moderate' and 'contextual'. Their findings show that there was "evidence of considerable employer awareness and presence at all [ten] UTCs. . . [all] demonstrated moderate and contextual employer input into young people's learning" (p. 2). They describe 'moderate' engagement as "employers contributed significantly to projects but with less emphasis on project development and ownership. Contextual involvement requires a commitment to provide information about the workplace and activities that help to inform young people about technical and employability knowledge and skills required by industry"(p. 9).

They also found a 'profound level' of employer engagement when employers took ownership of modules and units of the curriculum, becoming involved in the delivery of projects. Project-based learning offered the opportunity for employers to provide "authentic, engaging and complex questions, problems, or challenges"(McCrone et al. 2017).Such 'profound level' projects were employer-led, but were co-developed by UTC staff combining pedagogical and industrial expertise. In addition, the study identifies a number of other employer engagement activities that support the application of theory seen and observed by students in practice. These included, for example, students solving real-world problems, workplace visits, employers influencing the curriculum by providing information about the current skills needs and employers supporting UTCs with resources and high quality equipment. Based on their expertise, employers were able to advance students' technical knowledge and skills in line with current industry needs.

McCrone et al. (2017) clearly identify the positive influence of employer engagement on the sample of UTCs they studied. They stress the importance of establishing and maintaining high quality strategic employer engagement. Some advice offered by the interviewees to other UTCs was to "provide regular and sustained exposure to a range of industry partners" (p. 3). The advice of UTCs could be helpful to other types of schools and education providers, although whether this type of engagement could be replicated at scale remains open to question. The study also identified challenges to continuous, high quality employer engagement which may be overcome through a better understanding of how employers and UTCs operate and through greater mutual appreciation of UTCs' and employers' expertise. This may include, for example, UTC staff's detailed understanding of the curriculum, qualifications, assessment criteria and employers' awareness of current skills needs in the workplace and industry requirements (pp. 9–10).

The study clearly highlights that one of the most important employer contributions was the expertise they brought to project-based learning. This was also considered crucial in developing students' employability skills. However, employability skills and employer-led project-based learning are not recognised in the latest school/college accountability measures introduced by DfE. This is unfortunate since project-based production is an increasingly common method of working within modern workplaces (Eikoff and Warhurst, 2013; Billett, 2010). (See chapter 6 for a further discussion of project-based learning.) As Kettlewell et al. (2017) suggest: "The existing measures do not attempt to capture the value of employers being strongly engaged in UTCs or what successful outcomes may be achieved through doing this well" (p. 19). This particularly contradicts recent policy rhetoric asking for ever stronger employer engagement in education, which is clearly achieved by UTCs (Thorley, 2017).

Employer engagement: practical implications for awarding organisations

Ironically, what is often notable by its absence from the majority of discussions on qualification development is the role of experts in qualification design, development and assessment, namely the AOs. In this not so 'brave new world', they will be expected to tender to offer the technical qualifications designed by employers. Given the significant opportunity cost of competitively tendering for these licences, will they wish to play ball? What of the existing range of technical and vocational qualifications that they currently offer and that are valued by learners, including some of those still being re-designed (see Tech levels above)? Are they to be abandoned in yet another attempt to meet the so-called needs of employers?

In England, qualifications are designed and offered by a wide range of AOs. Education and training providers decide which qualifications they will offer learners. That choice will be governed by a number of factors, including the suitability of the qualification for intended learners; its cost; its eligibility for government funding; and the support provided by AOs to providers. Some of these bodies are registered charities; others are professional institutes or associations and some commercial businesses. Some are small sector specific bodies, offering just few qualifications; others are large cross-sector bodies, offering large numbers of vocational and academic qualifications which are delivered in schools, colleges and by private training organisations. The titles 'awarding organisation' and 'awarding body and exam board' tend to be used interchangeably; for the purposes of this discussion, we shall use the term 'awarding organisation' (AO).

AOs are experts in the design and development of qualifications. They approve centres (schools, colleges and training providers) that offer their qualifications to ensure the quality of the qualifications awarded (Federation of Awarding Bodies, 2017). They are experts in assessment design and continually monitor qualifications performance to ensure that results are robust, reliable and valid. The majority of AOs within the UK are regulated by Ofqual (for England), CCEA(for Northern Ireland), Welsh Government (for Wales) and SQA (for Scotland).

Whilst the foregoing sections of this chapter have described the long history of qualification reform in policy terms, what often appears to be a 'taken for granted' assumption is the role of AOs. Policy announcements outline proposed reforms with little mention of how this will impact qualification designers and developers and whether or not the proposals are actually feasible, in technical terms, deliverable operationally, and financially viable. The same approach is taken in terms of employer engagement; the expectation is that employers will wish to be involved. However, for them it is voluntary. For awarding organisations, although technically voluntary, involvement may be a matter of commercial survival. Most important of all is the potential impact that all this can have on those young people studying for the qualifications. For how long will these qualifications retain currency? Will achieving the qualifications ensure entry to employment or to further or higher education? Will studying these qualifications serve as preparation for life beyond school or college?

We now illustrate the impact of such continuous reform on AOs. The evidence has been gathered from in-depth, face-to-face interviews with stakeholder engagement managers within a large and long established AO in England offering a wide range of academic and vocational qualifications. Three senior managers were interviewed by the authors in early 2018. Each manager was responsible for engaging with a particular sector – for example, engineering or hospitality. In addition, publicly available summaries of consultation discussions held by DfE with AO representatives concerning current reform proposals were reviewed.

Respondents reported that, although required to do so within the context of the current reforms, it is "really difficult" to engage employers. Competition is fierce, not just from other AOs, but because other institutions and organisations are seeking to engage them – for example, schools, universities, charities and employer bodies like the Chambers of Commerce. A great deal of time and effort is expended on finding, approaching, recruiting and then keeping employers engaged, which was described in various ways as "stalking", "cajoling", "developing relationships at the top of an organisation in order to try and secure engagement further down the chain of command to functional managers". "For big companies cold calling is not an option, because reception is there to block." "You must have a face-to-face meeting."

Where there is a dedicated education liaison manager, or similar, then the job is a little easier. Similarly, if a company has a stance on corporate social responsibility, this can serve as a lever. For small and medium enterprises it is particularly challenging since there is no one with a designated responsibility for such work. In this case, link organisations, or partnerships, were seen as helpful – for example, County Councils' Economic Forum events or Local Enterprise Partnerships. Networking at conferences is another strategy, but costs of attending have to be weighed against potential 'hits'. The social media resource, LinkedIn, was found to be helpful; even so it was reported that "about ten per cent of approaches (by whatever means) were worthwhile". Once secured, these relationships were described as "a bit like dating"; relationships "need to be kept warm". It should be remembered that these are relationships with people, not necessarily with companies, and when the person moves on then the relationship with the company may be lost: "Unfortunately some people just do not get it."

Respondents described the expectation that employers should be involved in all aspects of qualification development as unrealistic. They are not experts in the technicalities and complexities of qualification design and development and particularly not in assessment. Although it was felt critical to involve employers in some way; for example, in terms of providing model content they should not be required to undertake things for which they have no knowledge or experience. Also, the extent and form of their contribution should be made clear from the outset to avoid disappointment. This confirms evidence reported by Huddleston and Laczik (2012) on the disappointments felt by many employers during the development of the discontinued 14–19 Diploma qualifications. They found it difficult to understand that model content is not a fully developed qualification.

Where employers' input is welcome and appropriate is in describing "current sector needs in terms of knowledge, skills and behaviours". They were also seen as helpful in suggesting possible realistic and relevant project topics; respondents had encountered some excellent examples provided by a company's young graduates. It was felt that employer endorsement brought credibility to a qualification (the proposal in Tech Levels described above). However, this should take the form of "solid letters of support, with reasons, and not simply a collection of autographs". Of course, it is schools and colleges that ultimately decide which qualifications to offer learners and that will be decided by things other than employer endorsement. However, it was suggested that for young people and their parents perhaps employer recognition could be important.

Some areas were seen as particularly challenging in terms of stakeholder engagement. One example given was the 'science community' because of its ubiquity. In other words: "Where do you go to get science input into a qualification because so many sectors have a scientific component in their qualifications and yet they are not seen as science qualifications?" A similar view was reported on English and maths because they are not sector specific but yet are requirements within many qualifications. An interesting example was provided from the performing arts sector; here, consortia of theatres had come together with the AO to help develop sector relevant qualifications.

The overriding view was that the pressure to engage employers in all aspects of education, and certainly within qualification development, has intensified since 2005. Expectations of employers were seen as too great and beyond their capacity, particularly within a voluntary system. Respondents felt that "employers are overloaded", and as a result some are now "asking for payment" for their involvement. "Big companies can afford to say no, SMEs cannot afford to say yes."

Sectors are very different in terms of what they expect and need from qualifications; each requires a tailored approach, hence the dedicated sector stakeholder engagement managers. Some sectors are dominated by a major employer that can dominate the debate to the exclusion of other, smaller voices. Awarding organisations have to manage these expectations if they are to keep employers engaged. But they also have to develop and design qualifications to tight government deadlines at considerable expense and, under the latest T level reform proposals, as part of a competitive tendering process.

Whilst respondents recognised that employer engagement was desirable to some extent within qualification development, this should be limited to what could reasonably be expected, what was manageable and what was within their competence. Given these pressures on AOs and their employer partners, one respondent suggested: "qualifications may be designed by those who turn up on the day." Clearly, this does not amount to 'putting employers at the heart of the system' or 'in the driving seat'; nor should it.

Conclusions

We have shown that calls for employer engagement in education generally, and more recently in qualifications development for post-16 students specifically, have featured as a *leitmotif* in education reform for over forty years. Over the past ten years this has intensified. We suggest that based on previous research evidence, and what is currently being proposed, the task is not straightforward and cannot guarantee an education and training system 'that meets the needs of employers'.

The reasons for this state of affairs stem from a fundamental misconception that 'reforming' qualifications is a *sine qua non* of curriculum reform from which all else will flow. This is clearly not the case. Employers, however well intentioned, do not have the technical capacity or competence to design qualifications, and their assessment methodologies and the majority are not experts in curriculum or pedagogy. However, the evidence suggests that they do have a role to play in terms of suggesting model content, endorsing the authenticity of tasks and assignments, of providing relevant context for project-based learning and, more crucially, being willing to employ those who hold such qualifications.

In a context of rapidly changing labour markets, specialist skills quickly become outdated and so notions of tightly defined 'pathways' and 'occupational maps' delineated by small groups of employers are unlikely to meet the needs of an entire sector, particularly those sectors characterised by SMEs and micro businesses with diverse skills needs. In these contexts transferable skills are more enduring and demanded. These are skills that are the most challenging to assess, even for assessment experts and even more so for those with no such background (Ahmed, 2015). Yet, these are the skills that employers often say they want and register disappointment when labour market entrants fail to meet expectations.

Policy in this area has been predicated upon a willingness of employers to engage voluntarily, but they have been asked to do so before, particularly in the now abandoned 14–19 Diplomas. Previous research has shown that some were disappointed to have been summarily dismissed; how willing they will be to engage in the current reforms remains to be seen. The same is true for AOs: policy based on the expectation that they will wish to expend considerable resource on competitively tendering for a licence to offer qualifications for which there is an unknown demand. This underlines the fundamental imbalance of power between stakeholders: government, business, awarding organisations and education providers.

If employers are to be engaged, then it is suggested that what is expected of them is de-scaled, structured and prioritised in such a way that what they can offer is relevant, realistic and adds value. In the latest round of reforms (T levels), employers are being asked to design qualifications, including assessment methodologies, develop industry-focused assignments, plan and host extended work placements and contribute to their assessment. It is unfortunate that there appears to be so little policy memory about the potential consequences.

References

Acquah, D.K., Limmer, H. and Malpass, D. (2017). I don't know where to find the careers adviser . . . he has disappeared: The impact of changes to careers advice on 14–16 year olds in University Technical Colleges and schools. *Research Papers in Education* 32(2): 197–216.

Ahmed, A. (2015). *Assessing 'hard to assess' skills: The future of assessment*. Manchester: AQA.

Atkins, M.J. (1999). Oven ready and self-basting: Taking stock of employability skills. *Teaching in Higher Education* 4(2): 267–280.

Barnett, R. (2004). Learning for an unknown future. *Higher Education Research and Development* 23(3): 247–260.

Billett, S. (ed). (2010). *Learning through practice: Models: Traditions, orientations, and approaches*. London: Springer.

Billett, S. (2014). *Mimetic learning at work: Learning in the circumstances of practice*.: Springer.

City and Guilds (2014). *Sense and instability: Three decades of skills and employment policy*. Available from: www.cityandguilds.com/~/media/Documents/news-insight/CGSkillsReport 2014%20pdf.ashx [accessed January 10th 2018].

DBIS and DfE. (2016). *Post-16 skills plan*. CM 9280. London: DfE.

DfE (2011). *Review of vocational education – The Wolf Report*. London: Department for Education.

DfE. (2015). *Vocational qualifications for 16–19 year olds: 2017 and 2018 performance tables, technical guidance for awarding organisations*. London: DfE.

DfE. (2017a). *Performance tables and technical and vocational qualifications*. Available from: www. gov.uk/government/publications/2019-performance-tables-technical-and-vocational-qualifications/tech-levels [accessed January 10th 2018].

DfE. (2017b). *Post-16 technical education reforms T level action plan*. Available from: www. gov.uk/government/uploads/system/uploads/attachment_data/file/650969/T_level_Action_Plan.pdf [accessed January 29th 2018].

DfE and BIS. (2016). *Report of the independent panel on technical education* ('The Sainsbury Review'). London: DfE.

DfES/DTI/HMT and DWP. (2005). *14–19 Education and skills*. London: HMSO.

Dynes, J.M. (2012). *14–19 Education reform under new labour: An exploration of how politics and the economy combine with educational goals to affect policy*. Unpublished Ph.D. thesis, University of Warwick.

Eikoff, D.R. and Warhurst, C. (2013). The promised land? Why social inequalities are systemic in the creative industries. *Employee Relations* 35(5): 495–508.

Ertl, H., Stanley, J., Huddleston, P., Stasz, C., Laczik, A. and Hayward, G. (2009). *Reviewing diploma development: An evaluation of the design of the diploma qualifications*. London: DCSF.

Ertl, H. and Stasz, C. (2010). Employing an 'employer-led' design? An evaluation of the development of diplomas. *Journal of Education and Work* 23(4): 301–317.

Evans, L. (2014). *Avoiding the same old mistakes: Lessons for reform of 14–19 education in England*. IPPR. Available from: www.ippr.org/publications/avoiding-the-same-old-mistakes-lessons-for-reform-of-14-19-education-in-england [accessed January 10th 2018].

Federation of Awarding Bodies (2017). *The qualification manager's handbook*. London: Federation of Awarding Bodies.

Fuller, A. and Unwin, L. (2003). Learning as apprentices in the contemporary UK workplace: Creating and managing expansive and restrictive participation. *Journal of Education and Work* 16(4): 407–426.

Gleeson, D. and Keep, E. (2004). Voice without accountability: The changing relationship between employers, the state and education in England. *Oxford Review of Education* 30(1): 37–63.

Haynes, G.S., Wade, P. and Lynch, S. (2013). Engaging employers with the 14–19 diplomas: The employer perspective. *Journal of Education and Work* 26(2): 219–239.

Hodgson, A. and Spours, K. (1997). *Dearing and beyond, 14–19 qualifications, frameworks and systems*. London: Kogan Page.

Hodgson, A. and Spours, K. (1999). *New Labour's educational agenda: Issues and policies for education and training from 14+*. London: Kogan Page.

Hogarth, T., Owen, D., Gambin, L., Hasluck, C., Lyonette, C. and Casey, B. (2009). *The equality impacts of the current recession*. Equality and Human Rights Commission Research Report No.47.

Huddleston, P. (2012). Engaging and linking with employers, in Huddleston, P. and Stanley, J. (eds.), *Work-related teaching and learning*. Abingdon: Routledge: 29–43.

Huddleston, P. (2017). A question of identity: Does it do what it says on the tin, in Loo, S. and Jamieson, J. (eds.), *Vocationalism in further and higher education policy, programmes and pedagogy*. Abingdon: Routledge: 53–65.

Huddleston, P. and Laczik, A. (2012). Successes and difficulties of employer engagement. The new diploma qualification. *Journal of Education and Work*. Special Edition 24(4): 403–421.

Jamieson, I. (1991). Corporate hegemony or pedagogic liberation? The schools-industry movement in England and Wales, in Dale, R. (ed.), *Training and employment towards a new vocationalism*. Oxford: Pergamon: 23–38.

Keep, E. (2015a). *Unlocking workplace skills: What is the role for employers?* (Policy Report). Oxford: Centre for Skills, Knowledge and Organisational Performance, Oxford University.

Keep, E. (2015b). Governance in English VET: On the functioning of a fractured 'system'. *Research in Comparative and International Education* 10(4): 464–475.

Kettlewell, K., Bernardinelli, D., Hillary, J. and Sumner, C. (2017). *University technical colleges: Beneath the headlines*. NFER contextual analysis. Slough: NFER.

Laczik, A. and Mayhew, K. (2015). Labour market developments and their significance for VET in England: Current concerns and debates. *Research in Comparative and International Education* 10(4): 558–575.

Laczik, A. and White, C. (2009). Employer engagement and the 14–19 diplomas. *Research in Post-compulsory Education* 14(4): 399–413.

McCrone, T., Martin, K., Sims, D. and Rush, C. (2017). *Evaluation of University Technical Colleges (UTCs)*. Interim report. Slough: NFER.

Panteia (2017). *Business cooperating with vocational education and training providers for quality skills and attractive futures*. Brussels: European Commission, Directorate-General for Employment, Social Affairs and Inclusion.

Raffe, D. (2013). *First count to five: Some principles for the reform of vocational qualifications in England*. Conference paper, SKOPE symposium on the Reform of Vocational Qualifications, Oxford. February.

Raffe, D. (2015). First count to five: Some principles for the reform of vocational qualifications in England. *Journal of Education and Work* 28(2): 147–164.

Stasz, C. (2011). *The purpose and validity of vocational qualifications*. Oxford: SKOPE.

Technical Education Matters (2011). Available from: www.Technical Education Matters.org 2011/11 [accessed January 10th 2018].

Thorley, C. (2017). *Tech transitions: UTCs, studio schools, and technical and vocational education in England's schools*. IPPR. Available from: www.ippr.org/publications/tech-transition [accessed January 10th 2018].

Tomlinson, S. (2005). *Education in a post-welfare society*. Maidenhead: Open University Press.

Vaughan, K. (2017). The role of apprenticeship in the cultivation of soft skills and dispositions. *Journal of Vocational Education and Training* 69 (4): 540–557.

Watts, A.G. (1985). Education and employment: The traditional bonds, in Dale, R. (ed.), *Training and employment towards a new vocationalism*. Oxford: Pergamon.

Chapter 2

Investigating how benefits of an industry-school partnership vary between industry sectors

Kerry Lee, Fatima Abdulghani and John Hope

Introduction

The fervour to ensure that education is authentic and mirroring the 'real-world' is now equally matched by industry's drive for corporate social responsibility. Partnerships between industry and schools are now becoming common practice, with the number of industry-school partnerships having grown rapidly over the last twenty years. This chapter investigates which industry sectors are supporting schools and why they are doing so. It begins with an explanation of the driving forces behind industry-school partnerships and the accompanying changes to the education system. This is followed by a methodology section which details the data collection and analysis utilised in this New Zealand study. The findings, discussion and conclusion identify the benefits to each industry sector as well as the value of further research for both education and industry sectors.

The driving force behind the increased need for industry-school partnerships

Socially responsible business: a brief history

For centuries, specific groups of the population have questioned the notion of businesses making money at any cost. In North America, Quakers are said to be the first investors to screen their investments according to their values and beliefs, and by 1758 Quakers were prohibited from participating or supporting any aspects of the slave trade (Dillenburg et al. 2003). In Europe and America, early adopters of this socially responsible investing model (SRI) were often motivated by religious reasons such as to avoid 'sinful' companies, for example, guns, tobacco, liquor. In the 1960s investors increasingly sought to address equality for women, civil rights and labour issues, and the term 'corporate social responsibility' became popular (Carroll and Shabana, 2010).

Three decades later, Elkington coined the phrase 'triple bottom line' (Henriques and Richardson, 2004). "Triple bottom line requires companies to not only consider financial profit and loss but also the effects on social and environmental concerns" (Lee, 2007, 67). Since this time the notion has grown in acceptance, with international standards being developed. The Global Reporting Initiative (GRI) has been the most widely accepted report template as it sets out a comprehensive set of guidelines, including the triple bottom line of reporting (Monaghan, 2004). The UK government "was the first to develop a properly integrated framework for bringing together the key economic, environmental and social elements" (Porritt, 2004). Australia followed suit and adopted triple bottom line principles, whilst in 2003 the New Zealand Ministry for the Environment began publishing material which focussed on triple bottom line reporting (Ministry for the Environment, 2003). Numerous national organisations began considering their social and environmental responsibilities and looking for ways in which they could contribute and add value to their communities. For example, New Zealand's largest fishing company identified the need to ensure society benefited as well as shareholders (stockholders). These benefits included ensuring at least 50% of full-time employees were engaged in some form of training under the New Zealand Qualification Authority (NZQA) framework. When this regime was introduced, over 90% of the staff opted for the company's free voluntary one hour per week session with an individual tutor to enhance their English. The company adopted a community programme titled "Take a kid fishing" (Sanford, 2006) as well as numerous school partnerships. These partnerships included working with the Foundation for Youth Development to write classroom-based lessons (Sanford, 2009), sponsoring local Science and Technology Fairs (Sanford, 2013) and working with youth offenders (Sanford, 2016). This is one of many examples where large and small industries have given both time and resources to support others' learning.

Whilst business has developed an ethos of community involvement, education has moved to increase its involvement with business. The following section outlines some of the political motives which may have influenced these changes to both education and business practice.

Political motives

Developing links between education and industry has been seen as a key tool to address economic and social policy goals. During times of economic uncertainty, interest in industry-school partnerships increases in value and importance (Huddleston and Stanley, 2013). By the middle of the 20th century an alignment was sought between the state education system in Britain and the divisions within the labour market (Ainley, 1990). The former UK Prime Minister Harold Wilson talked of the transformation that was needed in education to provide a workforce fit for the expanding post-war economy (The Guardian, 1963). In 1976, James Callaghan criticised state education's lack of engagement with industry needs and the failure to encourage the appropriate attitudes in students (Beckett, 2009). By the late 1980s and early 1990s, the emphasis on ensuring school leavers matched existing jobs had changed to a concern about students' attitudes and skills (Beckett, 2009). In this Thatcher era, an emphasis was placed on developing an enterprising culture and appreciation of small business (Ainley, 1990).

In Europe the potential impact of entrepreneurship as a key factor for European innovation, growth and success was highlighted by the Lisbon 2000 Agenda (Rodriguez et al. 2010). This and other initiatives to promote entrepreneurship resulted in a huge growth in business/school links. Overnight entrepreneurship and enterprise education were incorporated into European school curricula. Two years later, enterprise education programmes in English schools were evaluated. The Davies Review (Davies, 2002b) scrutinised the existence, strength and quality of industry-school links in terms of relevance to both the practicalities of work preparedness and the development of enterprise skills. This review also involved an analysis of how best to promote a better understanding of business in schools through enterprise education. Building capacity through forging partnerships between schools and businesses was believed to give students access to meaningful enterprise experiences, as well as work placements. This was seen as critical to effectively respond to the opportunities of the 21st century economy and its labour market challenges (Davies, 2002b). In 2010 the Organisation for Economic Co-operation and Development (OECD) published a report titled "Learning for Jobs" (Hoeckel and Schwartz, 2010), and in 2011 the Harvard School for Graduate Education produced a document titled "Pathways to Prosperity" (Symonds et al. 2011); both documents highlighted the need for employer engagement.

Industry-school partnerships

Industry-school partnerships can occur at all levels of education from kindergarten through to tertiary. These partnerships can be mutually beneficial to teachers, students and industry (Lonsdale et al. 2011; Mann et al. 2010). Partnerships can be at the school, teacher or student level (Burge et al. 2012) and may involve visits to businesses or employees visiting the kindergarten or school, whilst support may take the form of personnel time to provide mentoring for pupils or free resources for schools – for example, donations of equipment. In 1998, the Centre for Education and Industry (CEI) at the University of Warwick, UK identified at least forty activities ranging from primary schools to higher education institutions (HEIs) in which employers were asked to engage with education (Huddleston and Stanley, 2012). Partnerships can be beneficial to students vocationally, academically or personally (Lonsdale et al. 2011). Whilst notions of business, industry, organisations and institutions will be simply referred to as 'industry', the term 'partnership' will be used to define a collaborative relationship between industry and school.

A great deal of research has focused on the benefits of industry-school partnerships for schools and students (Breen, 2004; Dodd and Hynes, 2011; McLarty et al. 2010; Mann et al. 2010; Ehlen et al. 2015). These benefits include increased test scores (Blank et al. 2003), increased attendance rates (Sheldon and Epstein, 2002; Sheldon, 2007), changes in attitudes (Department for Children, 2008), clarity on career decisions (Harreveld and Singh, 2009) and fitter and healthier students (Phillips, 2010). However, researchers have yet to investigate which industry sectors are developing these partnerships and whether each sector experiences the same level of benefit. Exploring the benefits of partnerships across the industry sectors may enable schools to identify local businesses which could be potentially supportive and provide industries with an awareness of possible gains prior to any partnership commitment. This chapter outlines a New Zealand study which investigated the benefits to various industry sectors when they linked with schools.

Research methods

This exploratory research (Davidson and Tolich, 2003) utilised questionnaires as objective research tools to produce generalisable quantitative results (Harris and Brown, 2010). This research took a positivist (value-free) approach and only commenced after approval was gained from the University's ethics board. Participants were recruited via monthly newsletters sent by four New Zealand organisations which had databases to support industry-school partnerships. Of the 500 industries listed in these databases, forty participants responded and completed an online survey. Questions for the online survey were based on those used in an earlier, but similar, Australian study (Figgis, 1998), adapted for the New Zealand context. The questionnaire explored businesses' involvement with schools, as well as investigating benefits to the employees and the business as a whole. Data were analysed using Kruskal Wallis one-way analysis of variance (ANOVA) by ranks tests, Mann Whitney U tests, Chi Square tests and Fisher's Exact Probability tests.

Results and discussion

Data fell into four main sectors, with Business Trade/Banking/Financial being the largest sector with 16(40%) participants. The remaining participants were divided evenly amongst the Manufacturing/Construction sector 9 (22.5%), Computer/ IT/Telecommunications sector 8 (20%) and the Educational/Governmental and other services sector 7 (17.5%). The latter sector did not include schools but rather government and education agencies such as those established to support Māori achievement (New Zealand's indigenous peoples). These data reflect the diversity of the NZ industry sectors, especially within urban settings (Statistics New Zealand, 2013).

Proximity of the school to the industry can be very important to the establishment of the partnership (Hoff, 2002). A Kruskal Wallis Test revealed the difference between the four industry sectors in their interactions with schools to be significant (p < 0.05), χ^2 (3, 40) = 8.44, $p = 0.04$. No respondent in the computer/IT/telecommunications and business/banking/finance sectors linked solely with primary schools, but rather linked solely with secondary or both primary and secondary. Industries in the manufacturing/construction sector supported either primary (22%) or secondary schools (78%), but not both. Respondents from the manufacturing/construction (78%) and the business/banking/finance (69%) sectors strongly supported links with secondary schools. The seven industries in the education/government sector linked with primary (29%), secondary (29%) and both primary and secondary (42%).

A little under half of the industries (45%) linked with less than ten schools, whilst ten industries (25%) linked with more than fifty schools. This is in contrast to an urban American study, where 90% of industry participants linked with less than ten schools (Hoff, 2002). All representatives from the manufacturing/construction sector and 88% of the business/banking/finance sector stated that their organisation was linked to less than fifty schools, whilst an even spread of these links was demonstrated by the computer/IT/communications sector.

Time and clear communication is needed to develop successful school-industry partnerships (Barza, 2013; Davies, 2002a; Sanders, 2003). Face-to-face contact also contributes to successful relationships as it helps build a sense of trust (Storper and Venables, 2004). Some sectors linked with schools more frequently than others. The manufacturing/construction sector had the least interactions with schools. It not only linked with fewer schools than other sectors, but it also had the least regular contact (Table 2.1). In contrast the computer/IT/telecommunications sector tended to link more frequently with nearly half the participants, linking either daily or weekly. The business/banking/finance and education/government sectors both tended to make contact with schools on a monthly basis. This may be due to the support they provided, as both the education and business sectors tended to provide more personal support rather than financial (see Table 2.1).

Table 2.1 Frequency of visits to schools undertaken by each industry sector

Industry sectors	Approximately, how often did your organisation link with schools?			
	Daily (% of sector)	Weekly (% of sector)	Monthly (% of sector)	Annually (% of sector)
Manufacturing/ construction	0 (0%)	3 (33%)	2 (22%)	4 (45%)
Computer/IT/ telecommunications	2 (25%)	2 (25%)	2 (25%)	2 (25%)
Business/banking/ finance	1 (6%)	1 (6%)	12 (75%)	2 (13%)
Education/government	0 (0%)	2 (29%)	4 (57%)	1 (14%)
Total (% of total)	**3 (8%)**	**8 (20%)**	**20 (50%)**	**9 (22%)**

Industries supported schools in a wide range of activities. Mentoring (n=23, 57%), assisting students with mini enterprises (n=21, 52%) and allowing school visits to the industry (n=21, 52%) were interactions used by over half the respondents as shown in Figure 2.1. In 2010 YouGov research cited by Mann and Dawkins (2014, p. 15) reported that of the 2,198 high school participants, 76% 'wanted more' or the 'same amount' of visits to local businesses and 71% wanted mentoring. Mentoring can have a major impact on at-risk students as shown by Miller (1998, cited in Mann and Dawkins, 2014, p. 23), who found that 70% of borderline students at Key Stage 4 agreed that mentoring had affected their desire to do well at school.

Figure 2.1 also shows the least common interactions, which included taking part in curriculum development, providing technical knowledge, expertise and work-observations and providing teacher placements.

Table 2.2 identifies the most common school interactions for each sector. For example, the manufacturing sector (89%) tended to give donations, whilst for the education and government sector this was not a common practice. This sector included agencies established to support the indigenous population, and these organisations tended to work in schools via mentoring, mini enterprises, community projects, employee visits, product and services and problem solving.

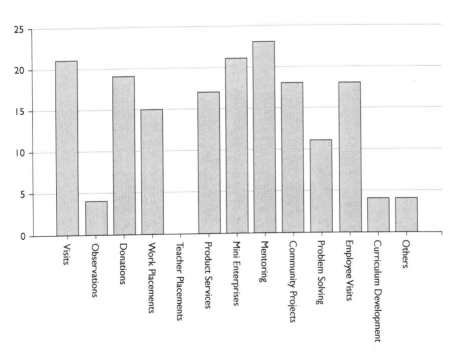

Figure 2.1 Frequency of interactions in industry-school partnerships

Table 2.2 The most common school interactions for each sector

Industry sectors	Mentoring	Mini-enterprises	Visits	Donations	Community Projects	Employee visits
Manufacturing/ construction	11%	22%	67%	89%	44%	44%
Computing/IT/ telecommun- ications	75%	63%	50%	63%	50%	25%
Business/banking/ finance	63%	56%	63%	38%	31%	44%
Education/ government	86%	72%	14%	0%	71%	72%
Percentage of 'yes' responses per type of interaction	**58%**	**53%**	**53%**	**48%**	**45%**	**45%**

It is therefore unsurprising that they were also the key sector offering support with curriculum development (43%).

Most common industry-school partnerships undertaken by businesses from each industry sector

All industry sectors were positive about their industry-school partnerships with the exception of the business/banking/finance sector, where four respondents (12%) stated they would not encourage others to link with schools.

Perceived benefits to the business

A 5-point Likert Scale (5 = very beneficial, 1= no benefits) was used to explore industry perceptions of the benefits of school partnerships. The results are presented in four categories: overall image and reputation of the industry, community networks, advertising and general benefits to employees.

Overall image and reputation of the industry

Reputation is very important for a business and a key driver for industry-school partnerships (Large, 1997). A Kruskal Wallis Test revealed a significant difference (p < 0.05) in perceived benefits to the image and reputation of the business across the four industry sectors, χ^2 (3,40) = 9.978, $p = 0.019$. This difference was attributed to the computer/IT/telecommunications sector which perceived higher benefits as determined by its highest overall ranking of 29.9. Follow up Mann-Whitney U tests were undertaken to investigate the significance of differences between the sectors. Businesses in the computer/IT/telecommunications sectors perceived more benefits than those in the manufacturing/

construction sector and the business/banking/financial sector, suggesting that the computer/IT/telecommunications sector has a significantly different perception of the benefits to their public image and reputation compared with other businesses. This difference is evident in   2.3 where 88% of the computer/IT/telecommunications sector report links which provide very beneficial advantages for their public image and reputation. This may be because the New Zealand computer/IT industry is currently lobbying the government for digital technology to be included in the national education curriculum (Parata, 2016). It also reflects the manufacturing and construction sector's insecurity about how to safely engage with schools, for example during on-site visits, or through the provision of pupil work experience. (Flynn et al. 2016).

Forming networks with the community

Visibility and community goodwill is anticipated as a benefit of many industry-school partnerships (Hoff, 2002). A Kruskal Wallis test revealed a significant difference across the four industry sectors $\chi^2 (3,40) = 12.528, p = 0.006$ in the perceived benefits to businesses of forming networks within the community. Businesses that belonged to the computer/IT/telecommunications sector and the educational/governmental sector both reported higher perceived benefits than the other industries. Follow up Mann Whitney U tests were conducted between the different sectors, applying Bonferroni adjustment to the alpha value ($p < 0.008$). Businesses in the computer/IT/telecommunications sector were more positive in their perception of the benefits of forming community networks than those in the manufacturing/construction sector and from businesses in the business/trade/banking/financial sector. These differences are evident in Table 2.3, where 88% of the computer/IT/telecommunications sector believed that linking with schools provided very beneficial advantages through forming networks in the community.

Table 2.3 Perceived benefits to business image/reputation across different industry sectors

How beneficial is it for your organisation's reputation/image to link with schools?

Industry sector	Not beneficial	Limited benefits	Some benefits	Beneficial	Very beneficial
Manufacturing/ construction	0%	11%	22%	45%	22%
Computing/IT/ telecommunications	0%	0%	0%	12%	88%
Business/banking/ financial	0%	6%	6%	63%	25%
Education/government	0%		14%	29%	57%
Total	0%	**5%**	**10%**	**42%**	**43%**

Industry advertising and benefits to personnel

Kruskal Wallis tests revealed no significant difference in the perceived benefits to the advertising of a business across the four industry sectors, χ^2 (3, 40) = 2.203, $p = 0.532$, and no significant difference between the industries' perception of benefits to their employees as a result of school partnership, χ^2 (3, 40) = 5.292, $p = 0.152$. Nor were differences identified between the different sectors in the perceived benefits for their employees' public speaking and communications levels, χ^2 (3, 40) = 3.653, $p = 0.301$, and employees' teamwork skills, χ^2 (3, 40) = 4.106, $p = 0.250$.

Discussion

The following discussion utilises the above findings to provide guidance for schools and businesses specific to each sector.

Industry sectors

Almost 23% of the participants represented the manufacturing and construction sector. Industries in this sector linked with a small number of schools (generally 1–9 schools) which were either primary or secondary, but never both. This may be because this sector developed fewer, but possibly closer relationships, with schools. This would enable them to establish safe workplace health and safety practices in order to specialise and support either primary or secondary more effectively.

It is worth noting that 89% of the manufacturing/construction businesses surveyed made donations and 67% supported visits (as shown in Table 2.4) whilst they were the only sector to foster workplace observations. This would suggest that schools wishing to source donations, visits or workplace observations should approach this sector. On the other hand, this sector felt they

Table 2.4 Perceived benefits to businesses from forming networks in the community across different industry sectors

How beneficial is it for your organisation to form networks within the community?

Industry sector	Not beneficial	Limited benefits	Some benefits	Beneficial	Very beneficial
Manufacturing/ construction	11%	0%	11%	67%	11%
Computing/IT/ telecommunications	0%	0%	0%	12%	88%
Business/banking/ financial	12%	6%	19%	38%	25%
Education/government	0%	0%	14%	14%	72%
Total	**7%**	**3%**	**13%**	**35%**	**42%**

gained less than other industry sectors (in terms of image and reputation, forming networks and advertising). In order to sustain long-term partnerships with industries from this sector, schools would need to be aware of these views and either ensure the industry is cognisant of all promotion undertaken by the school or ensure the business receives other benefits such as access to the school facilities and personnel or display material generated by students. If the governing board of the school is willing to promote the business as a way of 'giving back', the school could include an explanation and acknowledgement of the contribution made by the business in copies of class and school newsletters and parent information sheets which could also be sent to the business; alternatively, at the end of the year key personnel of the business-partnership could be invited to attend the school final assembly where their valuable contribution to the school would be acknowledged. Schools would also need to identify the amount of contact and interaction which was possible and desired by the industry, as many in this sector had minimal (annual) contact with schools. Whether this was because of an existing partnership arrangement, or the preference of the school or industry, is unclear. In contrast a number of manufacturing and construction industries maintained regular weekly contact. The reason for the difference between these two groups is not clear. To ensure the industry is not overwhelmed, the school would need to carefully plan the type, method and frequency of interactions.

The business, trade, banking and finance sector was the largest represented in this study. Nearly 69% of the school interactions in this industry sector were with secondary schools, with the majority (75%) of these interactions occurring on a monthly basis. Nearly 88% of this sector linked with less than fifty schools and commonly offered mentoring, visits, support with mini-enterprises and work placements (as shown in Table 2.4). Despite its strong representation in the survey, this was the least positive sector with regards to recommending school partnerships to others in the industry. For this reason it is advised that considerable effort is placed on ensuring the partnership is mutually beneficial. As responses were not detailed, further research is required to determine probable causes for this less positive view.

The education and government sector was the least represented (17.5%) amongst participants. This sector generally did not offer donations, workplace observations or teacher or work placements. However, for schools requiring support with mentoring, mini-enterprise, community projects, employee visits, problem solving or curriculum development, this may be the best sector to approach (as shown in Table 2.4). Representatives of this sector believed community networks were very beneficial, so approaching this sector could be the cheapest and quickest way to ensure mutual benefits are obtained. The education and government sector was also very supportive of partnerships with primary schools, and nearly 86% of interactions occurred on a weekly or monthly basis. National statistics identify that 23% of this sector perceived that they are hampered by government regulations (Statistics New Zealand, 2011). Schools could therefore be well advised to try to eliminate the need for time-consuming paperwork and red tape involved in the partnership.

One fifth of the participants represented the computing/IT/telecommunications sector, with many of these linking with large numbers of schools (25% linked with over 100 schools). This sector supported schools in many ways such as mentoring, mini-enterprises, providing products and services and donations, as well as supporting visits and community projects (as shown in Table 2.4). The sector tended to link with secondary schools, or both secondary and primary schools, but not solely primary schools. Industries that belonged to this sector perceived significantly greater benefits to business image and reputation, as well as forming networks within the community, compared to industries in other sectors. This may be partially attributed to recent changes in computing in New Zealand high schools in order to clarify the notion of computer science. A New Zealand study suggested that these perceptions could have changed as a result of high levels of support from industry organisations (Bell et al. 2012). This active engagement could explain why this sector perceived greater benefits to its image and to forming networks with the community than industries in other sectors.

A study undertaken by the New Zealand Education Review Office (ERO) in 1996 explored potential benefits (both tangible and intangible) to businesses. "Building a good reputation within the society" was listed under the intangible benefits. Tangible benefits to businesses from linking with schools included building a positive image through their contribution to the local community (Ministry of Education, 1993), although 'enhanced public relations' has proven very difficult to quantify (Figgis, 1998). All fifty-nine businesses in the Figgis' (1998) study, however, believed that business-school links were a cost-effective way of gaining the respect of their community, as did those in the New Zealand study.

Overall these findings are very encouraging and identify that all industry sectors surveyed were willing to support schools. Approximately 95% of the survey participants were willing to encourage other industries to form similar industry-school partnerships. This finding, however, cannot be generalised to all industries as it may be the result of the specificity of the sampling group and/ or the small sampling size, all participants being part of an email list of industries with established relationships with schools. Schools also need to recognise that they may gain more from the partnership than the industries (Education Review Office, 1996). Being aware of the need for reciprocity and keeping in mind the possible benefits to the industry can help ensure the relationship is symbiotic rather than parasitic, where both parties feel they have gained, thus increasing the chance of a sustained partnership.

This research highlights the need for further investigation into the associated benefits, the number of school partnerships and the reasons for each sector's linking with schools.

Conclusion

The results and discussion section has focussed on each industry sector. In this way it is anticipated that industries can easily see key findings and recommendations pertinent to their sector. Some of these industries may be in close proximity to schools keen to establish mutually beneficial and sustainable partnerships. The research also enables schools to identify which is the most suitable sector to approach for their specific needs, as well as highlighting which benefits need to be fostered by each sector to ensure long-term partnerships. This research also highlights the need for initial dialogue between school and business representatives in order to set objectives, define a programme of activities, nominate personnel to take responsibility for the activities, monitor outcomes and evaluate efficacy of programmes and areas for further development.

There are clear differences between the industry sectors, both in the types and frequency of industry-school interactions as well as the benefits each sector gains. A school that recognises these differences may more confidently anticipate favourable results by targeting approaches for partnerships to those sectors more likely to see the benefits. If schools are aware of the perceived benefits for the industry sector, they can place time and energy into ensuring these aspects of the partnership occur. Future research needs to be undertaken to determine how schools can ensure that industry receives value from the partnership. Whilst some benefits are a naturally occurring by-product of the partnership, there could be others that would result from better knowledge of the requirements of the industry. A longstanding (sustainable) partnership between school and industry should be a win-win for all parties, not just a charitable exercise on behalf of the business. The old adage applies: "There is no such thing as a free lunch", but a shared lunch can be a treat for everyone.

References

Ainley, P. (1990). *Training turns to enterprise: Vocational education in the market place*. London: Tufnell.

Barza, L. (2013). School-business partnerships: The case of the UAE. *Journal of Strategy and Management* 6: 180–189.

Beckett, A. (2009). *When the lights went out. Britain in the 1970s*. London: Faber & Faber.

Bell, T., Andreae, P. and Robins, A. (2012). *Computer science in NZ high schools: The first year of the new standards*. Proceedings of the 43rd ACM technical symposium on computer science education, New York, NY: ACM: 343–348.

Blank, M., Melaville, A. and Shah, B. (2003). *Making a difference: Research and practice in community schools* [online]. Washington, DC: Coalition for Community Schools. Available from: www.communityschools.org/assets/1/page/ccsfullreport.pdf [accessed October 2nd 2017].

Breen, J. (2004). Enterprise, entrepreneurship and small business: Where are the boundaries?. *International Journal of Entrepreneurship and Small Business* 1: 21–34.

Burge, B., Wilson, R. and Smith-Crallan, K. (2012). *Employer involvement in schools: A rapid review of UK and international evidence*. Slough: National Foundation for Educational Research.

Carroll, A. and Shabana, K. (2010). The business case for corporate social responsibility: a review of concepts, research and practice. *International Journal of Management Reviews* 12(1): 85–105. doi:10.1111/j.1468-2370.2009.00275.x.

Davidson, C. and Tolich, M. (2003). *Social science research in New Zealand: Many paths to understanding*. Prentice Hall, NZ: Pearson.

Davies, D. (2002a). The 10th school revisited: Are school/family/community partnerships on the reform agenda now?. *Phi Delta Kappan* 83: 388–392.

Davies, H. (2002b). *A review of enterprise and the economy in education*. Norwich: HMSO.

Department for Children, S.A.F. (2008). *Building stronger partnerships: Schools, colleges and children's and families' services: How employers can support you*. Nottingham: DCSF publications.

Dillenburg, S., Greene, T. and Erekson, H. (2003). Approaching socially responsible investment with a comprehensive ratings scheme: Total social impact. *Journal of Business Ethics* 43: 167.

Dodd, S. and Hynes, B. (2011). The impact of regional entrepreneurial contexts upon enterprise education. *Entrepreneurship & Regional Development: An International Journal* 24: 741–766.

Education Review Office. (1996). *School-business links*. Available from: www.ero.govt.nz/ero/publishing.nsf/print/school-business links [accessed April 20th 2009].

Ehlen, C., van der Klink, M. and Boshuizen, H. (2015). Unravelling the social dynamics of an industry – school partnership: Social capital as perspective for co-creation. Studies in continuing education; 1–25.

Figgis, J. (1998). *Benefits to business through school-industry partnerships*. Surry Hills: Dusseldorf Skills Forum.

Flynn, M., Pillay, H. and Watters, J. (2016). Industry – school partnerships: Boundary crossing to enable school to work transitions. *Journal of Education and Work* 29: 309–331.

The Guardian. (1963). *Wilson outlines his plans for 'new age'* [online]. The Guardian. Available from: www.theguardian.com/politics/2001/sep/19/labourconference.labour5 [accessed February 20th 2014].

Harreveld, B. and Singh, M. (2009). Contextualising learning at the education-training-work interface. *Education and Training* 51: 92–107.

Harris, L. and Brown, G. (2010). Mixing interview and questionnaire methods: Practical problems in aligning data. *Practical assessment, Research and Evaluation* 15: 1–19.

Henriques, A. and Richardson, J. (eds.). (2004). *The triple bottom line does it all add up? Assessing the sustainability of business and CSR*. London: Earthscan.

Hoeckel, K. and Schwartz, R. (2010). *Learning for jobs: OECD reviews of vocational education and training*. Austria: Organisation for Economic Co-operation and Development.

Hoff, D. (2002). School-business partnerships: It's the schools' turn to raise the grade! *School Community Journal* 12: 63–78.

Huddleston, P. and Stanley, J. eds. (2012). *Work-related teaching and learning: A guide for teachers and practitioners*. Abingdon: Routledge.

Large, S. (1997). Business sponsorship in British schools. *Business Ethics a European Review* 6: 189–194.

Lee, K. (2007). So what is the 'triple bottom line? *The International Journal of Diversity in Organisations, Communities and Nations* 6: 67–72.

Lonsdale, M., Deery, A., Clerke, S., Anderson, M., Curtin, E., Knight, P. and Bramich, M. (2011). *The benefits of school – business relationships. For: Department of Education, E. A. W. R.* Sydney: Australian Council for Educational Research.

Mann, A., and Dawkins, J. (2014). *Employer engagement in education*. Retrieved from: www.educationandemployers.org/research/taskforce-publications/teacher-and-pupil-voices-on-employer-engagement

Mann, A., Lopez, D. and Stanley, J. (2010). *What is to be gained through partnership?: Exploring the value of education-employer relationships*. 2nd ed. London: Education and Employers Taskforce.

Mclarty, L., Highley, H. and Alderson, S. (2010). *Evaluation of enterprise education in England*. London: Department of Education.

Ministry for the Environment. (2003). *Towards a triple bottom line: A report on our environmental and social performance*. Wellington: Ministry for the Environment.

Ministry of Education. (1993). *Working together: Building partnerships between schools and enterprises*. Wellington, NZ: Learning Media.

Monaghan, P. (2004). Put up or shut up, in Henriques, A. and Richardson, J. (eds.), *The triple bottom line does it all add up? Assessing the sustainability of business and CSR*. London: Earthscan.

Parata, H. (2016). *NZ curriculum to include digital technology* [online]. Wellington: New Zealand government. Available from: www.beehive.govt.nz/release/nz-curriculum-include-digital-technology [accessed October 10th 2016].

Phillips, K. (2010). *Unfolding opportunities: A baseline study of school business relationships in Australia*. Appendices to the final report. Appendix six- examples of school business relationships. Canberra: Department of Education, Employment and Workplace Relations.

Porritt, J. (2004). Locating the government's bottom line, in Henriques, A. and Richardson, J. (eds.), *The triple bottom line does it all add up? Assessing the sustainability of business and CSR*. London: Earthscan.

Rodriguez, R., Warmerdam, J. and Triomphe, C. (2010). *The Lisbon strategy 2000–2010: An analysis and evaluation of the methods used and results achieved*. Final report. Brussels: European Parliament, Directorate General for Internal Policies.

Sanders, M. (2003). Community involvement in schools from concept to practice. *Education and Urban Society* 35: 161–180.

Sanford. (2006). *Sanford: Triple bottom line report 2000/2001* [online]. Available from: www.sanford.co.nz [accessed January 20th 2006].

Sanford. (2009). *Sanford: Social sustainability* [online]. Available from: file:///users/klee171/desktop/international/data/sustainable-development-report-2009-published-16-december-2009.pdf [accessed September 28th 2017].

Sanford. (2013). *Sustainable development report 2013: From sea to food* [online]. Available from: file:///users/klee171/desktop/international/data/susatainable_development_report_2013_-_published_4_december_2013.pdf.pdf [accessed September 28th 2017].

Sanford. (2016). *Sustainable development report 2016: Uncompromising* [online]. Available from: file:///users/klee171/desktop/international/data/sanford-2016-annual-report-printed.pdf [accessed September 28th 2017].

Sheldon, S. (2007). Improving student attendance with school, family, and community partnerships. *The Journal of Educational Research* 100: 267–275.

Sheldon, S. and Epstein, J. (2002). Improving student behavior and school discipline with family and community involvement. *Education and Urban Society* 35: 4–26.

Statistics New Zealand. (2011). *Innovation in New Zealand: 2011* [online]. Wellington, NZ: New Zealand Government. Available from: www.stats.govt.nz/browse_for_stats/businesses/business_growth_and_innovation/innovation-in-new-zealand-2011.aspx [accessed February 14th 2014].

Statistics New Zealand. (2013). *New Zealand business demography statistics: At February 2013* [online]. Wellington, NZ: New Zealand Government. Available from: www.stats.govt. nz/browse_for_stats/businesses/business_characteristics/businessdemographystatistics_ hotpfeb13.aspx [accessed February 14th 2014].

Storper, M. and Venables, A. (2004). Buzz: Face-to-face contact and the urban economy. *Journal of Economic Geography* 4: 351–370.

Symonds, W., Schwartz, R. and Ferguson, R. (2011). *Pathways to prosperity: Meeting the challenge of preparing young Americans*. Cambridge, MA: Pathways to Prosperity Project at Harvard Graduate School of Education.

Chapter 3

Who is getting prepared?

Year 11 students' views on careers education and work experience in English secondary schools

Julie Moote and Louise Archer

As of 2017, securing independent careers advice for *all* pupils remains a statutory requirement for secondary schools in England while work experience is strongly encouraged but not mandatory. However, recent years have seen substantive changes to state funding and provision available to deliver these duties. In 2011, national funding for Connexions centres and Education Business Partnership Organisations, which had provided careers services and work experience placements to state schools, was terminated. Since then, widespread concern has been voiced regarding the consistency of provision as schools have struggled to meet the new requirements without additional, dedicated funding. Against this background, this chapter explores what careers education and work experience is being provided to students, from the student perspective.

It has been argued that the skills necessary to navigate transitions from education into work have never been so daunting or more valuable (Hooley et al. 2015; NCC, 2013). Indeed, it could be contended that young people have to navigate highly complex pathways through post-compulsory education, work and training, with a proliferation of choices and options offered by the 14–19 education system (Acquah et al. 2016), all while rapid technological advancements and social change are drastically transforming the labour market (Hooley et al. 2015; Independent Skills Taskforce, 2014; Mann and Huddleston, 2016). Work experience and careers education have been identified as key mechanisms for helping young people to develop the requisite knowledge and skills needed to enable them to plan and manage their lifelong career journeys beginning with transitions from education into initial employment (e.g. Moon et al. 2004; UKCES, 2009). Careers education and work experience have, moreover, been proposed as a means for improving the efficiency of education and helping to ensure an appropriately matched supply of young people to meet labour market needs (Palladino Schultheiss, 2005; OECD, 2004). Evidence suggests that careers education can result in a range of wider positive outcomes, such as promoting motivation and positive attitudes towards school learning enhanced self-awareness, clarifying career aspirations and reducing the proportion of young people becoming NEET (AIR UK, 2008; Hughes et al. 2016). Indeed, it has been suggested that careers education and employer engagement might be useful tools for promoting social equity (Archer et al. 2014) and are key for social mobility (Hutchinson, 2012; Mann et al. 2014; Deloitte 2010; OECD, 2004). For instance, research evidence suggests that when students have been exposed to substantial careers education from a young age, they are more likely to express broader career expectations and aspirations and are less likely to be constrained by societal and/or familial pressures to make early career compromises (Welde et al. 2016). In the same way, work experience has been proposed as a means to improve students' understanding of career opportunities and clarify aspirations through providing first-hand encounters with potential occupational futures (CBI, 2007; NCC, 2013).

However, despite the widespread hopes and promises regarding the potential of careers education and work experience, evidence suggests that, in practice, the benefits may be under-realised and failing to reach those most in need. For instance, research suggests that students in England from disadvantaged backgrounds may be getting 'lost' in the system from as young as 13 (DfE 2015, 2017). In particular, concerns in England have focused on how the termination of dedicated national funding and transferral of responsibility onto schools and teachers to deliver careers education and facilitate work experience under the Coalition government of 2010–15 has led to a decline in the quantity *and* quality (Acquah et al. 2016).

Equality within careers education and work experience

A wealth of evidence exists, showing that young people's aspirations and educational/occupational choices are patterned by ethnicity, gender, and social class (e.g. Archer et al. 2010). For example, research has documented how young people from Black and minority ethnic backgrounds are more likely to express aspirations for particular career routes (Archer et al. 2015; Hutchinson et al. 2011), often following 'safe', pragmatic routes into 'known' areas of employment as a way to mitigate wider inequalities (e.g. Archer and Francis, 2007). According to the UK Equal Opportunities Commission, 41% of pay gap differences can also be attributed to gendered patterns of career choice – although research also shows the complex mixture of factors that combine together to produce stereotypical patterns of aspiration (e.g. Francis, 2000). For instance, biases have been noted within career guidance practices and materials in relation to gender (Lufkin et al. 2007) and within teachers' and careers advisors' expectations for different communities of students, by ethnicity, class and gender (e.g. Archer and Francis, 2007; Archer et al. 2010). Uncertainty and unrealism in career aspirations and expectations, moreover, are both more widespread and more detrimental for those from poorer backgrounds (Yates et al. 2011). While students' educational and occupational choices may be broadly patterned according to social demographics, they are not fixed or determined by young people's backgrounds (Hutchinson, 2012). For instance, students' aspirations and decisions can be influenced by their experiences at home and school, exposure to employment through work experiences, encouragement from significant adults, or through planned career support activities (Archer et al. 2012; Blenkinsop et al. 2006; Mujtaba and Reiss, 2014).

As Richardson (1993) discusses, equality and diversity issues have not always been sufficiently acknowledged within the careers development literature. Indeed, some have argued that education and policy literature does not consider the 'dark side' of career education and employer engagement – its potential for reinforcing and reproducing social inequalities and/or encouraging the status quo instead of being drivers of social change and reform (e.g. Sultana, 2013). Moreover, while studies investigating students' experiences of and perspectives on careers education and work experience are growing in number (e.g. City and Guilds, 2013; Hutchinson, 2011), several of the high profile surveys and reports draw disproportionately on school leaders' and professionals' perceptions of provision (DfE, 2017; CDI, 2015; Mann, 2012). Hence in this chapter, we build on our previous work (Moote and Archer, 2017) to examine perceptions of the provision of careers information, advice and guidance and work experience expressed by Year 11 (aged 15/16) students, with a particular focus on how these experiences and views are shaped by social class, ethnicity and gender. In particular, we ask: which groups of students are reporting careers advice and work experience and how satisfied are students with the current provision? We adopt Hutchinson's (2013) conceptualisation of career-related learning, which comprises three parts: career education (including self-development, exploration and management); work-related learning (about types of work, developing skills *for* and *through* work); and careers information, advice and guidance (CIAG). The chapter focuses on the work-related learning and CIAG aspects of career-related learning and draws on a unique dataset to document current teenage perceptions held of CIAG provision and work experience in England. The findings illustrate the role of wider social contexts in shaping opportunities for employer engagement and career support. They show that young people might benefit from an extended period of more intensive support and exploration in their career choices which begins earlier, is more extensive and involves sustained work experience and careers education.

Methods

The ASPIRES 2 project is a 5-year longitudinal study funded by the UK's Economic and Social Research Council. It follows on from the initial ASPIRES study, which investigated children's science and career aspirations from age 10–14, with the present study extending the tracking of this cohort from 14–19 years old. The overall project employs a mixed methods approach in order to generate both a breadth and depth of data. This chapter reports on the first phase of the ASPIRES 2 study, which includes a survey and interviews with students age 15/16 years old (Year 11/Y11) with a particular focus on a subset of quantitative survey data gathered during the first phase of this 5-year study.

Survey overview and recruitment

A questionnaire exploring students' aspirations and science attitudes (DeWitt et al. 2011) was revised, validated and piloted with 532 students before being administered to a national sample of over 14,000 15-year-old students in Autumn 2014. Following data cleansing, 13,421 students remained in the sample for analysis. This sample was roughly proportional to the overall national distribution of schools in England by region, school type, attainment and free school meals (as a measure of socioeconomic status). See Moote and Archer (2017) for a detailed description of samples. A similar survey was also administered to a national cohort of 8,000 17-year-old (Year 13/Y13) students in Autumn 2016.

Of the 13,421 students, 46.7% were boys and 53.3% were girls. Among these students, 1,488 (11.1%) attended independent schools and 11,933 (88.9%) attended state schools. Ethnicities included: 75.9% White students, 9.7% South Asian (Indian, Pakistani, Bangladeshi heritage), 3.7% Black (Black African, Black Caribbean heritage), 1.5% Chinese or East Asian, .9% Middle Eastern, 4.8% mixed or other, and 3.4% preferred not to say. Parental occupation data was gathered on the survey as a broad indicator of social class, and students were assigned to the highest social class indicated by occupation (of either parent). Students came from a range of social class backgrounds, with 49.0% of students reporting having a parent in a professional or managerial occupation, 28.1% in a skilled occupation, 11.2% in a semi-skilled or unskilled occupation and 6.1% in some other job. Additionally, 5.7% of students had parents who were homemakers, unemployed or had an unknown occupation. The survey also contained a measure of cultural capital which serves as an indication of social advantage and disadvantage (e.g. Bourdieu, 1984) with a scale of -4 through 9, calculated on responses to items about parental education, approximate number of books in the home and frequency of museum visitation. The scores were grouped into categories, with 5.7% of students indicating very low levels of cultural capital (-4 through -1.5), 32.1% with low levels (-1–1), 28.3% medium (1.5–3.5), 17.7% high levels (4–6) and 16.0% very high levels (6.5–9) of cultural capital. For further justification for this scoring methodology, please refer to Archer et al. (2015).

Analyses

This chapter reports on students' responses to the following survey questions: 'Have you been provided with any information from school or career services relating to the jobs you are interested in?' and 'Have you participated in any work experience relating to the jobs you are interested in?' with discreet answer options (yes, no and don't know). Students were also asked how satisfied (or not) they were with the careers education they had received. Descriptive cross-tabulation (chi-squared) analyses were conducted to explore the dataset and find basic relationships. Analyses of adjusted residuals were also performed with Bonferroni corrections (see Moote and Archer, 2017 for detailed procedures). It is important to be clear that in this chapter we do not assume that the set of background factors investigated *fully* explains the variation in careers information and work experience reporting, but simply that they may be among the reasons for different patterns of response. We also acknowledge the potential for interaction between the background factors investigated, i.e. the possibility of individual factors working together with, or being mediated by, other background factors (e.g. Collins, 1999).

Results

Being mindful of Hutchinson's conceptualisation of CAIG and work-related learning as comprising multiple elements, we begin by outlining the range of careers education experiences students in our interview sample reported. As described in Moote and Archer (2017), most students reported one-to-one advice and guidance and/or group careers talks and events. Students reported meetings with both internal and external advisors, some sessions involving completing careers questionnaires. Similar findings were reported at Y13 with support activities ranging from career talks at school, one-to-one sessions, careers lessons led by teachers, and careers questionnaires. Due to the nature of the interview protocol, for work-related learning, findings relate specifically to work experience with students mainly reporting short opportunities for work, generally one or two weeks long.

Year 11 survey results also showed that students who reported receiving careers education were significantly more likely to report being happy with the provision, while students who did not report careers education were significantly more likely to be dissatisfied (χ^2(8, n=13404)=2122.785, p<.001, Cramer's V=.281). This dissatisfaction was also reported at Y13 with fewer than half of the 8,000 students sampled reporting that the career support they received from school/college or career services informed what they want to do in their future education and career. In Y11 interviews, students who had work experience underlined the value of these placements, reporting that the experience allowed them opportunities to work hands on in the field, identify careers they did not want to pursue, develop confidence and make professional contacts. Of the Y13 survey students who went on placement in Y12 or Y13, almost 90% reported that it was a worthwhile experience. Results from Y11 interviews showed that work experience was organised more often by parents and families than by schools, meaning that students from socially advantaged families were more likely to be able to arrange 'quality' work experiences and placements. Several students felt discouraged as their work experience was completely unrelated to their career aspirations and 'boring'. In the following section, Y11 survey analyses are presented, showing the patterned nature of students' self-reported experiences of careers provision and work experience participation.

Who received careers information and participated in work experience?

Less than two thirds of all students, 3,794 (62.5%), reported receiving careers information and even fewer (44.8%) had participated in work experience by Year 11. These results are mirrored in qualitative data with less than half of Year 11 students reporting work experience. Patterns of low participation seem to continue as Y13 survey results show again that less than half of the students sampled reported work experience in Y12 and Y13. These findings contrast studies conducted prior to the 2011 reforms, which showed that the great majority of teenagers in England participating in work experience (e.g. Mann and Kashefpakdel, 2014). A closer look at the cross-tabulation results for the background factors investigated show several important differences in careers information reporting and work experience participation, which will be discussed in turn. Results are summarised in Table 3.1.

Gender

A chi-square test for independence indicated a significant association between gender and careers information provision, $\chi^2(2, n=13415) = 35.886$, p<.001, with Phi indicating a small effect (.052). In other words, the difference observed in students' reporting that they had been provided with careers information between males and females was found to be statistically significant, with female students significantly less likely to report such provision by their school (females=60.3%; males=65.0%). Similar results were found relating to work experience (females=43.8%; males=46.0%), however smaller effect sizes were reported. The survey results also showed that boys were significantly more likely to report satisfaction with the careers support they had received ($\chi^2[4, n=13407] = 42.764$, p<.001, Phi=.056). These findings are mirrored in our interview data with girls being more likely to report dissatisfaction with careers advisors and work experience placements. Preliminary analyses from our Year 13 survey also suggest that girls are less happy with careers and significantly less likely to report that the support informed what they want to do in the future.

Ethnicity

The chi-square test for independence indicated a significant association between ethnicity and careers information provision, $\chi^2(12, n=13415) = 102.490$, p<.001, with Cramer's V indicating a small effect (.062). White students were significantly more likely to report 'yes' (63.8%). Similar results for ethnicity were found

Table 3.1 Careers information and work experience reporting among students by background characteristics

Characteristic	Careers information provision			Total	Work experience participation		
	Yes	No	Don't know		Yes	No	Don't know
	N (%)	N (%)	N (%)	N	N (%)	N (%)	N (%)
Overall Sample	8383 (62.5)	3794 (28.3)	1238 (9.2)	13415	6015 (44.8)	6847 (51.0)	553 (4.1)
Gender							
Male	4071 (65.0)*	1621 (25.9)*	572 (9.1)	6264	2880 (46.0)*	3100 (49.5)*	284 (4.5)
Female	4312 (60.3)	2173 (30.4)	666 (9.3)	7151	3135 (43.8)	3747 (52.4)	269 (3.8)
Ethnicity							
White	6492 (63.8)*	2832 (27.8)	854 (8.4)*	10178	4655 (45.7)*	5165 (50.7)	358 (3.5)*
Black	299 (59.7)	148 (29.5)	54 (10.8)	501	207 (41.3)	261 (52.1)	33 (6.6)
Asian	798 (61.1)	382 (29.3)	126 (9.7)	1306	543 (41.6)	686 (52.5)	77 (5.9)
Chinese	115 (56.1)	58 (28.3)	32 (15.6)*	205	74 (36.1)	118 (57.6)	13 (6.3)
Middle Eastern	71 (58.2)	30 (24.6)	21 (17.2)*	122	47 (38.5)	63 (51.6)	12 (9.8)
Other/mixed	376 (58.1)	209 (32.3)	62 (9.6)	647	292 (45.1)	336 (51.9)	19 (2.9)
Prefer not	232 (50.9)*	135 (29.6)	89 (19.5)*	456	197 (43.2)	218 (47.8)	41 (9.0)*
Cultural Capital							
Very low	407 (52.9)*	244 (31.7)	118 (15.3)*	769	314 (40.8)	385 (50.1)	70 (9.1)*
Low	2646 (61.4)	1194 (27.7)	470 (10.9)	4310	1928 (44.7)	2182 (50.6)	200 (4.6)
Medium	2408 (63.4)	1082 (28.5)	311 (8.2)	3801	1770 (46.6)	1897 (49.9)	134 (3.5)
High	1481 (62.2)	713 (29.9)	187 (7.9)	2381	1048 (44.0)	1253 (52.6)	80 (3.4)
Very high	1441 (66.9)*	561 (26.0)	152 (7.1)*	2154	955 (44.3)	1130 (52.5)	69 (3.2)
Post-16 Plans							
Full-time work	263 (51.8)*	170 (33.5)	75 (14.8)*	508	232 (45.7)	242 (47.6)	34 (6.7)
Part-time work	751 (58.4)*	402 (31.3)	132 (10.3)	1285	615 (47.9)	614 (47.8)	56 (4.4)
Apprenticeship	945 (65.1)	366 (25.2)	141 (9.7)	1452	788 (54.3)*	598 (41.2)	66 (4.5)
A-levels	5926 (64.4)*	2574 (28.0)	707 (7.7)*	9207	3985 (43.3)*	4930 (53.5)*	292 (3.2)*
Don't know	497 (51.9)*	279 (29.2)	181 (18.9)*	957	392 (41.0)	461 (48.2)	104 (10.9)*

* Indicates significance of the adjusted residual analyses at the Bonferroni corrected alpha level to control for multiple tests

relating to work experience; however, only one cell reached significance at adjusted alpha level. As with careers information provision, White students were significantly more likely (45.7%) to report work experience (Black=41.3%, Asian=41.6%, Chinese= 36.1%, Middle Eastern=38.5%).

Cultural capital

Results showed a statistically significant relationship between careers information reporting and cultural capital, $\chi^2(8, n=13415) = 93.893, p<.001$, Cramer's V=.059 (indicating a small effect for a large table). Post hoc analysis investigating adjusted residuals showed that students from advantaged social backgrounds (with very high levels of cultural capital) reported receiving career education significantly more than expected (cultural capital very high=66.9%, cultural capital high=62.2%), while students from less advantaged backgrounds (with very low cultural capital) reported receiving careers education significantly less (52.9%). Students in the very low cultural capital group were also significantly more likely to report being dissatisfied with the provision of career support ($\chi^2[16, n=13407] =98.113, p<.001$, Cramer's V=.043). For work experience, again only one cell reached significance after correcting for multiple tests. While not significant, students in the medium cultural capital group reported more work experience (46.6%) than the very low cultural capital group (40.8%). Results from our interview data also suggest that students from advantaged backgrounds were more likely to report placements organised by their parents and were less likely to report negative experiences.

Post-16 plans

The chi-square results also showed a significant association between post-16 plans and careers information receipt ($\chi^2[8, n=13409] =191.01, p<.001$, Cramer's V=.084). Survey results indicated that students planning to enrol in A–levels were significantly more likely to report receiving careers (64.4%), while students planning to pursue part-time work alongside further study were significantly less likely (58.4%). Students who were planning to enter full-time work or who were unsure of their post-16 plans were also significantly less likely to report receiving careers information (full-time=51.8%; don't know=51.9%). When these tests were repeated using the work experience data, while similar significant chi-square tests were reported, different trends emerged. Students intending on pursuing Apprenticeships (10.8% of the total Y11 sample) were significantly more likely than expected to report work experience (54.3%) while students pursuing A–levels were significantly less likely (43.3%). Less than half of students intending to pursue full-time work (48%) reported work experience. Students aspiring to science (42.7%) and law (41.6%) were the least likely to have had work experience while those aspiring to careers in the trades (56.2%), teaching (55.8%) or business (50.3%) were the most likely.

Discussion

Our findings provide insight into current career education and work experience provision in England from students' perspectives. Similar to the findings of Hutchinson (2013), the results document a variety of different forms of administration of career-related learning in England. Preliminary findings from our Year 13 data reported above suggest that this variety continues in later secondary years. The variety of support activities reported shows one of the impacts of shifting responsibility onto schools – national variations in provisions (Hutchinson et al. 2011). Our findings also provide a clearer picture of the types of support being offered, as reported by students, building on previous research conducted with school leadership and career professionals (CDI, 2015; Hutchinson, 2013).

Students often reported dissatisfaction with the work experience provided and complained that placements were often not well connected to their aspirations. Our interview findings also suggest that students from socially advantaged backgrounds may be more satisfied with their placements. This goes against current national guidelines that high quality, meaningful work experience opportunities should be provided for *all* students (DfE, 2015) and has also been reported elsewhere (Le Gallais and Hatcher, 2014). Recent findings have documented that, while students' career ambitions are the primary consideration when matching students to work experience placements, few schools/colleges are able to meet their aims due to difficulties including sourcing placements in certain employment sectors (DfE, 2017). The findings presented in this chapter further highlight the need for efforts to address this.

Students reported that schools are doing little to facilitate work placements, placing responsibility instead on families to use their connections. These findings have important implications for social mobility as such placements are heavily influenced by family social capital. A recent survey (DfE, 2017) found that, while the majority (88%) of schools/colleges administered work experience through a centralised system or a work experience coordinator, they took a largely student-led approach to actually setting up work experience. The DfE found that having supportive parents as well as good family connections facilitated this student-led approach. As discussed in our previous work (Moote and Archer, 2017), this self-referral system may be contributing to the patterned nature of provision and participation documented.

Does current provision meet statutory requirements?

In 2017, securing independent careers advice for *all* pupils remains a statutory requirement for secondary schools in England (whether following academic or technical curriculums). However, schools have struggled to meet new requirements without additional funding and widespread concern has been voiced (e.g. from Ofsted, the National Careers Council and the Education Select

Committee) regarding the consistency of provision (Hooley and Watts, 2011). The findings reported here provide reason for further concern, showing that less than two thirds of Year 11 students report receiving careers information. If accurate, these results suggest that schools may not be meeting the requirement to provide support and placements for *all* students. Likewise, while there is currently an expectation on schools to facilitate work experience (DfE, 2015; 2017), less than half the sample reported participating in such placements. Findings suggest that students largely hold positive perceptions of the benefits of work experience, yet it seems that many do not get to experience it in practice. These findings raise concerns given the wide array of positive student impacts of careers education and work experience discussed earlier (e.g. Hughes et al. 2016).

Previous findings (Moote and Archer, 2017) showed that there is a demand from students for more, better and earlier careers support, with analysis showing that students who reported receiving careers information were significantly more likely to report being happy with the provision. There is a real need for schools and policy makers to focus on improving access to these provisions. Quantitative results show, moreover, that students planning to enter work post-16, and those who did not know what they want to do post-16 (arguably two groups that need this support most) were significantly less likely to report having careers education and participating in work experience than their peers planning to stay in full-time education. An Ofsted survey conducted in 2013 similarly found that beyond CIAG often not being well coordinated, vocational training and apprenticeships were rarely promoted effectively in schools. Additionally, schools with sixth forms have been found to, at times, lack impartiality by encouraging young people to stay at the sixth form post-16, without informing them of other possible routes (Blenkinsop et al. 2006). It would be desirable, therefore, that more effort is dedicated to communicating the options and benefits of routes other than sixth form/university, including vocational options and apprenticeships (Vinson, 2014). While these results indicate that students intending to enrol in apprenticeships are more likely than expected to have had work experience, this is still relatively low (54.3%). This is particularly worrying if students are making/committing to training and career choices without having experience in their chosen field.

The patterned nature of careers information and work experience in England

Our data also highlights how certain groups are marginalised within the current careers information and work experience provision in England. For instance, boys reported significantly more support and placements than girls and were significantly more satisfied with the support they had received.

Ensuring that CIAG reaches female students in Year 11 is also essential considering that school transitions are particularly challenging for girls' self-perceptions (Symonds et al. 2014). Teachers and careers professionals must also be aware of potential gendered stereotypes relating to perceptions of ability as they play a role in fostering students' academic self-concepts, which can mediate career choice (e.g. Carlone, 2003). These judgements also extend to the home environment with research suggesting that gender preferences in parental aspirations emerge in late secondary school years, with parents expressing higher educational expectations for boys than girls (Bask et al. 2014).

These issues were also found to play out across social class and ethnicity, as results showed that students from less advantaged social backgrounds (with lower levels of cultural capital) received significantly less CIAG and work experience and reported being less satisfied with provision. Wider research has shown that students from socially disadvantaged backgrounds are more likely to attend schools that are less well-resourced and/or which have stretched resources (e.g. Caldas and Bankston, 1997). Qualitative data also showed that students from disadvantaged backgrounds seemed to be less likely to use self-referral models of careers provision (Moote and Archer, 2017) with several students from deprived backgrounds reporting difficulty in accessing services. It is argued that more needs to be done to ensure broader and more equitable provision.

In terms of ethnicity, White students were significantly more likely than minority ethnic students to report receiving careers information and work experience. As discussed in previous work (Moote and Archer, 2017), most students indicated in interview that they wanted and felt the need for more support to navigate the careers education system – this was especially the case for those from Black and South Asian backgrounds, who were more likely to report feeling 'scared' or 'unsure'. The need to acknowledge the potential for institutional racism and the present results raise questions around what might be putting off certain groups of students is also suggested.

Together, the results presented in this chapter show a complex picture of the interplay between several background factors, which contribute to a pattern of CIAG and work experience reporting that needs to be addressed. It is suggested, therefore, that an intersectional approach would be beneficial, to help further understand the finding that access, provision and uptake are structured/shaped by intersecting identities and inequalities (e.g. ethnicity, class and gender).

Recommendations for policy and practice

The present findings suggest that urgent attention needs to be given to acknowledging and redressing inequalities in terms of who is, and who is not, participating in careers education and work experience. Along with monitoring and ensuring that the provision reaches *all* students, school leaders could usefully develop equity agendas through performing equity audits looking at current access and availability of opportunities, encouraging teachers to actively adopt and advance an equity agenda and then together begin to address the processes that have reinforced the inequitable practices in schools and which are currently seen (Hamilton et al. 2015).

While the potential value of self-selecting/self-initiated resources is appreciated, data presented in this chapter is in line with the findings of Le Gallais and Hatcher (2014) and suggests that this structure may be contributing to the fragmented system of career provision and work experience in English secondary schools. Organisations should therefore take particular care with respect to schemes and opportunities that are offered on an 'opt in' basis to ensure that these do not contribute to the further reinforcement of patterns of unequal participation in careers education and work experience. This will have particular implications for various employer and related initiatives, often targeted at smaller or selected groups of students, or are offered just to those young people (or schools) who self-identify and/or express an interest (or as these results indicate, who have family connections to draw on). Through the recent debate about careers and employability discussed at the outset of this chapter, the focus has mainly been around career guidance professionals and employer engagement with teachers' roles often being overlooked (Hooley et al. 2015). The authors of this chapter agree with Hooley and colleagues who state that teachers should be at the heart of a long-term approach to improving careers support and work experience. This is especially the case as schools have primary responsibility to provide the support and considering the challenges of an 'overloaded curriculum'.

Conclusions

Careers education and work experience have the potential to be useful tools for promoting social equity and can be helpful for encouraging social mobility. Yet the findings presented in this chapter suggest the reality may be reproducing patterns of inequality. The chapter highlights a need for policy makers and practitioners to re-evaluate current provision and participation in England. Survey and interview findings suggest that some schools may not be meeting the requirement to provide impartial careers support for *all* students, or at least this provision is not *reaching* all students. Consequently, schools should be provided with dedicated resourcing to target, engage and support disadvantaged students, with the findings presented here suggesting that particular emphasis should be given to ensuring the participation of girls, minority ethnic students, working-class students, students in bottom sets and those who are unsure of their post-16 plans or who plan to leave education post-16. We also recommend that schools and organisations involved in delivery should monitor, evaluate and take steps to address inequalities in terms of which students do or do not access and participate in careers education and work experience.

References

Acquah, D.K., Limmer, H. and Malpass, D. (2016). 'I don't know where to find the careers adviser . . . he has disappeared': The impact of changes to careers advice on 14–16 year olds in University Technical Colleges and Schools. *Research Papers in Education*. Advance online publication. doi:10.1080/02671522.2016.1167234

AIR UK. (2008). *The involvement of business in education: A rapid evidence assessment of measureable impacts*. London: Department for Children, Schools and Family.

Archer, L., DeWitt, J., Osborne, J., Dillon, J., Willis, B. and Wong, B. (2010). 'Doing' science vs 'being' a scientist. *Science Education* 94(4), 617–639. doi: 10.1002/sce.20399.

Archer, L., DeWitt, J., Osborne, J., Dillon, J., Willis, B. and Wong, B. (2012). Science aspirations, capital, and family habitus: How families shape children's engagement and identification with Science. *American Educational Research Journal* 49(5): 881–908.

Archer, L., DeWitt, J. and Dillon, J. (2014). "It didn't really change my opinion": Exploring what works, what doesn't, and why in a school STEM careers intervention. Published online in *Research in Science and Technology Education*. doi: 10.1080/02635143.2013.865601.

Archer, L., Dawson, E., DeWitt, J., Seakins, A. and Wong, B. (2015). Science capital: A conceptual, methodological, and empirical argument for extending Bourdieusian notions of capital beyond the arts. *Journal of Research in Science Teaching* 52(7): 2–17.

Archer, L. and Francis, B. (2007). *Understanding minority ethnic achievement: Race, Gender, Class and "Success"*. London: Routledge.

Bask, M., Ferrer-Wreder, L., Salmela-Aro, K. and Bergman, L.R. (2014). Pathways to educational attainment in middle adulthood: The role of gender and parental educational expectations in adolescence, in Schoon, I. and Eccles, J.S. (eds.), *Gender differences in aspirations and attainment: A life course perspective*. Cambridge, MA: Cambridge University Press: 389–411.

Blenkinsop, S., McCrone, T., Wade, P. and Morris, M. (2006). *How do young people make choices at 14 and 16?*. Research Report 773. London: Department for Education and Skills.

Bourdieu, P. (1984). *Distinction: A social critique of the judgement of taste*. Cambridge, MA: Harvard University Press.

Caldas, J. and Bankston, C. (1997). Effect of school population socioeconomic status on individual academic achievement. *The Journal of Educational Research* 90(5): 269–277.

Carlone, H.B. (2003). (Re)producing good science students: Girls' participation in high school physics. *Journal of Women and Minorities in Science and Engineering* 9(1): 17–34.

CBI. (2007). *Time well spent: Embedding employability in work experience*. London: Confederation of British Industry.

CDI. (2015). *Survey of career education and guidance in schools and links with employers*. Stourbridge: Career Development Institute with Careers England.

City and Guilds. (2013). *Great expectations: Teenagers' career aspirations versus the reality of the UK jobs market*. EMSI.

Collins, P.H. (1999). Moving beyond gender: Intersectionality and scientific knowledge, in Marx Ferree, M., Lorber, J. and Hess, B. (eds.). *Revisioning gender*. CA: Sage Publications.

Deloitte. (2010). *Helping young people succeed - How employers can support careers education*. London: Education and Employers.

Department for Education. (2015). *Careers guidance and inspiration in schools: Statutory guidance for governing bodies, school leaders and school staff*. London: Department for Education.

Department for Education. (2017). *Work experience and related activities in schools and colleges*. London: Department for Education.

DeWitt, J., Osborne, J., Archer, L., Dillon, J., Willis, B. and. Wong, B. (2011). Young children's aspiration in science: The unequivocal, the uncertain and the unthinkable. *International Journal of Science Education* 35(6): 1037–1063.

Francis, B. (2000). The gendered subject: Students' subject preferences and discussions of gender and subject ability. *Oxford Review of Education* 26(1): 35–48.

Hamilton, A.F., Malin, J. and Hackman, D. (2015). Racial/Ethnic and gender equity patterns in Illinois high school career and technical education coursework. *Journal of Career and Technical Education* 30(1): 29–52.

Hooley, T. and Watts, A.G. (2011). *Careers work with young people: Collapse or transition?* Derby: International Centre for Guidance Studies, University of Derby.

Hooley, T., Watts, A.G. and Andrews, D. (2015). *Teachers and careers: The role of school teachers in delivering career and employability learning.* International Centre for Guidance Studies, University of Derby.

Hughes, D., Mann, A., Barnes, S.A., Baldauf, B. and McKeown, R. (2016). *Careers education: International literature review.* London: Education Endowment Foundation.

Hutchinson, J. (2011). Partnership, capital formation and equality and diversity: Learning from five case studies, in Barham, L. and Irving, B.A. (eds.), *Constructing the future. Diversity, inclusion and social justice.* Stourbridge: Institute of Career Guidance: 103–115.

Hutchinson, J. (2012). Career-related learning and science education: The changing landscape. *School Science Review* 94(346): 91–98.

Hutchinson, J. (2013). *School organisation and STEM career-related learning.* York: National STEM Centre.

Hutchinson, J., Rolfe, H., Moore, N., Bysshe, S. and Bentley, K. (2011). *All things being equal? Equality and diversity in careers education, information, advice and guidance.* Equality and Human Rights Commission.

Independent Skills Taskforce. (2014). *Qualifications matter: Improving the curriculum and assessment for all.* The third report of the independent Skills Taskforce. London: Labour Party.

Le Gallais, T. and Hatcher, R. (2014). How school work experience policies can widen student horizons or reproduce social inequality, in Mann, A., Stanley, J. and Archer, L. (eds.), *Employer engagement in education: Theories and evidence.* London: Routledge.

Lufkin, M., Wiberg, M., Jenkins, C., Lee Berardi, S., Beyer, T., Eardley, E. and Huss, J. (2007). Gender equity in career and technical education, in Klein, S.S. (ed.), *Handbook for achieving gender equity through education.* 2nd ed. Mahwah, NJ: Lawrence Erlbaum Associates: 421–443.

Mann, A. (2012). *Work experience: Impact and delivery – insights from the evidence.* London: Education and Employers Taskforce, UK Commission for Employment and Skills and Chartered Institute for Personnel and Development.

Mann, A. and Huddleston, P. (2016). Schools and the twenty-first century labour market: Perspectives on structural change. *British Journal of Guidance & Counselling* 45(2): 208–218.

Mann, A. and Kashefpakdel, E.T. (2014). The views of young Britons (aged 19–24) on their teenage experiences of school-mediated employer engagement, in Mann, Stanley, and Archer. (eds.), 2014. *Understanding Employer Engagement in Education: Theories and Evidence.* London: Routledge.

Moon, S., Lilley, R., Morgan, S., Gray, S. and Krechowiecka, I. (2004). A systematic review of recent research into the impact of careers education and guidance on transitions from key stage 3 to key stage 4 (1988–2003), in *Research Evidence in Education Library.* London: EPPI-Centre, Social Science Research Unit, Institute of Education, University of London.

Moote, J. and Archer, L. (2017). Failing to deliver? Exploring the current status of career education provision in England. *Research Papers in Education,* DOI: 10.1080/02671 522.2016.1271005

Mujtaba, T. and Reiss, M. (2014). A survey of psychological, motivational, family and perceptions of physics education factors that explain 15-year-old students' aspirations to study physics in post-compulsory English schools. *International Journal of Science and Mathematics Education* 12(2): 371–393.

NCC. (2013). *An aspirational nation: Creating a cultural change in careers provision.* England: National Careers Council.

OECD. (2004). *Career guidance and public policy: Bridging the gap.* Paris: Organisation for Economic Co-Operation and Development.

Ofsted. (2013) *Going in the right direction? Careers guidance in schools from September 2012.* Manchester: Office for Standards in Education.

Palladino Schultheiss, D.E. (2005). Elementary career intervention programs: Social action initiatives. *Journal of Career Development* 31(3): 185–194.

Richardson, M.S. (1993). Word in people's lives: A location for counselling psychologists. *Journal of Counseling Psychology* 40: 425–433.

Sultana, R.G. (2013). Career education: Past, present . . . But what prospects? *British Journal of Counselling* 41(1): 69–80. doi:10.1080/03069885.2012.739373

Symonds, J.E., Galton, M. and Hargreaves, L. (2014). Emerging gender differences in times of multiple transition, in I. Schoon, I and Eccles, J.S. (eds.), *Gender Differences in Aspirations and Attainment: A Life Course Perspective.* Cambridge, MA: Cambridge University Press: 101–122.

UKCES. (2009). *The employability challenge.* London: UK Commission for Employment and Skills.

Vinson, J. (2014). *Where is career advice going? The danger of personal bias in searching for the right path.* London: FE Week and ABC Awards. Available from: http://lsect.co.uk/where-is-careers-advise-going.pdf.

Welde, A.M.J., Bernes, K.B., Gunn, T.M. and Ross, S.A. (2016). Career education at the elementary school level: Student and intern teacher perspectives. *Journal of Career Development* 1–21.

Yates, S., Harris, A., Sabates, R. and Staff, J. (2011). Early occupational aspirations and fractured transitions: A study of entry into 'NEET' status in the UK. *Journal of Social Policy* 40(3): 513–534.

Chapter 4

Competences, capabilities and capitals

Conceptual paradigms in the educational-employment relationship

Michael Tomlinson

Employability and education policy

When schools and universities engage employers in the educational experiences they commonly do so to enhance the ultimate employment prospect of young people. This chapter explores three influential approaches to the analysis of the relationship between education and employment, broadly framed in terms of individuals' lifetime employability. These approaches, based on theories of competences, capabilities and capitals, have informed much thinking and discussion around individuals' relative employment outcomes. At one level, they provide an account of the relationship between education and the labour market in terms of the role of the former in shaping individuals' future employment. At another level, they offer an understanding of the relationship between individuals' agency and wider social structures in which employability-related experiences, actions and outcomes are located. From both perspectives, they present a theoretical lens through which episodes of employer engagement can be implicitly viewed.

In recent years, employees' progression in the labour market, and across most occupational strata, has commonly been framed in terms of a challenge for sustaining lifetime employability (Gazier, 1999; Clarke, 2008). This phenomenon is often associated with the decline of welfare-centred notions of full-term employment within single organisational locations and the advent of more individualised processes of career mobility. It emerges from the widely shared consensus that the labour market has changed in fundamental ways since the latter decades of the last century through the expansion of knowledge-service industries and digitalised modes of production, more fluid mobility of skilled labour across geo-political boundaries and an overall precariousness and intensification of work (Brown et al. 2011). Contemporary working life is increasingly conceived as moving relentlessly towards protean or self-managed career patterns whereby employees move more fluidly within and between labour markets and away from single organisations and specific jobs (Inkson et al. 2015). Whilst there is inevitable variance in the scale and direction of such developments, it is commonly accepted that employees' career mobility have become more complex and variegated, bringing with it the need to proactively manage the task of sustaining lifetime employment (Tomlinson, 2013).

This changing labour market context has had a significant bearing on the direction of educational policy. Governments across the OECD have looked to reform educational policies to meet the challenges presented by such change, largely under the remit of enriching the stock of human capital entering the labour market (Lauder et al. 2012). The alignment of education policy to increased economic demands and meeting the need of the knowledge economy while equipping learners with requisite skills has become a clear imperative amongst most national governments. In England, this is manifest in a number of economically-driven policy levers and developments (Woodin et al. 2013). These include the expansion of the post-compulsory sector, the raising of the age for compulsory participation in education or training age to eighteen, reform of vocational education, the massification and marketization of higher education, the introduction of tuition fees and the incorporation of skills-driven curricula.

Whilst economic, technological and political forces associated with employability may operate largely outside of formal educational institutions, their influence can be felt quite profoundly within. At the supply-side level, educational institutions are often enacted as key sites of labour market reproduction to be invested in and consumed in an increasingly market-driven environment. This now includes a diverse training market for vocational provision and a managed market within higher education. There has, moreover, been no shortage of skills-orientated policy frameworks over the last generation. In higher education, the Dearing report (1997) called upon universities to more actively develop graduates' employability skills in order for them to add value and secure favourable outcomes when in the labour market. Latterly, reports such as the Leitch review (2006) and Wolf Report (DfE, 2011) made an explicit connection between skills and economic prosperity, picturing raised qualifications as key indicators of enhanced skills levels.

At the demand-level, the contract between individuals and employers has shifted as individual employees are encouraged to view their career progression as an on-going personal and entrepreneurial project (Fenwick, 2003). However, often overlooked in debates around the role of education in enhancing individuals' employability are demand-side considerations relating to the ways in which individuals' potential, or job-entry, employability is then further realised by what employers offer in terms of training provision, workplace cultures and job design (Keep and Mayhew, 2010).

In spite of such noisy policy rhetoric, considerable ambiguity remains as to what constitutes an individual's employability, how this is manifested and played out in the labour market and the specific role played by education towards its enhancement. One of the central conceptual challenges in related discussions has been picking apart the distinctions between *employment* and *employability* (Holmes, 2013). The most obvious point of distinction is time-scale: individuals may be employable at job entry, but this does not necessarily predict longer-term job market outcomes or how their employability develops and is organisationally mediated. This in turn leads to a further distinction between what might be seen as process and outcome. If employability is understood principally as a formal and objective job-related outcome (for example, being in post after a finite time period), this leaves limited consideration of the processes – personal, social, institutional or otherwise – by which such outcomes are achieved. Three conceptual paradigms through which the problem of employability has been conceived – competencies, capabilities and capital – offer specific frameworks for understanding the problem of employability.

Competencies: employee functionality and the performance imperative

The concept of *competences* has been influential in explaining individuals' immediate labour market outcomes and has framed understandings of formal educational processes which potentially enhance learners' future employment outcomes. Competences are largely understood to be both supply-side driven and demand-orientated. The competences which educational institutions provide are seen to have a utility in the market, serving as productive resources in meeting economically efficient ends. Employee competences, sometimes defined more broadly in literature as *professional competences*, are developed within education and training contexts and then applied into workplaces in ways that enhance both individuals' and organisations' productive advantage (Mulder et al. 2009).

At an individual level, definitions of competences are often framed around the ways in which people draw upon formally or informally acquired learning which enables them to perform to, or exceed, demanded expectations in a work context. When considering what specifically constitutes competence at an individual level, attention has focused on individuals' functional capacities in terms of what an employee may be expected to execute towards the purposive end of fulfilling tangible job-related demands. Le Deist and Winterton (2005) have broken competences into three dominant categories: *functional, cognitive* and *social* competence. Functional competence is typically linked to technical performance and is oriented towards specific occupational tasks that enable the competence to be effectively executed. It is underpinned by broader sets of cognitive competences relating to individuals' knowledge (codified and tacit), conceptual understanding and other internal abilities which enable them to execute job-related tasks. Social competences are those which relate to the appropriate channelling of behaviours and attitudes towards desired outcomes. In attempting to fuse the different components of competence, these authors describe *meta-competences* which refer to not only the integration of cognitive, technical and social competences, but also the ability to access these and utilise them across multiple occupational domains.

The competence approach ascribes much significance to the role of formal learning in enhancing the levels of competences people can acquire and then utilise for productive benefit. This is largely based on the notion of learning as 'acquisition' (Hager and Hodkinson, 2009) whereby an individual internalises knowledge and technical understanding, which are applied to accomplish a range of specific occupational functions. In learning environments, curricula and pedagogies are largely transfer-based: the role of the learner is to acquire and reproduce technical knowledge applicable to a future workforce. This has also been influential on behavioural approaches to formal learning and assessment based on the logic that learners need to be directed towards the accomplishment of a 'learning outcome', often codified and manifested in a positive behavioural outcome. This approach has been strong within vocational education and training, linked to 'occupational standards' and the alignment of learning outcomes to occupational demands within a prescribed framework (Brockmann et al. 2008). Whilst this provides short-term outcomes which enables a learner to demonstrate set competencies, a criticism of this approach is that it does not readily equip learners with more holistic competences which are more broadly transferable across multiple domains.

Researchers such as Eraut (1998, 2007) have discussed how competences are largely socially mediated in terms of being derived from inter-organisational and inter-professional exchanges and being contained with often fluid professional spaces. This is what gives competences a clear context and organisational value. This is an important consideration given that competence is largely context-driven. At the organisational demand-level, competences can only genuinely be valued if they fulfil specified organizational problems and place genuine demands on the employee. Eraut highlights, for example, the importance of workplace cultures in framing and legitimising agreed competence-related behaviours which are largely channelled through social rather than purely technical occupational domains.

In focusing on the context in which competences are applied, appraised and given a clear cultural or occupational value, greater attention is given to demand-side characteristics rather than supply-side knowledge and skills developed within educational institutions. In adopting a demand-side, organisationally-rich account of competences, Lindberg and Rantatalo's (2016) explore the 'practice' dimensions of professional competence. Their research was based within the medical and police professions and focused on both managers' selection decisions and employees' initial career development and integration. They examined the ways in which judgements of competence were formed through the interactions between early career employees and significant others in the workplace. In this conceptual approach, competence becomes less about merely meeting objective criteria of job-specific demands, and instead is bound up in the symbolic and socio-cultural institutional constitution of a workplace. This entails interactions and relationship formations with significant others such as colleagues and managers who further mediate the enhancement and future deployment of competences. Thus, Lindberg and Rantatalo's research has illustrated how the performance and appraisal of employee competence is socially-orientated and largely based on the execution of appropriate behavioural competences within socially-rich occupational contexts.

Capabilities: functionings, value and enhanced human agency

A more recently discussed conceptual angle to employability, related to individuals' capacity to act in beneficial ways that add value to their employment experiences and outcomes, is the *capabilities* perspective associated with the work of Sen (1985, 1999; and Nussbaum, 2011). This departs from more functional approaches by placing closer attention on individuals' broadly conceived capacity for action towards the fulfilment of their personal potential. Capabilities are understood to embody broader ability sets than those which merely reference occupational demands. They are more than an extension of competences and instead embody sets of enabling dispositions which enhance people's scope for action and social engagement, and therefore, their overall social and economic functioning. The capabilities approach to personal and collective wellbeing also questions the assumption of classical economic growth models which explain employment outcomes as a function of educational attainment. Sen (1985) has disputed the premise that wellbeing and extended personal freedom are largely by-products of enhanced overall economic productivity. Rather, his account of capability, social and economic well being, including aspects related to the labour market, encompasses much more than an individual's ability to generate favourable economic returns.

In focusing on individuals' functional capabilities, attention is placed on the conversion of their potential or acquired capabilities to real and desirable outcomes in social and economic life. To Sen, individual capabilities constitute a set of *functionings*, defined as ways of acting and behaving that enable people to function freely and in ways which they have reason to value. Functionings are manifestations of individuals' acquired potentials. These range from the basic kind such as physical mobility and elementary reading to more complex forms, such as the formation of self-esteem and reflection or execution of advanced interpersonal negotiations. A significant dimension to *capability functionings* is people's capacity to choose and control the conditions around which they can act in desired or beneficial ways. The development of individual freedom, based on the fulfilment of outcomes that people have reason to value is central to the capability approach: without genuine freedom and choice capacity, capabilities may not necessarily have any effect on people's lives.

Capability functionings therefore require the genuine conversion of an individual's potential and acquired abilities to meaningful actions that enable them to function in significant areas of their lives, including the labour market. Thus, capabilities only function if they constitute a form which Sen (1999) has defined as *combined capabilities* – that is, the productively beneficial combination of internal capabilities and favourable social conditions that allow for the execution and further enhancement of people's potential internalised abilities. For example, internal capabilities which pertain to skills and knowledge such as a good working knowledge of ICT, need to be matched by conducive institutional conditions in order for individuals to become proficient and fully operable in that field. A person's aptitude for ICT remains a potential or partially fulfilled one, or indeed may become depreciated, unless there is a technological infrastructure that allows for its actual realisation.

The capability approach clearly has some salience for understanding employability and labour market integration. Whilst the approach does not establish an explicit hierarchical ordering of capabilities, it is clear that some set of capabilities functioning are likely to advantage individuals in economic life. Sen and Nussbaum have not made explicit references to the types of capability sets which have purchase in people's employment, arguing that capabilities should be seen in a holistic ways and not isolated to specific domains. However, a capability which emerges strongly is that of practical reason and judgement formation in terms of a person's informed choices and being able to take purposive measures towards fulfilling outcomes sought.

The analysis speaks to questions of agency and autonomy which are integral to people's ability to function and make both meaningful decisions and contributions. Agency is understood in the capabilities perspective as the enhanced scope for action or the capacity to choose multiple courses of action. The self-orchestration of one's life, including some discretionary control over one's career pathways, choice of employment and labour market outcomes is critical for enabling people to live the lives they choose to value. The exercising of agency to beneficial effect is reflected in enhanced decision-making and choices which, in the context of employment, can potentially result in economically productive outcomes. Motivation and choice are clearly interlinked in the capabilities approach, but one is often a precondition to the other. An individual may have choices, but these may be notional unless opportunities to pursue them are presented.

In terms of an individual's management of their employment outcomes and the enrichment of their employability, a distinction therefore emerges between choice and opportunity. People may have opportunities to pursue an employment pathway, but this is only meaningful if they are able to genuinely express the freedom of choice and possibility which their internal capabilities allow. The capabilities perspective consequently speaks to questions of value and values formation. The life of a school-leaver, graduate and early career professional extends well beyond the immediate career formation phases of the initial employment to include other life projects and goals. Accordingly, an individual's value, including the values they hold, is in no sense exclusively related to their economic capacity. Their abilities or potential to generate personal economic returns is only one value domain. Instead, individuals' capabilities encompass more holistic aspects of their development and personhood, including their capacity for reason, judgement and improved autonomy. Hence, if an individual values creativity or socially-orientated employment, then this becomes a guiding principle for their goals and actions.

Capitals – employability as resources, assets and dispositions

The final conceptual approach this chapter explores, one which has been used to explain individuals' relative opportunities and outcomes in the labour market, is the capital perspective. This approach has often been associated with the sociological work of Bourdieu (1986) and Coleman (1988), but also more recently been adapted by researchers with a more psycho-social orientation (Luthens et al. 2007. Capitals are often understood as key resources, accumulated through an individual's educational and social experiences, equipping them favourably when transitioning to, and integrating into, job markets. In Bourdieu's (1986) conceptualisation, the accumulation and deployment of capital confers advantages onto individuals, particularly when the value of one's capital is exchanged within an institutional setting, be that education or employment. Capitals can be derived from individuals' formal educational and socio-cultural experiences and impact on their subsequent educational and economic outcomes (Stanley and Mann, 2014).

Two forms of capital, *human* and *cultural*, have often been used to explain the relationship between education and labour market advantage and individuals' relative positioning within each life stage (Becker, 1993; Bourdieu, 1986). *Social capital* has also been applied when referring to relationships that further mobilise educationally-derived resources and credentials that help bridge relationships between educational and work contexts. Two newer forms have also emerged in recent analysis – *identity* and *psychological* capital – which conceptualise the ways in which people's relationships are further influenced by psychosocial resources and dispositions.

Many UK educational policy frameworks are underpinned by the logics of human capital theory: the raising of participation age, widening participation in Higher Education and more employability-focused curricula. Human capital is seen as the sum of individuals' educational knowledge and skills acquired through formal education and used for advantage in seeking employment (Becker, 1993. In short, higher levels of education and related qualifications represent a greater level of accumulated human capital which can be transferred to labour market. There are clear overlaps between human capital and competence approaches in explaining how formal educational experience can enhance labour market outcomes. Knowledge and skills acquired in formal education are both codified and embedded and adds to employees' productive capacity. The graduate, for example, is assumed to have access to employment that is not suited to a school-leaver because they have acquired exclusive knowledge which is better aligned to a specific professional field. The technical knowledge or hard skills which specific forms of education and training produce enable individuals to be more productive and command higher overall wage returns and labour market opportunities. Those not investing in additional forms of education are in possession of lower aggregate human capital which, in turn, potentially precludes them from entering employment which is seen to require higher overall technical knowledge as codified in qualifications.

There has been considerable criticism of the idea that enhanced educational knowledge and skills, on their own, can generate economic return and account for relative returns in the labour market. One of the main criticisms questions the presumed simple relationship between supply of education and its workplace demand. As critics have observed, a range of mediating factors influence this relationship, and the accumulation of human capital is only one contributory dimension (Keep and Mayhew, 2010; Lauder et al. 2012). Human capital on its own can only generate so much return, particularly in less certain and competitive labour market contexts when the relationship between educational supply and economic demand is less stable. More significantly, for human capital to influence employment outcomes, it needs to be socialised and mobilised through wider interactions and networks. Social capital theorists such as Coleman (1988) argue that social capital helps to mobilise human capital by creating a bridge between individuals' educational, social and labour market experiences and their access to job openings. The social ties possessed by school-leavers or graduates are potentially crucial in bringing them closer to targeted employment and therefore opening up opportunities.

Granovetter's (1973) concept of 'strong' and 'weak' ties helps make sense of the means by which social capital can mobilise human capital. Focusing on the level of strength of people's formal or informal connections and the quality and potential richness of these for equipping them for job market integration, Granovetter's work stresses strong ties on their own are not always influential, or can indeed be counter-advantageous (e.g. if family members have limited job market knowledge). Instead, the relatively thin spread of social connections and contacts, i.e. weak ties – for example, a wider span of significant other stakeholders such as emerging employer contacts – can be more influential. The accumulation of weak ties witnessed in dispersed social capital not only potentially enhances knowledge and information around job opportunities and how to access them, but also of the nature of jobs and what is needed to succeed in them.

Bourdieu used the concept of social capital somewhat differently from Coleman and Granovetter, emphasising the how social capital is further derived from existing socio-cultural experiences which individuals have relative access to. In order to establish and maintain ties, individuals need to acquire valued forms of cultural knowledge, behaviours and dispositions that make them attractive to employers: their *cultural capital*. In Bourdieu's conceptualising, cultural capital represents a body of culturally valued and embodied forms of knowledge and behaviours which is acquired through an individual's wider cultural milieu and then validated within educational and wider social field such as the labour market. Essentially, the more aligned someone's cultural capital is towards the culture of an employer organisation, the more advantageously it will equip then when trying to enter a given employment field. Whilst this concept is quite far-removed from the human capital approach, it similarly posits that higher levels of education advantage individuals in their future lives. This is because of its role in conferring higher status knowledge that signals relative markers of personal value which are exchangeable for economic returns.

Cultural capital is also not only relative between different groups of individuals, but also between individuals and is not only derived through education, but from individuals' class positioning, gender and ethnicity. One pertinent issue here is the way in which people's culturally-valued knowledge and dispositions are embodied and performed in ways which convey signals about prospective employee potential value in a given occupational domain. When individuals seek to enter an employment, most significantly in the recruitment process, the inter-personal dynamics they engage in have an inter-cultural dimension which is based on the transference of all-important cultural signals, codes and cues. Cultural capital is valued differently in different occupational fields and linked to the assumptions and dispositions that individuals form, what Bourdieu calls *habitus*. A significant finding from recent research on graduate employment in this area (Bathmaker et al. 2013; Burke, 2015) has been the ways in which graduates with differential levels of cultural capital are able to decode the 'rules of the game' or 'field rules' and fashion behaviours in ways that convey desirable potential.

Developments within the literature offer two relatively new forms of capital which provide closer attention to individuals' psycho-social relationship development and how this might influence their approaches to employment. The concept of *identity capital* has been developed by a number of authors (Coté, 2002; Schuller, 2004; Warin, 2015) and refers to the ways in which individuals' relationships to economic life are mediated by self-identities and personal narratives which provide a reflexive basis for future orientation and action. Identity capital is crucially formed through the self-concepts people carry about what kind of person they perceive themselves to be and wish to become, as well as their potential sense of agency as a prospective employee (Tomlinson, 2007).

The actual presentation of identities is witnessed not only through formal means such as Curriculum Vitaes, but is also embodied through presentation of constructed selves. As Holmes (2013) discusses in relation to graduates' negotiation of access to employment, young people feel the need to behave 'in ways that lead others to ascribe to them the identity of a person worthy of being employed' (p. 549). Identity capital is also the extent to which identities can be warranted and sustained at significant phases of individuals' working lives. For someone seeking to enter and integrate into a workplace, the challenge is being able to warrant identity claims that they are a suitable and credible employee. This is where the performance of one's credentials and purported abilities comes into play, including the recruitment process and early interactions with significant others such as line managers.

The final capital, one which again addresses people's direct and personal relationship to the job market is *psychological capital*, usually associated with the school of positive psychology (Seligman, 1998; Bandura, 1997). Psychological capital can be defined as the psycho-social resources which enable individuals to adapt and respond positively to inevitable labour market challenges. There are a number of potentially significant composites to this form of capital which are largely based on notions of resilience, adaptability and self-efficacy, all set within an increasingly challenging labour market (Luthans et al. 2007). The capital is perhaps best understood from the perspective of school-leavers and graduates entering increasingly precarious labour markets. This form of capital can clearly be advantageous if it enables new job entrants to approach the labour market proactively, aligning their goals and expectations with challenges encountered.

Discussion and overview: connecting structure and agency

This chapter has offered an oversight of three dominant approaches which offer differing, yet also overlapping, accounts of employability. They also provide an account of the interplay between education and future labour market outcomes, and each clearly offers some significant insights into individuals' relationship to employment and how positive and productive advantages can be generated that enhance individuals' employability. The chapter concludes by considering how each approach maps onto the agency-structure dynamic which is central to any analysis of individuals' educational and subsequent employment experiences.

In summary, competences can be viewed as having a functional utility value which is closely related to performance, practice and successful execution of a range of technical and demand-based occupational activities. At its crudest, competencies approaches depict agency in terms of behaviours which result in the effective execution of externally-derived criteria. The competent agent is one who is able to draw upon largely individually-centred ability sets in the shaping of both immediate as well as longer-terms employment outcomes. As individuals develop more competencies, their agential capacity extends and they are able to negotiate more complex external demands. Structure in this sense is one-dimensionally located outside individuals and provides the context for the application of internally-acquired skills-sets. Employment outcomes become contingent on the successful and routinised performance of behaviours resulting in personal and organisational advantage. However, broader, more contextually-sensitive competences approaches tend to conceive the agency-structure dynamic as more multi-faceted. Thus, when interpersonal and cultural dynamics mediate the ways in which competencies are channelled and appraised, agency constitutes more than technical-functional operation and also includes individual's behaviourally and social-orientated skills which are given meaning and legitimacy within different work settings. Structure correspondingly encompasses cultural dimensions, including the role of other agents and the relational properties of work interactions.

Capabilities can be seen as the enhanced developmental and existential capacity individuals have to become more empowered in the labour market, as well as the extended capacity to fulfil goals they value and desire. Agency is conceived in terms of individuals' empowerment to make decisions and pursue goals which lead to meaningful employment circumstances and outcomes. A successful agent in an employment context is one who is not only able to enhance their internal capabilities and utilisation functionings, but also the choices and outcomes that they have reason to value. Success in an employment context is a measure of how relevant this is to people's wellbeing and freedom. In the capabilities perspective, the agency and structure relationship is a measure of the extent to which internal capabilities become convertible and, by extension, operable, by dominant cultural, politico-economic and institutional arrangements. The development of an individual's agential capacity is reflected in the enhancement of capability sets which need to be promoted through favourable institutional conditions.

Different accounts of capital conceive agency and structure in different ways. As with the technicist competency approach, human capital takes a narrow view of agency: an individual is more functionally proficient and empowered in the labour market through having invested in further skills and knowledge. Structure here refers to an economic context which differentially rewards and values formal knowledge. Social and cultural capital approaches provide a more socialised account of the value and transfer of knowledge, paying attention to the wider socio-cultural milieus in which different forms of knowledge and competencies are rewarded. Bourdieu's theorising continues to provide a largely structural lens to educational and economic opportunities, particularly when class and gender are the main structural components in determining them. Agency to some extent reflects the effective mobilisation of cultural capital and awareness and understanding of how and where this can be achieved. However, overall, Bourdieu's approach provides a largely socialised account of agency and the parameters through which it is exercised: individuals act according to predetermined cultural arrangements which delimit the scope for their actions.

Accounts of identity and psychological capital, when related to more volatile and fluid contemporary economic contexts, provide a more elaborated notion of agency, including the reflexive capacities individuals have to develop an active sense of self around work and careers. The key element to such approaches is individuals' capacity not only to navigate career paths through the development of significant psycho-social resources, but the ability to present this into a narrative of one's employability. Proponents of traditional forms of capital may take these to be somewhat individualistic in their approach, but they nonetheless speak to more agential elements and the subjective mediation of an individual's relationship to employment. Employer engagement reflecting this approach would value the development of personal resiliency and understanding of labour market operation.

All approaches consequently carry educational implications. The complexities of the education-employment relationship are not always fully captured by the dominant supply-side, technicist and human capital approaches which have influenced policy. The preponderance of largely metrics-driven approaches to school and university students' formal achievement reflects the value given to measures of the purported skills developed within institutions. Employment outcomes are conceived not only as reflections of an individual's enhanced capacity to find employment, but also the effectiveness of institutional provision towards this end. In a competencies approach, this is construed as the development of key functional abilities, including knowing how to find suitable employment, which may have an immediate bearing on post-education outcomes. From an employer engagement perspective, a competencies approach has driven historic patterns of teenage work experience where placements have been historically designed as *a taste of real work* to enable the development and application of skills demanded within specific occupations.

A capabilities perspective might argue that such outcomes signal the enrichment of individuals' capability sets as manifested in their expanded range of functionings. This may include their ability to make informed choices, seek opportunities and pursue pathways that they value. However, this approach would clearly question both the measure of value (i.e. finding employment) and the institutional means through which this is promoted, particularly when success criteria are reducible to student performance. Supporters of this approach such as Hinchliffe (2002) have argued that capabilities are developed through multiple contexts and are not confined to formal provision. In schools and universities, capabilities may also be promoted through pastoral, social and political arenas which help enrich broader aspects of a person. The object of value in the capabilities approach is the freedom of people to develop and live creative and fulfilled lives. This is clearly not also confined to material or status-referenced outcomes such as employment success. The overall goal of education is empowering individuals' towards self-authorising in their lives, including how its relationship to labour market matters and in ways that they can potentially value.

When looking at curricula and assessment issues, capabilities advocates often look to guard against largely top-down, norm-referenced approaches, including standardised assessment. The object of learning must move beyond employability outcomes, based on the end goals of optimising utility value, so that students come to value their personal development. It calls for more nuanced, qualitative and self-referenced evaluation systems that track wider aspects of student development, including measures of wellbeing, creativity and social engagement. As Hinchliffe and Jolly (2011) illustrate, it is these markers, rather than lists of skills, which employers use to judge prospective employees. These are also what will add value to their actual involvement in economic life. Hoffman's account, in this collection, of an ethnographic approach to critical and individualised understanding of employability within specific occupational setting is illustrative of a related employer engagement approach.

Capital formation is clearly challenging in educational provision, including the core issue of how far capitals can be taught or formally acquired. One solution to concerns about employability has been the move to increase people's participation in formal education which is seen to add value to their skills, knowledge and future productivity. An extension of this logic is the acquisition of the relevant skills which are seen to count in the labour market. In Bourdieusian terms, relative labour market outcomes reflects the reproduction function of formal education, enmeshed as it is in the values, codes and cultural praxis of middle classes. The link between education and employment is a largely reproductive one which explains why those who have acquired stronger cultural and social capital experience more favourable labour market outcomes. This reworks and adapts itself in mass educational systems and continues as an intensification of competition and signalling between different employees and more stringent and discriminate selection approaches by employers. In this context, related employer engagement would recognise structural contexts and harness workplace interventions to broaden and challenge the assumptions and expectations of young people.

References

Bandura, A. (1997). *Self-efficacy: The exercise of control.* New York, NY: Freeman.

Bathmaker, A.M., Ingram, N. and Waller, R. (2013). Higher education, social class and the mobilisation of capitals: Recognising and playing the game. *British Journal of Sociology of Education* 34(5/6): 723–743.

Becker, G. (1993) *Human Capital: Theoretical and empirical analysis with special reference to education* (3rd Edition). Chicago: University of Chicago Press.

Bourdieu, P. (1986). The forms of capital, in Richardson, J. (ed.), *Handbook for theory and research for the sociology of education.* Westport, CT: Greenwood.

Brockmann, M., Clarke, L., Mehaut, P. and Winch, C. (2008). Competency-based Vocational Education and Training (VET): The cases of England and France in a comparative perspective. *Vocations and Learning* 1(3): 227–244.

Brown, P., Lauder, H. and Ashton, D. (2011). *The global auction.* Oxford: Oxford University Press.

Burke, C. (2015). *Culture, capital and graduate futures: Degrees of class.* London: Routledge.

Clarke, M. (2008). Understanding and managing employability in changing career contexts. *Journal of European Industrial Training* 32(4): 258–284.

Coleman, J. (1988). Social capital in the creation of human capital. *America Journal of Sociology* 94: 95–120.

Coté, J. (2002). The role of identity capital in the transition to adulthood: The individualization thesis examined. *Journal of Youth Studies* 5(2): 117–134.

DfE. (2011). *Review of vocational education - The Wolf Report*. London: Department for Education.

Eraut, M. (1998). Concept of competence. *Journal of Interprofessional Care* 12(2): 127–139.

Eraut, M. (2007). *Early career learning at work: Insights into professional development during the first job*. Swindon: Economic and Social Science Research Council.

Fenwick, T. (2003). Flexibility and individualisation in adult education work: The case of portfolio educators. *Journal of Education and Work* 16(2): 165–184.

Gazier, B. (1999) *Employability: Concepts and policies*. InforMisep Reports No. 67068, Birmingham: European Employment Observatory.

Granovetter, M.S. (1973). The strength of weak ties. *American Journal of Sociology* 78(6): 1360–1380.

Hager, P. and Hodkinson, P. (2009) Moving beyond the metaphor of transfer of learning. *British Educational Research Journal* 35(4): 619–638.

Hinchliffe, G. (2002). Situating skills. *Journal of Philosophy of Education* 36(2): 187–205.

Hinchliffe, G. and Jolly, A. (2011). Graduate Identity and Employability. *British Educational Research Journal* 37(4): 563–584.

Holmes, L. (2013). Competing perspectives on graduate employability: Possession, position or process? *Studies in Higher Education* 38(4): 538–554.

Inkson, K., Dries, N. and Arnold, J. (2015). *Understanding careers*. 2nd ed. London: Sage Publications.

Keep, E. and Mayhew, K. (2010). Moving beyond skills as social and economic panacea. *Work, Employment and Society* 24(3): 565–577.

Lauder, H., Brown, P. and Tholen, G. (2012). The global auction model, skills bias theory and graduate incomes, in Lauder, H. (ed.), *Educating for the knowledge economy*? London: Routledge.

Le Deist, F-D. and Winterton, J. (2005). What is competence?. *Human Resource Development International* 8(1): 27–46.

Leitch Report. (2006). *Prosperity for all in the global economy – world class skills*. Norwich: HMSO.

Lindberg, O. and. Rantatalo, O. (2016). Competence in professional practice: A practice theory analysis of police and doctors. *Human Relations*. doi:0018726714532666

Luthans, F., Youseff, C. and Avolio, B. (2007). *Psychological capital: Developing the human competitive edge*. Oxford: Oxford University Press.

Mulder, M., Gulikers, J., Biemans, H. and Wasselink, R. (2009). The new competence concept in higher education: Error or enrichment? *European Journal of Industrial Training* 33(8/9): 755–770.

Nussbaum, M. (2011). *Creating capabilities: The human development approach*. Cambridge, MA: Cambridge University Press.

Schuller, T. (2004). Three capitals, in Schuller, T. et al. (eds.), *The benefits of learning: The impact of education on health, family and social policy*. London: Routledge.

Seligman, M. (1998). *Learned optimism*. New York, NY: Pocket Books.

Sen, A. (1985). Well-being, agency and freedom. *Journal of Philosophy* LXXXII(4): 169–221.

Sen, A. (1999). *Development as freedom*. Oxford: Oxford University Press.

Stanley, J. and Mann, A. (2014). Towards a theoretical framework for employer engagement, in Mann, A., Stanley, J. and Archer, L. (eds.), *Understanding employer engagement in education: Theories and evidence*. London: Routledge.

Tomlinson, M. (2007). Graduate employability and student attitudes and orientations to the labour market. *Journal of Education and Work* 20(4): 285–304.

Tomlinson, M. (2013). *Education, work and identity*. London: Bloomsbury.

Warin, J. (2015). Identity capital: An application from a longitudinal ethnographic study of self-construction during the years of school. *British Journal of Sociology of Education* 36(5): 689–706.

Woodin, T., McCulloch, G. and Cowan, S. (2013). Raising the participation age in historic perspective: Policy learning from the past? *British Educational Research Journal* 39(4): 635–553.

Chapter 5

Socialised social capital?

The capacity of schools to use careers provision to compensate for social capital deficiencies among teenagers

Anthony Mann, Elnaz Kashefpakdel and Christian Percy[1]

Introduction

Social capital, equality and careers provision

It has long been understood that the social context within which a young person exists can influence the outcomes they enjoy through childhood and adult life. Conceptualised as social capital, over recent years, the idea has attracted the interest of policy makers and researchers interested in understanding the comparative success of young people within both education and transitions into ultimate employment. Understood as a phenomenon which exists essentially within social relationships, social capital is conceived of as a resource in which individuals may wittingly or unwittingly invest in order to gain later benefits. While a complex and contested idea (Halpern, 2005; Field, 2008), three forms of social capital have been particularly widely used across sociological and policy literature:

bonding giving individuals a strong sense of identity and common purpose often located within families and ethnic groups characterised by a strong sense of mutual obligation;

bridging whereby individuals with different social and economic experiences are connected, enabling access to new information and experiences; and

linking which speaks to relations between individuals of different social positions across hierarchies of power, social status and wealth. (OECD, 2001)

Scholars have described and measured variations in the character and extent of social relationships experienced by young people in such terms and found a range of well-evidenced impacts. As the OECD states: 'Access to information and influence through social networks ... confers private benefits on individuals and in some cases can be used by individuals or groups to exclude others and reinforce dominance or privilege' (OECD, 2001: 41–42). In sociologist

James Coleman's famous study of US religious schools, evidence was presented that social relations within and beyond families shaping young people's sense of community norms and expectations to lead to greater engagement and success in education than peers from similarly disadvantaged backgrounds (Coleman, 1988). The character of an individual's social capital, moreover, has been seen as of significant advantage within the competition for jobs in the labour market. In contrast to the work of Coleman which looked at the influence of tightly bonded communities sharing the same ideas and values, the work of Mark Granovetter (1973) has emphasised the value of variation in social networks (bridging social capital). Articulated as the 'strength of weak ties', the American scholar has mapped the ways in which broad and varied individual networks (knowing lots of different people who know different things) bestow important advantage in the search for paid employment. To Granovetter, such networks acted as channels through which 'non-redundant trusted information' concerning employment opportunities could easily flow, connecting individuals with opportunities to which they were well suited. Applying the insight to a youth perspective, Jokisaari has drawn on Granovetter from a Finnish perspective, to understand how relationships between teenagers and adult contacts occupying economic roles as supervisors (a form of linking social capital) influence economic benefits enjoyed by the young people as they move themselves into full-time employment (Jokisaari, 2007).

Within the realm of careers provision, scholars and policy makers have identified aspects of employer engagement in education as a means of influencing the access of young people to forms of social capital. After all, it is a distinctive element of any episode of school-mediated employer engagement that a young person will encounter individuals possessing knowledge and experiences which is different from that which they enjoy themselves. From a policy perspective, the UK Social Mobility and Child Poverty Commission has, for example, often turned to social capital as a convenient theoretical model for explaining, in part, how similarly talented young people can expect different educational and economic outcomes (Ashley et al. 2015). Launching a fund to create new relations between adult mentors and school-based 'struggling teens' in 2016, then Prime Minister David Cameron pointed to the power of social relations:

> Many people can look back at their younger selves and point to someone, perhaps a parent or teacher, a sports coach, or their first boss, and say 'that's the person who found my passion. They're the ones who made the difference.' But if you haven't ever had someone in your life who really believes in you, who sees your potential and helps bring it to the fore, the sands of time can drain away, and your talents can remain hidden.[2]

Scholars have stressed the efficacy of school-managed mentoring programmes in building social capital (Hooley, 2016; Linnehan, 2004), but also found evidence in other employer engagement activities such as work experience and career talks. Raffo and Reeves (2000), Mann and Percy (2014), Norris and Francis (2014), and Kashefpakdel and Percy (2016) have all drawn on Granovetter to make sense of the outcomes they observe experienced by young people as a result of their engagement.

However, it is by no means certain that increased access to social capital will always serve to enhance the economic prospects of young people. Social capital is understood to have a darker side – being described as a mechanism which can exclude as well as include, reinforcing inequalities as well as challenging them. In particular, forms of bonded social capital have been associated with patterns of social reproduction, whether in elite or disadvantaged communities (Bourdieu with Wacquant 1992). Young people living within closely knit communities, for example, can have aspirations limited or closed off through the imposition of community norms or feel significant obligations to contribute to family incomes by sacrificing educational opportunities for early entry to the labour market (van Deth and Sonja Zmerli, 2010; Afridi, 2011; Field, 2003; McCabe et al. 2013).

While many studies consider the influence of social capital emerging from what might be seen as natural or organic social relationships, for example, within families, this chapter focuses on the capacity of educational institutions to shape the social capital available to young people and explores how young people, of different social backgrounds, respond to such experiences.

Two US studies provide insight to the unpredictable character of change linked to work-related experiences. Neumark and Rothstein (2005) explore the influence of participation in US work-related activities and programmes which routinely require new relations with people from the economic community (job shadowing, mentoring, cooperative education, school enterprises, technical preparation provision and internships/apprenticeships). Drawing on US longitudinal databases tracking a population of teenagers into adulthood, the authors build on earlier analysis which had demonstrated positive economic and educational returns related to participation in such activities to divide their cohort into two groups based on predicted progression to higher education. The study found effect sizes to be greater in many cases for young men in the more disadvantaged half of the sample than for their more privileged peers, while for young women it tended to be the more advantaged participants who gained most from the interventions.

Erickson et al. (2009) also draw on US longitudinal data to explore whether the character of social relations can be seen to influence the outcomes of young people. The authors looked at the influence of informal mentors ('non-parental adults who take a special interest in the lives of youth' including teachers, youth workers, relatives and employers). Finding both that access to informal mentors was statistically related to better educational outcomes and that young people reporting such access were commonly from more privileged social backgrounds, Erickson and colleagues find that it is young people from more advantaged backgrounds who are both more likely to access such support and to take advantage of it. They argue: 'Contrary to usual expectations, much of the evidence shows that [informal] mentoring relationships that develop naturally have the potential to contributing to – rather than reducing – social inequality" (p. 359). The authors conclude that government should intervene to encourage formal mentoring programmes for low-income students without access to informal mentors.

From a UK perspective, Stanley and Mann (2014) among others, have argued that preceding levels of human, social and cultural capital influence pupil access to work experience placements, whether due to the influence of family ties in sourcing placements (Le Gallais and Hatcher, 2014) or familial and societal norms gendering decision-making (Francis et al. 2005). As the OECD state at the head of this chapter, the social context of engagement in work-related activities serves to shape the experience of them, and this might serve to enhance or reduce social inequalities (see also, Jones et al. 2016).

Analytical approach

In this study, we explore the relationship between access to school-mediated forms of social capital and outcomes related to its possession in the social context of the recipient. Drawing on the data from the British Cohort Study, we build on earlier work by Kashefpakdel and Percy (2016) which demonstrated links between adult wage premiums and teenage participation in school-mediated career talks with people from outside of school.

In that work, data were collected concerning the participation of young people between the ages of 14 and 16 in 'career talks with people from outside of school.' The teenagers reported on whether they had participated in such career talks at either age 14–15 or at 15–16, how many career talks they had experienced and whether they had found them helpful or not. Kashefpakdel and Percy then, with a standard series of controls in place to account for social background, academic aptitude, local environment and demographics, explored relationships with earnings, when in full-time employment, at age 26. They found that participation in careers talks with people from outside of school at age 14–15 was related to a wage premium of 0.8% per career talk – a finding that was statistically significant at the 1% level. When the career talks were felt at the time to have been 'very helpful', the size of impact associated with each talk grew to 1.6%. For teenagers reporting on career talks at ages 15–16, while a directionally positive relationship was identified between participation in such careers activities and higher earnings at age 26, the relationship was not found to be statistically significant. However, where the teenagers reported the talks to have been 'very helpful', higher earnings of 0.7% per career talk were detected with a significance level of 5%.

The current paper returns to this analysis and introduces new data. The paper looks at the characteristics of young people who engaged in career talks and explores whether social background influences the level of later adult premiums received. Following Leonard (2005), the chapter explores whether access to school-mediated forms of social capital interact with existing levels of social advantage to multiply effects of comparative privilege. Reflecting the terminology of Erickson et al. (2009), the paper asks: do such new episodes of social capital serve to complement or exacerbate existing family-rooted inequality or can they serve as a compensatory mechanism, reducing inequalities? Put another way, do those who have least access to useful work-related networks through their immediate networks have most to gain from school-mediated interventions?

Analysis of data from the British Cohort Study allows a comparison of what might be described as 'proxy' social capital and 'real' social capital. The term 'proxy' social capital is used to describe interactions between young people and the givers, in this case, of careers talks. 'Proxy' describes a form of social interaction which is enabled by schools within what can routinely be expected to have been transient encounters. Such encounters mimic the character of trusted information exchange typically observed within examples of bonded or bridging social capital, proving recipients with information considered to be authentic and trustworthy. In the analysis that follows, outcomes related to such 'proxy' social capital are compared to those observed in relationship to 'real' social capital – that is, relationships which are rooted in family connections. Questions within the British Cohort Study enable such a comparison to take place.

Data

This paper uses the British Cohort Study 1970 (known as BCS70) which follows the lives of approximately 17,000 individuals from birth to age 42. The cohort study surveys people after birth at ages 5, 10, 16, 26, 30, 34, 38 and 42. Since its start, the cohort members have been asked about their health, education, employment and social and economic status (UK Data Service, 2016). In their earlier paper, Kashefpakdel and Percy (2016) set out the value of this dataset in evaluating the impact of a specific intervention on economic outcomes. Following their methodology, information on young people was gathered from 1986 when participants were mostly aged 16 and from their earnings in 1996 when they were mostly 26 years old. Other socio-economic factors including academic ability and parental social class are collected from birth to age 26.

It is these data that allow the hypothesis to be tested that access to information and insights via a social network mediated by schools could in fact compete with access to social capital provided by family and friends. This test is made possible by two questions in the 1986 survey: young people were asked at age 16 whether (1) they knew a contact through their family or friends who could help get them a job ('real social capital') and (2) they had taken part in careers talks with outside speakers organised by their schools ('proxy social capital').

Of 4,806 BSC1970 respondents in 1986, 59.4% said they had no access to this 'real social capital.' When asked whether someone in their family or anyone else they know could help them find paid employment, three-fifths of the sample replied negatively. In the discussion that follows, the earnings outcomes at age 26 of the two-fifths of study participants who can be described as recipients (or at least perceived themselves to be the recipients) of such 'real social capital' are explored. They are directly compared to the outcomes enjoyed by cohort participants reporting access to 'proxy social capital.' This is the group of young people who in 1986 testified that they had taken part in careers talks with people from outside of their school, as previously analysed by Kashefpakdel and Percy (2016). The BSC1970 questionnaire asked students whether they had received any such talks at ages 14–15 and 15–16, and if yes, how many they had received. The frequency distribution of career talks at age 14–16 is presented in Figure 5.1. In total, 66% of respondents took part in (at least one) career talk with people from outside school.

The outcome variable used in the analysis is weekly income at age 26 if the cohort member was in full time employment at that time. Individuals in full time employment only are used to ensure fair, like-for-like comparisons are made. The average earnings reported in 1996 was £215 a week with a standard deviation of approximately £100. The main statistical drivers of income at age 26 overall were, as suggested by past literature (for example, Hendricks et al. 2015), academic ability and parental social class. The 1996 earnings frequency distribution is given at Figure 5.2.

The following analysis aims firstly to investigate whether young people who believed that they had access to family networks, who could provide them with a job opportunity, benefit from a wage premium when they enter the labour market compared to their peers with no such networks. Secondly, in light of the findings of the first analysis, the paper explores whether relationships exist between teenage participation in career talks at school and possession of the 'real' social capital embodied in extended family networks.

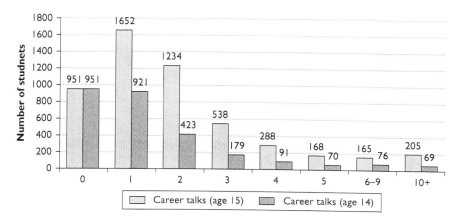

Figure 5.1 Distribution of career talk participation

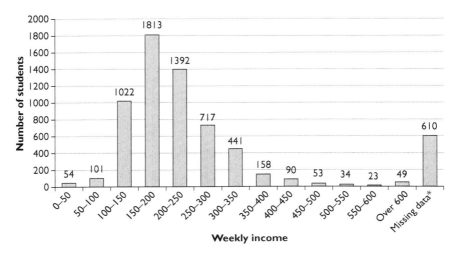

Figure 5.2 Distribution of weekly earnings (full time workers only), age 26 full sample (1996)

Method

Control variables

As with any study exploring variation in labour market performance, it is crucial to account for background variables in the analysis, as particular effects might otherwise distort or disguise findings. For instance, it is possible that individuals from wealthier socio-economic backgrounds are more likely to attend schools which included a diet of career talks within their provision, but such individuals can also be expected to go on to earn more due to other social advantages or better school performance. Hence, it is important to include a control for individuals' family background. In general, BCS allows for a rich number of background variables (from birth to age 16). Drawing on the well-established literature on school-to-work transitions and employment outcomes, variables across several key categories were identified and considered for inclusion: socio-economic status, academic ability/attainment, home learning environment, demographics and attitudinal characteristics (see, for example, Schoon and Polek, 2011; Yates et al. 2011).

Basic demographic data on gender was available in a straightforward fashion from the BCS survey results. Academic attainment was captured through identification of the highest qualification achieved by age 26, including both vocational and academic qualifications to allow comparison of individuals across different types of qualification. Mathematics score is a derived variable using an individual's grade at O-level/CSE, the two most common national qualifications undertaken at age 16 in 1986. Households were asked whether the cohort member had sat an examination in Mathematics at age 16, at what level and what mark they achieved.

The third category represents the early home learning environment and draws on data collected from early age, including the number of weekday evenings spent watching television. The fourth category addresses one of the most important set of background variables, family socio-economic status, and this was captured by parental social class at age 16 (measured by the Registrar General Social Class Scale and based on the occupation of the parents) and whether respondents resided in council-owned accommodation.

The final control applied is one for the level of deprivation at the local education authority (LEA) level, allowing an account to be made of local labour market conditions within tests for variations in earnings. To derive an average rate of economically active participation for those aged 16 and above in each of the 120 LEAs recorded in the dataset, the NOMIS census results from 1991 are used. This control is necessary to account for the exogenous difficulty in finding employment for those young people who seek work in the same local authority area where they went to school. Provided a similar relationship obtains on average within the LEAs, the control for localised unemployment allows adjustments to be made for this bias.

Finally, as suggested by Schoon and Lyons-Amos (2017), a measurement of young people's attitudinal characteristics is included in the model. Specifically, drawing on a wider literature, Schoon and Lyons-Amos focus on young people's stated future intentions as a representation for agency, measured by education expectation. Using the British Cohort Study, this variable is captured by asking young people at age 16 whether they expected to leave education or stay from September 1986. The use of these important control variables translates into a reduction in sample size for the final analysis.

Estimation method

Since the dependant variable, income at age 26, is a continuous variable, a linear least squares regression model is applied using SPSS v21. In order to obtain a better fit model and in line with common econometric practice for wage regressions, the natural log transform of the income variable is adopted. This transformation makes the positively skewed distribution of income more normal.

Results

Are the recipients of 'real' and 'proxy' social capital different?

A cross tabulation of participants in school-mediated careers talks and individuals believing that their social networks would help them find employment after leaving school is given in Tables 5.1 and 5.2 below. Some 40% of respondents felt that their social networks would help find employment. The confidence in the power of relationships to deliver such economic outcomes is clearly related to parental social class – nearly 60% of young people raised in the highest socio-economic group, as characterised by the Goldthorpe class schema (Evans, 1992), agreed with the statement, with proportions agreeing falling in direct relationship to level of social class as measured by the reported social status of the participants' mothers. Less than one third of young people from the lowest

Table 5.1 Socio-economic status background of teenagers, aged 16, believing that they will be able to find a job through their network of family and friends. British Cohort Study.

Social class * Family contact able to help you get job. Cross tabulation using Chi-Squared

P-value: 0.00		Family contact able to help get a job		Total
		No	Yes	
I Professional occupations	%	41.2%	58.8%	100.0%
II Managerial/technical occupations	%	54.0%	46.0%	100.0%
III Skilled non manual occupations	%	57.0%	43.0%	100.0%
III Skilled manual occupations	%	66.2%	33.8%	100.0%
IV Semi-skilled occupations	%	65.7%	34.3%	100.0%
V Unskilled occupations	%	68.5%	31.5%	100.0%
Total	Count	1230	838	2068
	%	59.5%	40.5%	100.0%

Table 5.2 Socio-economic status of teenagers, aged 16, who participated in careers talks with people from outside of school. British Cohort Study.

Social class * Careers talks from people outside school. Cross tabulation using Chi-Squared

P-value: 0.01		Careers talks from people outside school		Total
		No	Yes	
I Professional occupations	%	33.3%	66.7%	100.0%
II Managerial/technical occupations	%	17.4%	82.6%	100.0%
III Skilled non manual occupations	%	16.9%	83.1%	100.0%
III Skilled manual occupations	%	12.0%	88.0%	100.0%
IV Semi-skilled occupations	%	13.0%	87.0%	100.0%
V Unskilled occupations	%	10.7%	89.3%	100.0%
Total	Count	396	2155	2551
	%	15.5%	84.5%	100.0%

socio-economic group agreed that people they knew could help them find a job after leaving education.

Turning to participation in careers talks with people from outside of school, the relationship with social class is reversed (Table 5.1). It is those young people from the highest socio-economic groups who are least likely to report having taken part in the activity (67%) and their peers from the lowest socio-economic groups who reported the highest levels of engagement (89%).

'Real' vs. 'proxy' social capital

The first analysis looks at the association between confidence in having access to a network of family and friends believed to be helpful in getting a job after school, i.e. 'real' social capital, and wage outcomes at age 26 with control variables in place. Core control variables were prioritised for inclusion in the model based on the strength of relationship in a direct regression on wage, following a similar approach to Kashefpakdel and Percy (2016) with the addition of the educational expectation variable.

The analysis indicates that those individuals who reported access to 'real' social capital as teenagers earn as adults, on average, 4.3% more than comparable peers who felt that they had no access through their networks of family and friends to people who could help get them a job after leaving education. The correlation is significant at the 5% level (N = 1,234). This finding represents the average effects across all those who responded to this question of social capital access at age 16 and also provided answers for the other control variables included.

In the second stage of the analysis, those participants who responded negatively to the 'real' social capital access question at age 16 (59% of young people in the BCS sample) were isolated. The analysis was designed to explore whether

Table 5.3 Regression results: 'real' social capital against in wage

Model 1 N=1,234 R²: 18.1%	Unstandardized coefficients		Sig.
	B	Std. error	
(Constant)	4.759	0.205	0
Gender	0.169	0.022	0
Highest qualification achieved	0.035	0.009	0
Mother social class	−0.013	0.006	0.019
Math score	−0.053	0.008	0
Local unemployment index	0.983	0.321	0.002
No of days watched TV	−0.003	0.006	0.593
Education expectation	−0.033	0.028	0.237
Cognitive assessment	0.021	0.01	0.026
'Real' social capital	**0.043**	**0.021**	**0.043**

individuals without access to real-world networks of helpful family and friends would respond in different ways, following their engagement in school-mediated career talks, to peers who felt that individuals known to them would be able to help find employment. Table 5.4 shows the result of the regression analysis between career talks by people from outside school and income at age 26, for young people who felt that they did not have access to 'real' social capital.

The result of the regression shows that, for young people who did not believe they had access to 'real' social capital, participation in career talks organised by schools and given by people from outside school was, on average, extremely beneficial. Those who said they had participated in career talks between the age of 14 and 16 earned 8.5%, on average, more compared to their peers at age 26 who reported no such participation as teenagers. The relationship is statistically significant at the 5% level (N = 691). This is nearly twice the level of wage premium experienced by young adults who entered full time employment with access to 'real' social capital. This does not necessarily mean that those with 'proxy' social capital earn, on average, more than those with 'real' social capital (as measured by these simple yes/no dummy variables). For instance, the starting points (the constant terms) are different between Model 1 and Model 2, and the background variables have different effects in the two different models. Further work could explore such direct comparisons in more detail.

In keeping with earlier work by Kashefpakdel and Percy (2016), an important variation of impact related to the age at which careers talks were undertaken. In the case of young people reporting no access to 'real' social capital as teenagers, participation in career talks at a younger age did show some impact on later earnings. The regression results between number of careers talks at age 14–15 and later income shows that young people enjoyed a 1.5% wage premium for

Table 5.4 Regression results: participants in career talks lacking 'real' social capital against ln wage

Model 2 N=691 R²: 19.5%	Unstandardized coefficients		Sig.
	B	Std. error	
(Constant)	4.389	0.276	0.000
Gender	0.160	0.029	0.000
Highest qualification achieved	0.041	0.013	0.001
Mother social class	−0.011	0.008	0.158
Math score	−0.052	0.010	0.000
Local unemployment index	1.433	0.428	0.001
No of days watched TV	0.000	0.007	0.962
Education expectation	−0.044	0.038	0.255
Cognitive assessment	0.017	0.013	0.184
Career talk from people outside school ('proxy' social capital)	**0.085**	**0.038**	**0.023**

each talk they attended (significant at 10% level) for each extra talk when in full time employment at age 26. The relationship between the number of career talks at age 15–16 and later income is not significant.

To understand whether young people with access to 'real' social capital benefited in similar ways, the analysis was repeated. The relationship was found to be no longer significant. The correlation disappeared for this group of respondents (N=481). When the analysis considers only those young people who declared their possession of social networks able to enable employment opportunities, no impacts on later earnings are detected in relation to teenage participation in careers talks.

Discussion

The analysis presented in this chapter explores the impact of school-mediated action to enhance the work-related social capital of teenagers in the context of existing levels of family-based social relationships. The chapters specifically ask: can careers-related action to enhance teenage access to social capital be designed to reduce social inequality?

The paper draws on data from the British Cohort Study 1970 to consider the impact of two forms of social capital encountered by teenagers. In the first analysis, the impact of 'real' social capital is tested. The Cohort Study asks teenagers at age 16 whether they felt confident that they knew people through their network of family and families who would be able to help them get a job after leaving school. Looking at relations with earnings, when in full-time employment at age 26, young people claiming such helpful contacts earn, on average, 4.3% more than peers – after controls are put in place for demographics, social background and academic performance. The study provides no further information about the nature of the relationships described. In the OECD's simple categorisation of forms of social capital, it can be reasonably expected that young people had in mind forms of *bonding* or *linking* social capital when responding to the question. In stating that they knew somebody able to help find employment through their network, it is possible to imagine teenagers reflecting on contacts who both felt sufficiently close to the participant to want to help them and who possessed positions of some economic authority – i.e. individuals with some influence over recruitment processes. It is perhaps unsurprising, therefore, that the two-fifths of the sample who responded positively to question were drawn disproportionately from higher status social backgrounds.

In this first analysis, a validation of social capital theory is offered: who you know does matter to your economic outcomes. A social relationship can be seen to transform into a cash return. In the second analysis, a different type of relationship is considered. Whereas cohort participants claiming access to 'real' social capital might be expected to be engaged in a long-term, multi-faceted relationship with one or more individuals able to help in the search for employment, those teenagers who took part in careers talks with people from outside of school cannot be expected to have enjoyed such vivid relationships. Rather, their engagement with careers speakers can expect to have been of very short duration. In conceptual terms, these individuals can be better seen as recipients of *bridging* social capital: that through their careers talks, they encountered individuals from backgrounds and possessing knowledge outside of their immediate circles. Following Raffo and Reeves (2000), Mann and Percy (2014), Stanley and Mann (2014), Jones et al. (2016) and Erickson et al. (2009), it is easy to imagine such participants gaining insight to what Granovetter (1973) labels 'non-redundant, trusted information' about jobs and careers. It is hard to imagine them gaining further active help in securing employment. As made clear in Kashefpakdel and Percy's 2016 study, at the time of the talks many teenagers described them as 'helpful' or 'very helpful' and they were proved to be right, enjoying high wage premiums at age 26.

In this analysis, the social characteristics of teenagers participating in teenage careers talks are set out and in contrast to the recipients of 'real' social capital, these consumers of 'proxy' social capital are disproportionately drawn from lower socio-economic groups. The analysis shows that school-mediated careers-related action can act to enhance teenage access to social capital as measured through adult economic outcomes. Moreover, the advantages linked to participation in career talks are significant, competing very favourably with the extent of social capital resource possessed within families. Teenagers who engaged in careers talks but who lacked 'real' social capital can be seen to earn 8.5% more than those who did not engage in careers talks, an impressive premium in comparison to that associated with having 'real' social capital.

In the final analysis, a comparison is made of the wage returns enjoyed by careers talks' participants by their status in relation to possession of 'real' social capital. The analysis finds no evidence of adult wage premiums where teenagers were already confident that they possessed personal networks of individuals able to help secure later employment. The data points, consequently, to a deficit model, suggesting that young people lacking economically useful social networks can compensate for their absence through school-mediated initiatives. The findings point towards *bridging* style social capital being, as argued by Granovetter and his followers, as a particularly powerful driver of ultimate economic gain.

The data provide little explanatory insight into why such distinct patterns of outcomes should be observed. One possibility is that teenagers who feel that they possess strong existing networks linked to employment exhibit a greater degree of complacency than peers when thinking about their working futures and feel poorly motivated to engage with the subject of career talks, so increasing the risks of sub-optimal progression through continuing education and training.

Conclusion

This chapter has drawn on data from the 1970 British Cohort Study to compare forms of social capital encountered by teenagers and explored their impact on earnings at age 26. The chapter questions whether schools can intervene in the lives of young people to enhance their access to social capital of ultimate economic value – and finds that they can. Comparing a family-based 'real' form of social capital with a school-mediated 'proxy' form, it is seen that those who lack real social capital gain higher average wage returns from school-mediated social capital than their more advantaged peers gain from their family-based ties, once academic achievements, background characteristics and local environment are controlled for. The comparison suggests that it is access to reliable, authentic, diverse sources of new and useful information about the labour market ('non-redundant trusted information') that has impact on some economic outcomes. It is telling that among young people with useful family-based ties, the wage premium correlated with school-mediated activities was no longer significant. This suggests both it is young people from lower socio-economic groups who have most to gain from participation in school-mediated careers talks. In this way, the careers intervention can be seen to close the gap in adult economic outcomes. By consequence, the results suggest that policy makers intent on reducing social inequalities should prioritise such activities on those young people possessing the weakest social networks. Taking advantage of the willingness of individuals to volunteer to provide careers talks in schools, schools can be imagined as turning an archetypally private resource (possession of expert knowledge about discrete elements of the labour market) into a public one. Few obstacles can be imagined as standing in the way of the donors of social capital sharing the useful information they possess about the world of work with family members. Access to such private sources of social capital is inequitably distributed, naturally reflecting economic inequalities within societies. This study suggests that government, schools and other public actors have it in their power to harness and channel (or in other words, socialise) such social capital as a mechanism to compensate, in some part, for preceding levels of inequality.

The study will, it is hoped, prompt further research, if in recognition that it does include some significant limitations. Data are old – relating to a cohort of young people who turned 16 in 1986 and 26 in 1996. Data are also limited both about what young people were thinking when they considered whether they had access to individuals able to help them into employment after leaving education and what the participants actually experienced when they participated in careers talks. However, the British Cohort Study does include a rich series of controls and ask questions enabling such comparative work to take place, providing findings of genuine interest to all those who seek to capture and enhance the delivery of careers provision as a vehicle for social justice.

Notes

1 The authors are grateful to Tristram Hooley, Ronald Sultana and Rie Thomsen for their comments on an earlier draft of this chapter.
2 'Prime Minister to announce new generation of mentors to help struggling teens'. Available from: www.gov.uk/government/news/prime-minister-to-announce-new-generation-of-mentors-to-help-struggling-teens. [accessed February 20th 2017].

References

Afridi, A. (2011). *Social networks: Their role in addressing poverty*. York: Joseph Rowntree Foundation.

Ashley, L., Duberley, J., Sommerlad, H. and Scholaios, D. (2015). *A qualitative evaluation of non-educational barriers to the elite professions*. London: Social Mobility and Child Poverty Commission.

Bourdieu, P. and Wacquant, L.J.D. (1992). *An invitation to reflexive sociology*. Chicago and London: University of Chicago Press

Coleman, J.S. (1988). Social capital in the creation of human capital. *American Journal of Sociology* 94: S95–S120.

Erickson, L.D., McDonald, S. and Elder, Jr. G.H. (2009). Informal mentors and education: Complementary or compensatory resources? *Sociology of Education* 82: 344–367.

Evans, G. (1992). Testing the validity of the goldthorpe class schema. *European Sociological Review* 8(3): 211–232.

Field, J. (2008). *Social Capital*. London: Routledge.

Francis, B., Osgood, J., Dalgety, J. and Archer, L. (2005). *Gender equality in work experience placements for young people. Occupational segregation: Working paper series No. 27*. Manchester: Equal Opportunities Commission.

Granovetter, M. (1973). The strength of weak ties. *American Journal of Sociology* 78(6): 1360–1380.

Halpern, D. (2005). *Social Capital*. London: Polity

Hendricks G., Savahl S., Mathews K., Raats C., Jaffer L., Matzdorff A., Dekel B., Larke C., Magodyo T., Gesselleen M. and Pedro A. (2015) Influences on life aspirations among adolescents in a low income community in Cape Town, South Africa. *Journal of Psychology in Africa* 25(4): 320–326.

Hooley, T. (2016). *Effective employer mentoring: Lessons from the evidence*. London: The Careers and Enterprise Company.

Jokisaari, M. (2007). From newcomer to insider? Social networks and socialisation into working life, in Helve, H. and Bynner, J. (eds.), *Youth and Social Capital*. London: Tufnell Press.

Jones, S., Mann, A. and Morris, K. (2016). The "Employer Engagement Cycle" in secondary education: Analysing the testimonies of young British adults. *Journal of Education and Work* 29(7): 834–856.

Kashefpakdel, E. and Percy, C. (2016). Career education that works: An economic analysis using the British cohort study. *Journal of Education and Work* 30(3): 217–234.

Le Gallais, T. and Hatcher, R. (2014). How school work experience policies can widen student horizons or reproduce social inequality, in Mann, A., Stanley, J. and Archer, L. (eds.), *Understanding employer engagement in education: Theories and evidence*. London: Routledge.

Leonard, M. (2005). Children, childhood and social capital: Exploring the links. *Sociology* 39(4): 605–622.

McCabe, A., Gilchrist, A., Harris, K., Afridi, A. and Kyprianou, P. (2013). *Making the links: Poverty, ethnicity and social networks*. York: Joseph Rowntree Foundation.

Mann, A. and Percy, C. (2014). Employer engagement in British secondary education: Wage earning outcomes experienced by young adults. *Journal of Education and Work* 27(5): 496–523.

Linnehan, F. (2004). The relation of source credibility and message frequency to program evaluation and self-confidence of students in a job shadowing program. *Journal of Vocational Education Research* 29(1): 67–81.

Neumark, D. and Rothstein, D. (2005). *Do school-to-work programs help the 'Forgotten Half'?* Cambridge, MA: National Bureau of Economic Research.

Norris, E. and Francis, F. (2014). The impact of financial and cultural capital on FE students' education and employment progression, in Mann, A., Stanley, J. and Archer, L. (eds.), *Understanding employer engagement in education: Theories and evidence.* London: Routledge.

OECD. (2001). *The well-being of nations: Human and social capital.* Paris: Organisation for Economic Co-Operation and Development.

Raffo, C. and Reeves, M. (2000). Youth transitions and social exclusion: Developments in social capital theory. *Journal of Youth Studies* 3(2): 147–166.

Schoon, I. and Lyons-Amos, Mark. (2017). A socio-ecological model of agency: The role of structure and agency in shaping education and employment transitions in England. *Journal of Longitudinal and Lifecourse Studies.* doi:10.14301/llcs.v8i1.404

Schoon, I. and Polek, E. (2011). Teenage career aspirations and adult career attainment: The role of gender, social background and general cognitive ability. *International Journal of Behavioral Development* 35(3): 210–217.

Stanley, J. and Mann, A. (2014). A theoretical framework for employer engagement, in Mann, A., Stanley, J. and Archer, L. (eds.), *Understanding employer engagement in education: Theories and evidence.* London: Routledge.

UK Data Service. (2016). *April 2015–March 2016.* London: UK Data Service.

Van Deth, J.W. and Zmerli, S. (2010). Introduction: Civicness, equality, and democracy – A "Dark Side" of social capital? *American Behavioral Scientist* 53(5): 631–639.

Yates, S., Harris, A., Sabates, R. and Staff, J. (2011). Early occupational aspirations and fractured transitions: A study of entry into 'NEET' status in the UK. *Journal of Social Policy* 40(3): 513–534.

Chapter 6

Tell it like it is

Education and employer engagement, freelance and self-employment

Prue Huddleston and Heidi Ashton

Background

Calls for employer engagement within education are nothing new; the clarion call has gone out for over a century fuelled by complaints from employers concerning the lack of preparedness of young people for entering the labour market (Huddleston, 2013). Over 30 years ago, Jamieson (1985) described a situation amounting to a 'scapegoating' of young people for the presumed shortcomings of the education system; the language has not changed much since. There are many reasons for this assumed state of affairs, all of which cannot be set at the door of either the education system in general or at young people in particular. Yet the persistence of familiar rhetoric around 'low skills', 'poor productivity', 'skills shortages' and lack of 'global competitiveness' have dominated policy debate for over 30 years. In the context of the Sainsbury Review (DfE and BIS, 2016) and the resulting Post-16 Skills Plan (DBIS and DfE, 2016), the well-rehearsed themes have emerged as an all too familiar reprise to 'put employers at the heart of the system' (DBIS and DfE, 2016).

This is too simplistic a response to a complex and complicated challenge. To talk about employers as if they were an homogeneous group with the same needs and demands for labour is to fall into a trap of 'common sense', or 'everybody knows', generalisation. Organisations purporting to represent the views of employers will only represent the views of a particular group, or sector, of employers, or even of those who bothered to answer the questionnaire or respond to the consultation. Responses will reflect the size of the organisation, its field of operation, its product market, its perceived skills shortages (Huddleston and Keep, 1999). They should not be taken as unilateral endorsement of a poor state of affairs within the education system (for a fuller discussion see chapter 1 in this volume).

Of particular concern is the rhetoric appears to rely upon an out-dated concept of employment, one rooted in the belief that most jobs are in large corporations, dominated by engineering, manufacturing or financial services. This is clearly no longer the case in the UK. Recent statistics published by the Office for National Statistics (ONS) suggest that 15.1% of all people in work are currently self-employed or freelance.[1] Furthermore, the Office has reported continued growth with numbers increasing by 144,000 in the three months up to January 2017 (ONS, 2017). These workers are often invisible, lying outside of general statistical analysis and with limited detailed data on the group; nevertheless, this growth has been seen as a 'defining characteristic' of the UK's recent economic recovery (ONS, 2016). The term 'self-employed' is itself somewhat contested, although it generally encompasses freelancers, sole traders and those employing others in micro businesses. A recent study for the Association of Independent Professionals and the Self-Employed found that freelancers alone contributed £119 billion to the UK economy in 2016 (Jenkins, 2017).

> Self-employment accounts for nearly half of all jobs created since the economic downturn of 2008 . . . it may not be long before freelancers, sole-traders and micro-entrepreneurs outnumber the public sector workforce.
>
> (RSA, 2017)

This is why questions about the appropriateness, or not, of careers education and guidance need to be addressed as a matter of urgency. The preparation of young people for life beyond education needs to take account of the changed reality of the workplace, one increasingly characterised by precarity (Fleming, 2017; Standing, 2014), short-term or zero hours contracts, temporary work and self-employment. A 'job for life' is no longer the experience of most workers: 'Now a typical worker – more likely to be a woman – can anticipate having nine employers before reaching the age of 30' (Standing, ibid. 62).

What is available in our schools and colleges in terms of the curriculum offered, careers education and guidance proffered, and its links with potential employment and employers should more accurately reflect what is happening in the world beyond education. Put simply, they should 'tell it like it is'. Presenting images of 'jobs for life', traditional professional routes and focusing only on employment within a limited range of sectors is to do a disservice to young people and deny them opportunities to experience a wider range of engagement with the world beyond school. This is urgent because it restricts opportunities for young people to learn about the potential variety of labour market opportunities.

An area of the economy which is increasingly important and where self-employment is commonplace is the creative and cultural sector. Arguably, barriers to young people gaining relevant and useful insight into this sector before leaving education is particularly acute, not only because careers provision has so little to say about self-employment, but because of the narrowing of the English school curriculum since 2010. Many creative opportunities have been reduced, if not excised, from the National Curriculum in England, particularly at key stage 4 (age 14–16). For example, the 'English Baccalaureate (EBacc) measure', an indicator against which schools' performances are measured, includes five subjects: English, mathematics, science, a language, history or geography. Whilst there is opportunity within the curriculum to pursue other subjects as well, the perverse consequences have been for schools to concentrate their efforts on improving performance in these subjects at the expense of others (Baker, 2017; Henley, 2012; Warwick Commission, 2015). A report published by the Education Policy Institute (EPI) stated that:

> 53.5% of pupils took at least one arts subject in 2016, the lowest figure of the past 10 years. In 2007, 55.6% of pupils were entered for at least one arts subject, a proportion that steadily increased to 57.1% in 2014 before dropping more steeply since then. Provisional data from 2017 indicate the decline of recent years is set to continue.
>
> (Johnes, 2017, 7)

What can we learn from the creative and cultural sector?

We argue that the creative and cultural sector (a diverse sector offering a wide range of occupations across art and design, performing arts, fashion, media, IT, marketing and publishing) is a rich source of evidence and expertise, often providing role models to which young people can relate, and reflecting the realities of much of the modern labour market. It makes a significant contribution to the UK economy. In January 2016, the UK Department for Culture, Media and Sport (DCMS, 2016a) reported that the creative industries collectively contribute £92 billion a year to the UK economy. If creative jobs in other sectors are factored in, this contribution increases to £249 billion (DCMS, 2016b). As such, the sector is hailed as one of the UK's greatest success stories (DCMS, 2016a). The sector grew by 8.9% in 2014, more than any of the other 'Blue Book' industries and almost twice as fast as the UK economy as a whole (ONS, 2015). It has been one of the few growth sectors following the 2008 recession – the gross value added (GVA) has increased by 15.6% compared with 5.4% for the UK economy as a whole (DCMS, 2016a).

In terms of employment, the creative economy accounts for around 2.8 million jobs. Between 2013 and 2014, jobs in the sector increased by 5% compared with an increase of 2.1% for the wider UK economy (DCMS, 2016a). In 2014, the export of services from the creative industries was valued at £19.8 billion, up 10.9% on the previous year and accounting for 9% of the UK's total export services in that year (DCMS, 2016a). On March 13, 2015, the DCMS tweeted, 'Our creative industries are growing stronger each year, creating more jobs and driving economic growth.' The recent Bazalgette Review of the Creative Industries predicts that the creative industries could be worth £128.4 billion to the UK economy by 2025 and could help to create up to one million jobs by 2030. (Bazalgette, 2017)

In terms of wider societal benefits, the most recent government survey on arts participation 'Taking Part Year 12 (2016–2017)', an annual survey conducted for DCMS by Ipsos Mori, found that 76.1% of adults had engaged in the arts during the year (Ipsos Mori, 2017). One Dance UK, the main industry body for dance, reports that 'the arts contribute significantly to education, health and wellbeing, community cohesion, social mobility and diversity' (One Dance UK, 2017, 1).

The sector itself is characterised by a large proportion of self-employed workers. The music, performing and visual arts sub-sector has a particularly high proportion of self-employed workers with more than 7 in 10 jobs being held by those who are self-employed or freelance. This is due in part to the project-based mode of production that proliferates in the sector (Caves, 2000; Eikoff and Warhurst, 2013; Lahiff and Guile, 2016). Work organised in this way exposes workers to numerous short-term contracts, requiring them to adapt and develop their range of skills and abilities according to the demands of each project. This also puts the onus of developing skills on the worker. Workers have to work hard to obtain employment and maintain and build an evolving portfolio of skills. It is little surprise, therefore, that the DCMS reports a varied but overall lower rate of skills provision by companies within the creative industries. Clearly, there is little need to do so when workers will do it for themselves. Moreover, those micro and small businesses which do exist rarely possess a dedicated training function. Despite this, the research also states that businesses within the sector were less likely to report a 'skills gap' – only 12% of organisations across the entire sector reported a skills shortage compared with 15.6% of those outside the sector.

Outside their primary source of employment many freelance workers also find themselves diversifying and using their skills resourcefully beyond the sector in order to find employment between projects. Research into freelance workers in dance, music and film, for example, suggests a range of employment areas including photography, shop work, administrative jobs and, commonly, teaching (Ashton and Ashton, 2015; Banks and Hesmondhalgh, 2009; Hesmondhalgh and Baker, 2009).

Such workers have to keep their networks current and have a keen commercial awareness of their field. They need to update their skills accordingly and market themselves effectively for work. They have to be able to present themselves and their work quickly and engagingly in portfolios, show reels and auditions and carefully manage their finances. This requires a range of skills, both creative and administrative, in addition to a strong work ethic, good team-working skills and confidence. As one freelance dancer interviewed for this study summed up particularly succinctly, 'We adapt very, very quickly because we have to.'

As we have demonstrated above, self-employed and freelance workers are not exclusive to the creative industries; an increase in freelancing and self-employment generally can be found across sectors. The UK labour market as a whole has seen a significant growth in self-employment. This argues the case for a more realistic presentation of modern labour markets within schools not only within careers provision, but in terms of pedagogic approaches – for example, through group and teamwork, problem solving within realistic contexts and engagement with freelance workers from across sectors (including former pupils).

The project-based mode of production, for example, is becoming increasingly popular beyond the creative industries because of the flexibility it affords to organisations (Sahara et al. 2015; Brown et al. 2011; Boltanski and Chiapello, 2005). With this type of work, however, comes greater uncertainty and precarity. There is some discussion over the extent to which this is beneficial or damaging for workers in terms of employment rights, security and flexibility (Banks, 2016; Hennekam and Bennett, 2017; Oakley, 2006), but research in the area highlights the range of skills required and developed by this group of workers.

The UK Skills Employment Survey (SES) found that self-employed people made greater use of some skills than regularly employed peers, including self-planning, client communication and problem solving. Furthermore, self-employed workers reported greater levels of task variety, requiring the ability to adapt and demonstrate resilience (Baumberg and Meager, 2015). As seen above, there has been a significant increase in self-employed and freelance workers, with forecasts predicting continued growth in these types of employment. We are only beginning to understand the area of skills development amongst this group of workers, but there could be lessons here for the organisation of school curricula, pedagogical approaches and assessment.

Testimonies of creative workers

We draw on data from a group of workers predominantly located within the music, performing and visual arts sub-sector of the creative industries to examine the range of skills developed.[2] The data derive from on-going ethnographic research into the nature of work in dance-related industries with a focus on professional, freelance dancers. Data include interviews with working professionals about their experiences in both training and work, in addition to fieldwork within the freelance dance community. What we find is that there are a number of important skills gained through engagement with these creative activities that are transferable to other employment contexts and settings. Furthermore, we see a significant gap between the skills required for this type of work and those most commonly developed in the formal education system.

The following case study of freelance dancers provides an insight into the range and diversity of skills and issues inherent in these types of occupations. Focusing on one group within the sector enables us to build upon the statistical evidence provided by researchers such as Baumberg and Meager (2015). (See also Chapter 7 in this volume for further discussion regarding skills development for freelancers within the music technology industry).

The approach is eclectic in terms of data collection. Commencing in 2012, data have been collected through 43 semi-structured interviews with dancers in the UK and the USA (24 from the UK and 19 from the USA),[3] participant observation at work sites such as dance rehearsal studios, theatres and events and engagement with the community via social media and social events. One of the authors remains active within the freelance dance community. The other is an external examiner on a UK undergraduate dance education programme.

Participant observation in the field provided further opportunities to record relevant conversations and observations in context. This left a great deal to chance, but the conversations that were recorded arose organically within the community (see Atkinson et al., 2007). This aspect of data collection was gained through complete immersion with the researcher accepted as an 'insider'. This connection and acceptance within the dance community enabled the researcher to be overt in the recording of data with dancers who were generally interested in the research. Whilst there are many disadvantages to being an insider (ibid), these were mitigated through the further analysis of data with the co-author in relation to the issues discussed herein and located within a reading of other ethnographic studies and wider academic and public literature.

The findings reported here draw upon the responses provided by the 24 UK respondents.

Skills, not qualifications

Freelance dancers, like many others in the creative sector – film makers, music technicians, lighting designers – engage in work across the creative industries. Dancers may be in a music video or pop tour, dancing on television, at events, in theatres, on cruise ships, dancing for advertising campaigns, in films or providing motion capture for the games industry. Their work is dependent upon numerous short-term contracts that can range from a day to several months. This means that not only do they need to engage in other paid work outside the creative industries between contracts, but they must also work hard to get work and maintain a profile within the industry. As with other freelance workers (Hesmondhalgh, 2012; Banks, 2016), they are also responsible for maintaining and developing their skills and at their own expense.

Previous research has shown that dancers generally train for around 10 years before becoming professionals (Ashton and Ashton, 2015; Ijdens and Langenberg, 2008). The majority of professional dancers do not perform regularly beyond the age of 40. Injuries can take a substantial toll on the dancer's career. The training is intense and entry into both professional training and work within the profession is by audition only. Academic qualifications have no bearing or influence either in terms of gaining access to professional training or subsequent work. Success is dependent upon performance in an audition, networks obtained through vocationally-oriented training and work within the industry. Decisions to call someone for audition will be influenced by a personal portfolio, including a performance video (show reel) or at the suggestion of another professional who is familiar with the dancer's work.

Different worlds

A striking finding in the data was the ways in which those entering the dance profession felt removed and different from the 'norm'. This was reinforced by expectations of professionals at school in relation to the student's transition into work.

> Careers was hilarious. . . . .You had to go on a computer and answer all these
> questions. I think it was like 50 questions or something . . . and then it would
> print off what career would be suited to you and I had none! [Laughter]!
> I was like why don't they just put that I want to be a performer? . . . and
> then going to sit with, you know, the woman in the library, going to me
> what would you like to do? I was like oh no, I am sorted, because at that
> point I had already auditioned for a college and got in. I knew I was going
> and she said what GCSEs are you taking? I was like well I am just taking
> the normal ones and then I am going to a performing arts college and she
> literally was like, what? You know you need a career, you need to do your
> A levels, she just didn't get it . . . And they (the school) did not support me
> in the slightest! They were just full on against it like you are making a big
> mistake. I remember them calling my mum as well and saying you know we
> think your daughter needs to kind of open her eyes and see the real world.

A fundamental lack of understanding pervaded experiences of mainstream
schools. Those in education providing advice and guidance on careers did
not encourage or impart knowledge of the creative industries in general, or
specifically in dance. Neither did they provide information about opportunities available in related sectors which utilise creativity and the transferable skill
set obtained by those pursuing creative careers. This supports anecdotal evidence given by creative professionals such as actors, film-makers, musicians and
designers in interviews and biographies.

Freelance dancers found themselves effectively alienated from mainstream
education, experiencing a fundamental difference in both an understanding and
value of employment in the creative industries. Within the UK, for example,
UCAS points (entry requirements for admission to higher education) and other
mainstream academic qualifications are not relevant for this sub-sector. Entry
into further education and training is not determined by academic grades but
rather through the performance of skills in an audition and the demonstration
of a desire to develop these skills further. The lack of support or understanding
of the skills required to gain entry into this sector is felt to be a 'different world'
from that of mainstream education.

> Often I found they [teachers] kind of didn't like get it. Because it's such
> a completely different type of thing, it's a different kind of world almost.
> I remember . . . you know, I suppose I was sixth form age, to do with
> whether I would need like UCAS points or things to be able to go on and
> I had to explain . . . it's not quite like that, you know, you have an audition,
> it's completely different.

The use of portfolios, show reels, auditions and other creative forms of demon-strating work and abilities are commonplace for entry into education and jobs in the creative industries. Work is demonstrated in a direct way.[4] Presenting oneself and one's work is important, and the ability and skill required to dem-onstrate one's talents in these ways are rarely perceived by professional dancers as being developed through school experiences. When academic qualifications are so highly valued in schools, there is a danger that other skills, such as pre-senting oneself and one's work, are considered peripheral or even irrelevant.[5]

This difference between the skills and talents valued within the education system and those valued by industry and required by freelance workers within the creative and cultural sector was clearly evident and often profound. This led to a sense of alienation and disconnection from the school system in relation to the chosen profession.

> I got quite good grades in my GCSEs. They assumed I would be pushing more because all my family are pharmacists they thought I would push more for that side of things if I didn't go into dancing, which they all thought I wouldn't because they kept saying it's a hard world, you won't be good enough. It's like how do you know, you have never seen me dance! They had never seen me dance. They were just thinking little girl from Hull, she is nowhere near London; it's never going to work out for her. They just didn't understand.

Whilst there is an understanding and acknowledgement that life as a freelance dancer is very tough, there is a lack of knowledge and understanding of the sector as a whole. Not only is there little understanding about the specific skills of the individual, but also the range of opportunities available and the skills and competencies gained during this type of training. The assumption, therefore, was that the entire venture, in the eyes of those in education, was unrealistic and unattainable. Incidentally, this dancer went on to have a very long and lucrative career working across theatre and television.

This lack of understanding was experienced by all the freelance dancers interviewed. Their creative skills were often not only misunderstood by their schools, but also experienced as under-valued and not taken seriously.

> The careers talk went like this: 'Oh . . . what do you want to do?' I am going to be a dancer. 'No. What are you going to do as a career?' No. I am going to be a dancer. 'No. That's your hobby. What are you going to do for your job?' I am going to be a dancer. In the end I think I kind of got in a bit of a mood because this careers person . . . just was like 'no that's not a career'. And I was trying to make her see, yeah it was.

There was a clear sense that professionals in the education system were part of a different world from those training to enter a profession as a freelance worker in the creative industries. Dancers left school with a sense that those outside the profession did not understand the way in which the profession is structured, the ways in which work is obtained, the skills and abilities that are valued by the profession and the skills and abilities required to obtain employment.

Working across boundaries

In contrast to the organisation of the school curriculum, particularly since the introduction of the post-2010 curriculum reforms, those working in the creative and cultural sector are required to work across boundaries, not in subject silos. Inter-disciplinary research and development is increasingly important in all fields of endeavour, yet school targets, league tables and even institutional arrangements are subject based. One of the many perverse effects of this accountability regime results in certain subjects being offered only if pupil numbers are financially viable or if the subject is included in the EBacc measure (see above).

This tendency also has a perverse effect on the supply of teachers in creative subjects; the UK Warwick Commission reported an 11% drop in teachers of art and design since 2010, with similar falls in numbers of specialist teachers of drama and dance (Warwick Commission, 2015). One Dance UK recently reported (One Dance UK, 2017) that the number of candidates who took GCSE Dance in 2016 fell by 9% compared to the previous year and by 32% compared to 2010, when the EBacc was first announced. As award-winning writer of children's literature Meg Roscoff has suggested, the British government's obsession with 'fact-based' education has encouraged the study of so-called 'hard subjects' – science, mathematics – as sure routes to secure employment in 'business, law, banking and finance' (Guardian, September, 2017) to the exclusion of creative activity. The official statistics presented in our opening section suggest that 'secure employment' is a fast disappearing *modus vivendi* and that jobs in the creative and cultural sector are, in fact, increasing.

> While the compelling need for creativity, care and compassion across the world has been growing, the greatest global educational trend of the past two decades ran completely contrary to it, driven by the promise of short-term results.
>
> (Hargreaves, 2016, 36)

School assessment, particularly that required by public examinations, is inimical to the sorts of approaches required by those working within the creative and cultural sector where project-based work, portfolio, performance, show reels, videos and artefacts are the metrics of recruitment, selection and assessment. In the latest round of qualification reforms, still working their way through the secondary education system, there is a renewed emphasis on terminal written examinations and a reduction in the permitted amount of coursework assessment, even in drama. This low trust environment is not conducive to experimental assessment design, such as project-based work, group work, live performance or the production of craft artefacts.

Creativity is not in a closed mental box, along with arts. It can and should apply to every area of the curriculum (and even to personal relationships). Both arts and sciences require creativity and imagination.

(Best, 1992, 3)

Outreach activities by creative and cultural enterprises make a significant contribution in helping young people develop creativity – an attribute very highly prized by employers (CBI, 2011, 2012; UKCES, 2009). Often this provision has to be squeezed into crowded curriculum time, or may be too expensive for a school's budget to afford. In a recent article in The Stage (January 2018), Andrew Lloyd Webber denounced the practice of a state school charging pupils to take a GCSE music course, stating that all arts subjects should be taught free in English state schools. In this environment, creative and cultural activities and engagement remain the prerogative of the well off.

Working to get work

Dancers were very aware of the importance of networks. As freelancers, they worked hard to increase networks and were proactive in finding and creating opportunities. There was also a sense of kinship and mutual support – dancers would often advertise opportunities within the dance community and offer work, where they could, to colleagues who, in turn, would reciprocate. Reliant upon numerous and various short-term contracts, dancers described working hard to maintain opportunities to work between dance contracts, to live, pay rent, attend auditions and, above all, stay fit.

When people are unemployed, you put out the feelers and say do you need a teacher, promo work, anything?

These freelance workers also had a keen understanding of how social media can be used to enhance opportunities and promote work in which they are involved. They demonstrated how to harness social media and utilise it for marketing purposes to secure employment. As freelance dancers often work globally, social media is particularly useful as a platform to share advice and work-related information. This ability to employ social media to enhance social capital for employment purposes is also found in other freelance occupations in the creative industries. In film and television, for example, Facebook sites are often used to find camera operators, sound technicians, project managers, runners and other technical and administrative staff. The importance of developing and maintaining social and professional networks is long established within the sector and, of course, pre-dates the introduction of Facebook (Blair, 2003, 2001). Facebook has just facilitated this tendency and is reflected in the findings of Lahiff and Guile (2016) in their study of media apprentices:

[T]hese networks of contacts are critical in the sense that without these and the where-with-all needed to develop networks, apprentices cannot hope to develop occupational practices that will sustain them in the sector beyond apprenticeship.

(p. 317)

Our findings also highlighted a sophisticated awareness of the commercial aspects of the industry, market forces and how to increase employability. Again, skill development is left to the individual. With no large organisation to invest in the individual and their skills and with the requirements of the industry constantly developing and evolving, freelancers have to be versatile and proactive in up-skilling and maintaining relevance in their industry.

You've kind of got to be versatile if you want to keep working; you've got to be able to rise to anything that's thrown at you.

This is achieved at their own expense. A collaborative and collegial approach is taken through mutual understanding and reciprocal exchanges. Teamwork and mutual support is crucial.

You're learning from each other all the time.

Within this market awareness, the dancers interviewed exhibited a very strong sense of themselves as 'a business', where the consequences of errors are stark and can be detrimental to the networks essential for employment (Blair, 2001). For freelancers, if you make a mistake, you personally will pay the price. If a dancer does not perform well on a job, it is unlikely that the choreographer will work with them again as the choreographer will also be exposed. It is the choreographer's name and work which is on display or hired by the client. Teamwork, reliability and consistency in their work become essential.

It's not like . . . I am an accountant and I messed up on a decimal place here or there and I can go back and fix it. I am . . . my product is myself.

Freelancers also demonstrated great resilience and an ability to adapt their skills to different contexts. It is not uncommon for freelance dancers to run a business in parallel with their dance work. Examples from interviewees included dog walking, creating coasters from film, choreographing wedding dances, opening dance and performing arts schools, developing and editing show reels and, of course, teaching and coaching.

We set up the business because we had bills and we needed to have some control over money coming in. Just to have something coming in really.

Here, a move that would seem precarious in terms of income to some is a source of stability to these portfolio workers. Those who do not start their own business adapt and work in a range of jobs in order to pay for living costs, dance classes and auditions whilst between jobs. A clear sense of resilience and a 'can do' attitude is evident throughout the data.

> I'd get a kind of fill in job, you know, just keep getting the money in, keep myself fit and keep going to the auditions.

Freelance dancers are required to demonstrate high-level capacities to adapt and survive, whatever their circumstances, finding creative solutions to problems and employing a diverse range of skills in a variety of occupations. This capacity is not confined to the world of dancers, but characterises 'ways of working' within the creative and cultural sector more broadly and, it is suggested, will become increasingly common, and essential, in labour markets dominated by freelance work and self-employment.

Conclusions

We have argued that those responsible for education, both policy and practice, need to provide young people with a more realistic picture of the changing nature of employment and working practices, particularly self-employment and freelance work. At a time when government is urging employers to 'sit at the heart of the system' (DBIS and DfE, 2016), it is essential that employers adequately and accurately represent the realities of modern workplaces. This is true in terms of the influence they might have on the curriculum, the development of qualifications and in the images they portray of current working practices and opportunities. It is important that any discussion of 'employer engagement' within education policy rhetoric includes those who work for no one but themselves and who are forming ever-greater proportions of the 21st century labour force.

We have also described how the current secondary school curriculum in England provides fewer opportunities than previously for pupils to access a broad range of creative and cultural experiences. Yet the creative and cultural sector provides a wide range of employment opportunities that go far beyond actor, artist, dancer, designer or musician. It is a sector of the economy that has shown significant growth in the face of economic downturn. The participants in this research experienced somewhat negative responses, often driven by ignorance, from teachers and careers professionals about their proposed career choices. Yet it has also been demonstrated that those working within the creative and cultural sector exhibit those skills, attributes, attitudes and behaviours that employers say they are looking for in young people. These include resilience, independence, networking and communication skills, an ability to undertake project-based work, self-management and sound financial management skills to survive in hard times. What is delivered by the education system and what employers say they want is not necessarily the same, particularly within some sectors.

Exposure to creative and cultural opportunities within the curriculum is important, not because the intention is to turn pupils into professional dancers, musicians, designers and film–makers, but because such exposure offers enriching and fulfilling experiences on a personal and societal level in terms of skills development, health and well-being. It also provides insights into the changing nature of labour markets, including labour relations, which have a wider significance beyond the creative and cultural sector. Those working within our education system, in particular policy makers, at every level should recognise that creative and cultural activities can provide opportunities for young people not available elsewhere in the curriculum; for many these are also unavailable at home or within their wider community.

Those who work in the sector also provide role models to whom young people can relate and who are engaged in activities in which they are interested. Education professionals and policy makers need to recognise the importance of other influences beyond school that shape young people's identities and interests. These will ultimately affect their career choices, as we saw with our case study respondents. The creative and cultural sector can provide opportunities to individuals who do not thrive within the conventional school curriculum, but we argue that it can provide opportunities for all as part of an entitlement to a rich and balanced curriculum that offers a vision of a wider world beyond formal education. Encouraging engagement between the creative industries and education is vital to ensure that the work of the sector is recognised and celebrated and is better understood by young people and education professionals.

> An attraction strategy is needed to inform and excite young people, their teachers and parents about careers in the Creative Industries.
>
> (Bazalgette, 2017, 6)

Everyone engaged in the education and development of young people has a duty to 'tell it like it is' in terms of the advice and guidance they offer, the images they project and the messages they broadcast concerning 21st century labour markets. They should also allow a voice to young people, who often know much more about 'how it is' than we give them credit for.

Notes

1 The terms 'freelance' and 'self-employed' are often used interchangeably, particularly in statistical analysis, although the latter can include those who employ others on an ad hoc basis.
2 Whilst predominantly located in the music, performing and visual arts sub sector freelance dancers work across a range of sub sectors such as; advertising and marketing, IT software and computer services (gaming especially), fashion design and film, TV, video, radio and photography.
3 The sample consisted of 15 male and 28 female dancers between the ages of 21 and 44. This gender differentiation is reflective of the industry as a whole with women making up around 70% of the workforce (Ijdens and Langenberg, 2008)
4 Problems such as social inequalities and bias have been found to create barriers to entry into some creative subjects limiting access and the ability of some to demonstrate such skills in the preferred manner. These issues are beyond the scope of this paper. See Banks, 2017; McRobbie, 2016; Archer, 2000 for further discussion.

5 It is interesting to note that assessment of speaking skills within the General Certificate of Secondary Education (GCSE) English qualification has been removed in the latest round of qualification 'reforms'. Yet, it is hard to conceive of any area of employment, particularly in customer facing roles, where the ability to present oneself and to relate to others is not important and highly valued.

References

Archer, M. (2000) *Being human: The problem of agency*. Cambridge: Cambridge University Press.

Ashton, H. and Ashton, D. (2015). 'Bring on the dancers': Reconceptualising the transition from school to work. *Journal of Education and Work* 29(7): 747–766.

Atkinson, P., Delamont, S., Coffey, A., Lofland, J. and Lofland, L. (2007). *Handbook of ethnography*. London: Sage Publications.

Baker, K. (2017). 14–19 *education a new baccalaureate*. London: Edge Foundation.

Banks, M. (2016). *Creative justice: Cultural industries, work and inequality*. London: Rowman and Littlefield.

Banks, M. and Hesmondhalgh, D. (2009). Looking for work in creative industries policy. *International Journal of Cultural Policy* 15(4): 415–430.

Baumberg, B. and Meager, N. (2015). Job quality and the self-employed, in Felstead, A., Gallie, D. and Green, F. (eds.), *Unequal Britain at work*. Oxford: Oxford University Press.

Bazalgette, P. (2017). *An independent review of the creative industries*. London: DCMS/DBEIS.

Best, D. (1992). *The rationality of feeling understanding the arts in education*. London: Falmer Press.

Blair, H. (2001). You are only as good as your last job: The labour process and the labour market in the British film industry. *Work Employment and Society* 15(1): 149–169.

Blair, H. (2003). Winning and losing in flexible labour markets: The formation and operation of networks of interdependence in the UK film industry. *Sociology* 37(4): 677–694.

Boltanski, L. and Chiapello, E. (2005). *The new spirit of capitalism*. London: Verso.

Brown, P., Lauder, H. and Ashton, D. (2011). *The global auction: The broken promises of education, jobs and income*. Oxford: Oxford University Press.

Caves, R. (2000). *Creative industries: Contracts between art and commerce*. Boston, MA: Harvard University Press.

CBI. (2011). *Skills for the creative industries: Investing in the talents of our people*. London: CBI.

CBI. (2012). *First steps: A new approach for our schools*. London: CBI.

DBIS and DfE. (2016). *Post-16 skills plan*. CM 9280. London: DfE.

DCMS. (2016a). *Creative industries economic estimates – Jan 2016*. London: DCMS.

DCMS. (2016b). *Creative industries economic estimates – Nov 2016*. London: DCMS.

DfE and BIS. (2016). *Report of the independent panel on technical education*. ('The Sainsbury Review'). London: DfE.

Eikoff, D. and Warhurst, C. (2013). The promised land? Why social inequalities are systemic in the creative industries. *Employee Relations* 35(5): 495–508.

Fleming, P. (2017). *The death of homo economicus*. London: Pluto Press.

Hargreaves, A. (2016). Blooming teachers. *RSA Journal* 1: 34–39.

Henley, D. (2012). *Cultural education in England: Independent review by Darren Henley for the department for culture, media and sport and the department for education*. London: DCMS/DBEIS.

Hennekam, S. and Bennett, D. (2017). Creative industries work across multiple contexts: Common themes and challenges. *Personnel Review* 46(1): 68–85.

Hesmondhalgh, D. (2012). *The cultural industries*. London: Sage Publications.

Hesmondhalgh, D. and Baker, S. (2009). 'A very complicated version of freedom': Conditions and experiences of creative labour in three cultural industries. *Poetics* 38(1): 4–20.

Huddleston, P. (2013). Engaging and linking with employers, in Huddleston, P. and Stanley, J. (eds.), *Work-related teaching and learning guide for teachers and practitioners*. Abingdon: Routledge.

Huddleston, P. and Keep, E. (1999). What do employers want from education? A question more easily asked than answered, in Cramphorn, J. (ed.), *The role of partnership in economic regeneration and development*. Coventry: University of Warwick: 38–49.

Ijdens, T. and Langenberg, B. (2008). *Dancers keep moving*. Report for the IOTPD.

Ipsos Mori. (2017). *Taking part survey year 12 (2016–2017)*. London: DCMS/DBEIS. Available from: www.gov.uk/taking-part-survey/technical report [accessed November 20th 2017].

Jamieson, I. (1985). Corporate hegemony or pedagogic liberation? The schools–industry movement in England and Wales, in Dale, R. (ed.), *Education, training and employment: Towards a new vocationalism*. Oxford: Pergamon in Association with the Open University Press: 23–38.

Jenkins, K. (2017). *Exploring the UK freelance workforce in 2016*. London: The Association of Independent Professionals and the Self-Employed.

Johnes, R. (2017). *Entries to arts subjects at Key Stage 4*. London: Education Policy Institute.

Lahiff, A. and Guile, D. (2016). 'It's not like a normal 9 to 5!': The learning journeys of media production apprentices in distributed working conditions. *Journal of Vocational Education & Training* 68(3): 302–319.

McRobbie, A. (2016) *Be creative: Making a living in the new culture industries*. Cambridge: Polity Press.

Oakley, K. (2006). Include us out — economic development and social policy in the creative industries. *Cultural Trends* 14(4): 283–302.

Office for National Statistics. (2015). *United kingdiom national accounts, the blue book: 2015 edition*. Available from: www.ons.gov.uk/economy/grossdomesticproductgdp/compendium/unitedkingdomnationalaccountsthebluebook/2015-10-30 [accessed January 16th 2018].

Office for National Statistics. (2016). *Trends in self-employment in the UK: 2001 to 2015*. Available from: www.ons.gov.uk/employmentandlabourmarket/peopleinwork/employmentand employeetypes/articles/trendsinselfemploymentintheuk/2001to2015 [accessed October 10th 2017].

Office for National Statistics. (2017). *UK labour market: Mar 2017*. Available from: www.ons. gov.uk/employmentandlabourmarket/peopleinwork/employmentandemployeetypes/bulletins/uklabourmarket/mar2017#employment [accessed October 10th 2017].

One Dance UK. (2017). *Dance manifesto*. London: One Dance.

Roscoff, M. (2017). Why Richard Dawkins and the government are wrong to be skeptical of storytelling. *Point of View, Guardian Review*, September 16th: 10.

RSA. (2017). *The entrepreneurial audit*. Available from: www.thersa.org/entrepreneurial-audit [accessed November 15th 2017].

Sahara, N., Bound, H., Karmel, A. and Sivalingam, M. (2015). *Masters of their destiny? Identities, learning and development of freelance workers in Singapore's technical theatre industry*. Singapore: Institute for Adult Learning.

Standing, G. (2014). *The precariat the new dangerous class*. London: Bloomsbury.

The Stage. (2018). *Andrew Lloyd Webber speaks out against schools charge for music GCSE*, January 9th. Available from: www.thestage.co.uk [accessed January 12th 2018].

UKCES. (2009). *The employability challenge*. Wath-upon-Dearne: UKCES.

Warwick Commission. (2015). *Enriching Britain, culture, creativity and growth, the 2015*. Report by the Warwick Commission on the Future of Cultural Value. Coventry: University of Warwick.

Chapter 7

'Selling the dream'

Stakeholder perceptions of the translation of employability policy into university strategy

Roy Priest

Introduction

The extent to which universities should prepare graduates for the workplace has been a particular focus of policy impacting across higher education over the last 20 years (Holmes, 2015). This is the result of a number of factors: changes to the ways in which higher education is funded in the UK and the subsequent cultural shift towards students being perceived as consumers of degree courses; ease of access to the results of metrics by which universities can be compared (Arora, 2015); the pace of technological change in the workplace and the impact that this has had on the requirements of employers when recruiting graduates (QAA, 2014).

Employability is a contentious issue, and there is no single definition in the context of higher education. Atkins (1999) underlined the lack of clarity around the term, highlighting the mix of nomenclature for skills related to employability such as 'transferable', 'core', 'key' etc. He also noted confusion around the classification of skill types such as technical competencies and personal attributes. The vagaries around the concept of employability have undermined various attempts to apply academic underpinning to evolving theories (Rajan, 2000).

The definition of employability as adopted by the UK's Enhancing Student Employability Co-ordination Team (ESECT) in 2005 has been widely accepted. The USEM model was developed in response to criticisms over the perceived lack of academic underpinning for previous attempts at defining employability and consists of the following inter-related aspects:

> Understanding; Skilful practices in context (deliberately so labelled in order to avoid the undesirable connotations of 'skills', and to acknowledge the situatedness of practice and performance); (self-) Efficacy and personal qualities; and Metacognition.
>
> (Yorke, 2010, 5)

Government reports Dearing (1997), Lambert (2003) and Wilson (2012) emphasised the importance of universities and employers working in partnership and have acted as a catalyst for research and change across the sector. The Dearing Report (1997) updated the overall aim of higher education to that of sustaining a learning society. The report advocated closer collaboration between universities and industry. Recommendations related to employability were made more specific with a call for individual programme specifications to focus on the development of key skills related to:

> Communication, numeracy, the use of information technology and learning how to learn.
>
> (Dearing, 1997, 372)

The Lambert Review (2003) emphasised sector-wide accountability, encouraging greater transparency in the comparative outcomes of individual courses in terms of graduate destinations. This review also emphasised the importance of informal interactions between business and higher education. The Wilson Review (2012) was unequivocal regarding the responsibility being placed on universities to enhance graduate employability. Students need to be supported in the development of skills related to employability and staff need to be trained to support this process.

The impact of such Government intervention has resulted in policy-driven strategies being pursued by universities that typically advocate an integrated approach for the enhancement of graduate employability. There remain issues around bringing together the cultures of academia and employers (Lowden et al. 2011). Whilst the now ubiquitous university employability statements typically espouse mutually beneficial, on-going relationships between higher education and industry, they do not necessarily present a coherent message (HEFCE, 2011). Furthermore, Archer and Davison (2008) contend that the messages being promoted by universities do not necessarily reflect the requirements of industry.

Findings suggest divisions within academia as to how universities should react to the changing environment (Boden and Nedeva, 2010). Various models and frameworks for the development of employability as part of an undergraduate experience have been developed (UKCES, 2009; HEA, 2015), typically emphasising an embedded approach to delivery.

Expert critics such as Tomlinson (2010), Collini (2011), Holmes (2015) and Teichler (2014) counter established attitudes. The work of Holmes in particular challenges the validity of prevailing assumptions borne out of the 'skills agenda' instead focusing on the development of context-specific individual graduate identities (Holmes, 2015). Such identities are socially constructed and borne out of negotiation.

Whilst considerable research into various aspects of graduate employability has been published in recent years, an under-explored area is stakeholder perceptions of this dynamic environment in which the expectations placed on different stakeholder groups is evolving.

This research explores issues around the enhancement of graduate employability in a particular setting: BSc Music Technology courses. Such highly vocational degrees offer an opportunity to investigate perceptions in the context of courses that typically highlight the development of skills and attributes carefully aligned to the requirements of employers. The perspectives of the following key stakeholder groups were considered for this study: individuals working at policy level, academic staff, students and employers.

Research approach

The size of the four stakeholder sample groups was carefully considered in order to generate an appropriate level of credible research material. A purposive approach to sampling was chosen in order to exploit the potential of research contacts in the audio industry and academia. For the student survey, volunteer sampling was adopted, as access to individuals at different universities was not possible. Although the approach to data collection does not allow for generalisability, it does provide insight into the opinions of the target groups.

Following a qualitative methodology, the research investigated the perspectives of stakeholders through semi-structured interviews, focus groups and a survey. Eight semi-structured in-depth interviews were carried out with individuals working at policy level. Interviewees included senior university management from four universities and a representative from the Department for Business, Innovation and Skills (DBIS). One respondent was from a national employer-led organisation tasked with ensuring that industry is able to access the skills required for future development and another from a network organisation focused on recording achievement in further and higher education. This group also included an individual from an independent professional body representing graduate recruiters in the UK.

The views of students were drawn from Music Technology (BSc) courses at a further five universities. Sixty-three students drawn from across these institutions completed an online survey, and this was supplemented by data from three focus groups. Feedback from academic staff was captured via a focus group with three staff at one institution and eight at another. This was supplemented by a further one-to-one interview with an academic from a third institution.

Fourteen face-to-face interviews were carried out with employers from a range of organisations, from micro employers to small to medium-sized enterprises.

The semi-structured interviews provided the opportunity for interviewees to have some ownership of the direction of the discussions, which helped to elicit in-depth responses. Interviews were recorded and transcribed, subject to the agreement of the respondents. Fieldwork was carried out between May 2013 and June 2014. In keeping with standard ethical research guidelines, all participating individuals were guaranteed anonymity.

Findings

What is the purpose of a university education?

Feedback collected via this study would suggest that there is a level of common understanding as to the purpose of a university education across those working at policy level, employers and academics, emphasising a holistic approach to the value of a university education and the opportunities for self-transformation. However, there was evidence of a difference of view between the perceptions of students when compared to other stakeholder groups.

Employers stated that degree courses can act as a bridge in that they prepare students for the workplace, providing opportunities for developing a foundation of knowledge, honing skills and supporting students as they consider which particular career path to pursue.

Two individuals working at policy level highlighted the continued importance of education for education's sake. This notion is still recognised by the academic staff personally, although they perceive that this view is not held by current students, and this was borne out in the feedback from students. An employer commented on how the culture of higher education has changed and lamented the passing of an era when a university experience provided the opportunity to explore possibilities unfettered by the constraints of preparing for graduate employment.

A level of scepticism was noted amongst academics:

> We're producing what people call a graduate. Companies now, they say, oh, we need a graduate for this job, and universities, across the board, are producing people that fit what the company wants. Well, is that a real graduate?
>
> (Academic Staff, University A)

Whilst academic staff supported the notion of self-transformation, importance was placed on managing student expectations. Though a degree experience can be seen as a rite of passage, the benefits of a university education should not be overplayed to students. The commercial environment in which universities now operate can create a conflict of interests: academics are encouraged to 'sell' their courses in a highly competitive environment but are aware that over-stating the benefits can lead to dissatisfaction and disengagement amongst students:

> You can't promise a world of work experience for these kids, . . . So what are you guaranteeing them? You're guaranteeing that they're doing something they enjoy, and they achieve a level of learning, and that's it. And that was all it was.
>
> (Academic Staff, University A)

The findings of this study would indicate that in the context of Music Technology BSc programmes, students tend to have a prescriptive view of the purpose of higher education. Feedback from the survey indicates that students consider the prime purpose of a university education is to develop knowledge and skills in a particular area, and this is closely linked to the belief that the experience gained through a degree will enhance their prospects of getting a job, ideally related to the subject area of their degree. Another important theme was the perception that a degree could enhance earning potential. Such themes are illustrated in responses from the student survey. Students were asked to consider the purpose of a university education:

> To acquire some highly technical, marketable and worthwhile skills.
>
> To get an in-depth understanding of a subject and the qualifications to prove capability to prospective employers, enabling the graduate to more easily get a decent job in that field.
>
> Natural progression to further yourself from A-levels. Study a more specific area that hopefully leads into a job and enables you to progress up the ladder of 'success' with a bit more knowledge and speed than peers. Hopefully earn a better wage quicker and give you the ability to make a decent and effective start to career . . . Whilst at the same time having an awesome few years!

Similar views were expressed in the student focus groups where students perceived the purpose of a university education as a fast track for career development. Degrees were undertaken in order to obtain competitive advantage in the jobs market.

Some students noted how their views had evolved during their course, and they came to appreciate the importance of personal contacts. The experience of having undertaken a degree and, in particular, exposure to industry through a placement, can lead to cynicism, however:

> I used to think that, when I came to university, it's to get an edge over everyone else, but from working in industry and getting jobs while I'm here, it's just all down to experience [. . .]. It's not really about what you've done at university, it's about who you know [. . .].

What are stakeholder perceptions of employability?

Definitions of employability as offered by those working at policy level resonate with widely accepted models. This study found that at a policy level, employability is perceived as a combination of having the appropriate level of knowledge and skills, a positive attitude and appropriate workplace behaviour in order for an individual to be worthy of investment by an employer.

Views of those working at policy level included the interpretation of employability as being about personal empowerment. A university education offers the opportunity to develop knowledge, skills and approaches to problem solving and the ability to cope with change, to 'future-proof' a graduate as they navigate a career in a highly dynamic business environment.

Feedback from academics focused on employability being about having a positive attitude, tenacity and strong transferable skills, as well as being able to gain an appreciation of the wider industry they wish to enter as graduates. Academics emphasised the importance of students gaining an appreciation of how the knowledge that they have gained through their studies translates into the commercial world.

One academic felt strongly that it is the responsibility of the university to be aware of the particular skills required by employers; skills that are not necessarily recognised by applicants to an undergraduate degree:

> In some ways, I'm proud of having hoodwinked people into coming on to the Music Tech course, and giving them skills they didn't actually realise they wanted, and actually done them a favour.
>
> (Academic Staff, University B)

Employers' interpretations of what is meant by employability tended to focus on the graduate as a resource: what value a particular individual can bring to an organisation and the speed of return on investment. One employer highlighted the importance of interpersonal skills, to the extent that they can be more important than job specific skills.

The findings of this study would suggest that students can have a fairly narrow view as to what is meant by employability. Students tended to interpret graduate employability as the extent to which a degree makes an individual more attractive as a potential employee; the competitive advantage that comes with such a qualification. For many of the student respondents to this study, employability is simply about how successful graduates are in terms of finding a job. A few students considered employability to be about the ease of translation of degree knowledge into the context of the workplace.

Analysis of data collected for this research demonstrated that there was general agreement across the four stakeholder groups as to what attributes employers require from graduates, and this broadly reflects the findings of the CBI (2009) which focused on self-management; team working; business and customer awareness; problem solving; communication and literacy; numeracy and applied information technology. However, the findings of this study highlighted variances in emphasis across the stakeholder groups.

Survey feedback from students indicated that the respondents perceived previous experience to be the main priority for employers; this was also highlighted in discussions with employers. In contrast, previous experience was not mentioned by academics regarding the requirements of employers. In wider discussions, whilst academics typically acknowledge the benefits of students gaining work experience and work placements in particular; this is not necessarily a key focus for an academic. Supporting students in the pursuance of such work-based learning is resource-intensive, and whilst course marketing typically highlights the availability of such internships, student respondents spoke of frustration with the lack of support for such opportunities once on the course. Such unfulfilled expectations can lead to disenchantment amongst students.

Students tended to focus on the importance of learning to use particular software or hardware. However, employer requirements for specific attributes such as technical skills can be ambiguous. An academic contended:

> Learn how to learn. That's all they're interested in. If you know how to learn, you're OK. Many technical skills will be defunct.
>
> (Academic Staff, University A)

An employer spoke of how he had witnessed the broadcast sector change over the last twenty years, from taking on graduates from a broad range of courses and training them within the organisation towards a strategy of selecting graduates from more specifically vocational degrees. Part of the reason given for this is the growth of specialisation in this sector.

The importance of communication skills was highlighted by employers, academics and those working at policy level. However, the findings of the survey indicate that students do not perceive the importance of areas of the curriculum related to transferable skills. If students do not perceive the value of such skills, they may become disengaged with the learning.

Interpersonal skills and the ability to work as part of a team were perceived as comparatively less important by students. Typically, students experience group work as part of their studies but it may be that they do not perceive how this translates into the context of the workplace.

In contrast to the comparatively low perception by students of the importance of creativity to employers, an academic highlighted the importance of employers seeking graduates that can demonstrate creative flair. Whilst the exploration of science and technology is fundamental to BSc Music Technology courses, the teaching tends to encourage creativity:

> I think companies who want to have the cutting edge over other companies need individuals who can do that thinking outside the box, who can do more unusual things, and can work with things perhaps in a non-traditional manner.
>
> (Academic Staff, University C)

The ability to 'add value' to an organisation was emphasised by three employers, but this issue was not reflected in feedback from academics, those working at policy level or students. This underpins the employer view of investing in graduates as a resource for which they need to see a return on investment. One employer commented:

> It's simple [. . .]. Value added, yeah? . . .if you want to get a salary of twenty thousand you need to make that for the company or save them at least sixty,

yeah? The only reason a job exists in the first place is because that person adds value or saves time from someone else.

(Employer, Live Events Production)

It may be perceived that there is a dichotomy between students' perceptions of an industry and reality. One employer emphasised the need for students to spend time in a particular professional environment in order to appreciate the reality of possible career paths. In the context of this highly specialised sector, new recruits can have unrealistic expectations of their potential to obtain prestigious roles that are currently monopolised by a very small number of highly experienced individuals. In the 'hard sell' of vocational courses, students can be disappointed by the reality of their level of entry into an organisation and their potential career progression. The importance of managing student expectations was emphasised.

An academic considered the influence of politically driven changes within higher education and how this has influenced the current focus in this area. He felt strongly that the rise in prominence of employability across the sector in recent years was welcomed, as without it going to university:

Just becomes that rite of passage where you just do it for the sake of doing it, and, as I say, I think that's fine, but I don't think people have the time or the money to afford that sort of luxury anymore.

(Academic Staff, University C)

Stakeholder perceptions of universities' employability strategies

Respondents from the four stakeholder groups agreed that universities do have some level of responsibility to prepare students in terms of graduate employability. However, perspectives on how this is delivered differed.

An individual working at policy level highlighted the importance of clarity in the way in which degrees are presented to potential applicants. Problems can occur when students misinterpret the ethos of the university to which they are applying. This emphasis on the importance of the ways in which universities describe their courses was echoed by an employer. He felt that in such a highly competitive environment, universities might exaggerate the benefits of their courses and mislead students.

At policy level, differences appeared in terms of the perceived role of the university as a facilitator for graduate employment. It was noted by one senior manager that whilst universities have a responsibility to prepare graduates for the world of work, this responsibility does not extend to actually securing them a job:

Employability, yes, employment, no.

(Policy Level, Senior University Management, University D)

In contrast, a senior manager at another university stated that her institution was following a more commercial approach. At the end of a term the university careers service transforms into an employment agency, moving from general support and advice to proactively seeking to match graduates to employers.

Overall, students indicated that they wanted an embedded approach to the delivery of employability-related material, ideally borne out of interactions with industry. Those working at policy level also tended to emphasise the importance of embedding employability across the curriculum:

> I think they have to be embedded. I think one of the biggest challenges [...] is, engaging students with what can be quite abstract concepts, no matter how committed the [...] undergraduate is. [...] if you can teach them skills of communication, teamworking, resilience and leadership, etc, etc, through the discipline, that is in my experience by far the best way to do it. So students learn these things without knowing that they're learning them [...].
> (Policy Level, Senior University Management, University D)

One individual working at policy level highlighted issues around cascading centrally derived employability strategies across individual courses and the need to take a holistic approach to individual programme development.

Academics were mindful of pressures on curriculum time and some also expressed cynicism over some employability-related initiatives that lacked credibility and academic rigour. Laudable as the intentions of some schemes might be, without the discipline and culture of the workplace they can lack credibility. In his opinion, the key employability-related skills are 'self-discipline, persistence, punctuality, attentiveness' and that such skills need to be learnt tacitly.

Comparing his university's employability-related awards to 'swimming badges', one academic argued that a university's demand for student progression means that such an initiative becomes a tick-box exercise. As an example of this he referred to efforts to recognise team-working skills which, if not achieved through group-based activities, could be evidenced through an individual piece of work, 'because you can't let them fail'.

Students also expressed concern that approaches to develop transferrable skills within a course can lack credibility:

> In all the group exercises ... there isn't the sense of leadership [in the workplace] you would have this clear sense of management. You know what you have to do, and if you don't do it, then the consequences are maybe a little bit harsher than maybe you get a bad grade, and a bad peer assessment.
> (Student, Final Year, ex-Placement, University B)

An employer also voiced concern that teamwork within a university course does not reflect the commercial world where typically a team would include at least one experienced individual.

The importance of developing an appreciation of workplace practices within courses was highlighted by individuals working at policy level. Individual employers, and those working at policy level, emphasised that there needs to be greater collaboration between academia and university careers departments and between HEIs and employers. One of the employers highlighted the importance of enhancing students' confidence through the teaching of foundation skills, developed in collaboration with industry professionals. He argued that such underpinning knowledge remains vital even in the face of rapid technology-driven change.

Students spoke of their experience of working with employers on coursework and highlighted the importance of the level at which such interactions occur in order to maximise the potential for learning. One student had been involved in a project with a local company in his first year and felt that neither he nor his colleagues were at the right stage in the course to fully appreciate the potential of such collaboration.

An individual working at policy level also highlighted that placements and work experience were beneficial to students in terms of developing their employability. This was echoed in feedback from employers. Employers highlighted the potential of placements to give students some industrial experience, not least in terms of the discipline of the workplace, but also the potential to start building a network of industrial contacts.

An individual working at policy level suggested that in order for tutors to be able to teach in a credible way that supports the enhancement of student employability, they need time for personal development. Courses need to adapt in line with a dynamic industrial environment. He questioned how academic staff could be expected to keep abreast of evolving sector skills requirements if their time is taken up with teaching.

Feedback from individuals working at policy level would support the view that there needs to be closer collaboration between higher education and industry. One employer emphasised that interactions with employers allow academics an opportunity to ensure that their course content remains relevant and up-to-date.

Overall, students were very positive about the potential benefits of closer collaboration between universities and companies, although some expressed reservations. There was some reticence about employers being involved in delivery, and, in particular, there was concern over the potential for the influence of specific companies leading to a narrowing of the curriculum.

There was evidence of reticence from some academics about engaging with industry, as they may have no experience of the culture of the commercial workplace. A senior university manager highlighted cultural divisions and reservations from academic staff:

> You mention 'employers', and suddenly sometimes people glaze over, as if it's a category of person they don't usually come across,. . .we're not accustomed to this group of people, and also we're not accustomed to what their values, what their perceptions are. . .
>
> (Policy Level, Senior Management, University E)

Negative perceptions of higher education within companies were also noted as a possible obstacle:

> And there's often a tendency to see HE as this passive kind of blob out there that just needs to sort itself out, and then industry will benefit.
>
> (Policy Level, Industry Skills Body)

However, he went on to contend that greater interaction between business and higher education could help to break down possible misconceptions. In his experience, when companies engage with universities through facilitating guest lectures or workshops, they tend to have a more positive attitude towards higher education.

Interviewees were asked how relationships between employers and universities could best be supported. Employers were positive about the role of brokers in nurturing these relationships:

> I think there is a role for brokers . . . I think the forming of a proposition that is of mutual benefit does actually take some work. It has to be dynamic, it has to be very flexible, and I think you should expect it to change. But the idea that there is an interstitial between . . . that just breaks down that standoff.
>
> (Employer, Broadcast Industry, SME)

An employer noted that companies can be sensitive to being used by universities to support course marketing or metrics; mutual respect and benefit is crucial to the success of such schemes.

Another employer from an SME in the broadcast industry considered the fragmented nature of the sector. He contended that whilst higher education can be seen to have centrally-derived policy, the broadcast sector does not have a unifying body as it did in the past through trade bodies. A university manager highlighted the issue of working with a diverse group of SMEs:

> It's quite difficult to talk to representative employers and for them to be representative of the whole general . . . And I think they're very, very focused on their needs.
>
> (Policy Level, Senior University Management, University F)

One employer highlighted how the language and culture of higher education can be off-putting to employers. When asked about how relationships between employers and universities could best be brokered he responded:

> Sorry but the wording of that question makes my skin curl. That is bureaucrat speak, yeah? Like, again and I speak the language, I get what they're saying and I can write like that too, like this whole process and how you broker it, 'partnerships', all these words . . . pick up the phone, get two decent intelligent human beings who get it to have a chat and if you want to put that down as a policy that's fine.
>
> (Employer, Live Events Production)

Suggestions from academics also highlighted the importance of a tailored approach to building relationships with industry and the benefits of flexibility and informality. Informality was also supported by students who perceived a group discussion as an alternative to 'being talked at'. Students thought smaller groups would be more conducive to open discussions.

All stakeholders were asked if they knew of any initiatives or organisations engaged in creating closer links between universities and graduate employers. Overall, amongst students and employers there is a general lack of awareness of such initiatives. This was highlighted by an individual working at policy level:

> It absolutely matters, because that's meant to be a quality mark, and meant to be a mark of relevance for that particular industry. So if employers aren't aware of it, and students aren't aware of it, then it's meaningless.
> (Policy Level, Publicly Funded, Industry-led Organisation)

A senior university manager was asked: "Do you think that employers are sufficiently aware of changes related to employability that have been rolled out across higher education?"

> They're confused by it. They're totally confused by it. Totally, totally confused . . . it's very difficult to get the message out there, because each company is an individual[. . .] One big company doesn't represent, one small company doesn't.
> (Policy Level, Senior University Management, University F)

Another individual working at policy level on behalf of graduate employers was asked the same question, and he acknowledged that as part of his role he was responsible for raising awareness. In his experience he had witnessed a cultural shift whereby higher managers in universities are now much more engaged with supporting industrial engagement. He spoke of urging the employers that his organisation represents to reconsider their preconceptions of higher education as the sector is rapidly evolving.

A manager in a university stated that in her experience employers were keen to share their skills and that typically they want to 'give something back':

> Engagement is not an issue. They want to engage with students, they want to make a difference, and they want to see students employed, many of them . . . you know, because they remember their own experience . . . and also because they've got kids.
> (Policy Level, Senior University Management, University G)

Students do not necessarily feel that they need to be directly involved in course-related discussions between the university and employers. In a forum discussion, a small group of students indicated that students cannot necessarily see the wider context and would tend to complain about resources and module content:

> I don't think the students are qualified to say what is needed in the industry, or what they want. It's not about what they want, it's about what the industry wants.
>
> (Final Year Student, University A)

Conclusions

Whilst established theory suggests that there is a lack of clarity in terms of the attributes employers require when recruiting graduates (Hinchliffe and Jolly, 2009), evidence gathered through this research offers new insight into the limited perceptions expressed by students studying Music Technology degree courses when compared to feedback from those working at policy level, academic staff and employers.

Some students expressed a narrow view of the purpose of a university education, typically focusing on the perceived competitive advantage of having a degree. Taking such a utilitarian view of the value of a degree experience can feed into a passive approach to education. Feedback from students suggests that they do not place as high a value on transferable skills as the other stakeholder groups. Such disconnection can lead to disenchantment with elements of programmes that are overtly related to employability.

Responses from academic staff highlighted concerns over the credibility of schemes designed to enhance employability. Lees (2002) underlined the importance of staff commitment for the success of any changes within the curriculum in higher education. In the context of this particular course type, academics at different institutions expressed concern that a focus on enhancing employability could be at the expense of core teaching. A lack of genuine commitment can serve to undermine the success of new approaches.

This study offers new knowledge in terms of the importance of managing student expectations in the context of this particular course type. In a highly competitive market, universities emphasise the benefits of their programmes to prospective students. The enhancement of graduate employability is now a key element of course marketing (Pegg et al. 2012), and universities typically espouse having close links with industry. In the context of the courses explored for this research, such links can be seen to be tenuous. Not only can this give rise to student disengagement, but the impact of changes in consumer law (Arora, 2015) means that universities need to be consistent in the way their courses are marketed and delivered.

Current theory would suggest that cultural differences between higher education and industry are a key barrier to closer collaboration (Hogarth et al. 2007; Lambert, 2003; Wedgwood, 2008; Wilson, 2012), and this was borne out in this study. Discussions focused on the need to bridge cultural differences through greater sensitivity between academics and employers.

References

Archer, W. and Davison, J. (2008). *Graduate employability: What do employers think and want?* London: The Council for Industry and Higher Education.

Arora, N. (2015). *CMA advises universities and students on consumer law*. [online]. Available from: www.gov.uk/government/news/cma-advises-universities-and-students-on-consumer-law [Accessed October 12th 2015].

Atkins, M.J. (1999). Oven ready and self-basting: Taking stock of employability skills. *Teaching in Higher Education* 4(2): 267–280.

Boden, R. and Nedeva, M. (2010). Employing discourse: Universities and graduate 'employability'. *Journal of Education Policy* 25(1): 37–54.

CBI. (2009). *Future fit – preparing graduates for the world of work*. London: Confederation of British Industry.

Collini, S. (2011). 'From Robbins to McKinsey', Review of higher education: Students at the heart of the system. *London Review of Books* 33(16): 9–14.

Dearing, R. (1997). *Higher education in the learning society, report of the national committee of enquiry into higher education*. London: Her Majesty's Stationery Office.

HEA. (2015). *Framework for embedding employability in higher education*. York: Higher Education Academy.

HEFCE. (2011). *Employability statements – A review for HEFCE by the higher education academy of the submissions to the unistats website (for prospective entrants from September 2011 onwards)*. London: Higher Education Funding Council for England.

Hinchliffe, G. and Jolly, A. (2009). *Employer concepts of graduate employability*. York: The Higher Education Academy.

Hogarth, T., Winterbotham, M., Hasluck, C., Carter, K., Daniel, W., Green, A. and Morrison, J. (2007). *Employer and university engagement in the use and development of graduate level skills – Main Report*. Warwick: Institute for Employment Research.

Holmes, L. (2015). Becoming a graduate: The warranting of an emergent identity. *Education & Training* 57(2): 219–238.

Lambert, R. (2003). *Lambert review of business-university collaboration: Final report*. London: HM Treasury.

Lees, D. (2002). *Graduate employability – literature review*. Exeter: University of Exeter, LTSN Generic Centre.

Lowden, K., Hall, S., Elliot, D. and Lewin, J. (2011). *Employers' perceptions of the employability skills of new graduates*. London: Edge Foundation.

Pegg, A., Waldock, J., Hendy-Isaac, S. and Lawton, R. (2012). *Pedagogy for employability*. York: Higher Education Academy.

QAA. (2014). *Higher education review: Themes for 2015–16*. Gloucester: The Quality Assurance Agency for Higher Education.

Rajan, A. (2000). *Employability: Bridging the gap between rhetoric and reality', first report: Employer's perspective*. Kent: Centre for Research in Employment & Technology in Europe.

Teichler, U. (2014). Possible futures for higher education: Challenges for higher education research', in Shin, J. C. and Teichler, U. (eds.), *The future of the post-massified university at the crossroads: Restructuring systems and functions*. Dordrecht: Springer.

Tomlinson, M. (2010). Investing in the self: Structure, agency and identity in graduates' employability. *Education, Knowledge and Economy* 4(2): 73–88.

UKCES. (2009). *The employability challenge*. London: UK Commission for Employment and Skills.

Wedgwood, M. (2008). *Higher education for the workforce barriers and facilitators to employer engagement*. London: Department for Innovation, Universities and Skills.

Wilson, T. (2012). *A review of business-university collaboration*. London: Department for Business, Innovation and Skills.

Yorke, M. (2010). Employability: Aligning the message, the medium and academic values. *Journal of Teaching and Learning for Graduate* Employability 1(1): 2–12.

Chapter 8

'My brother's football teammate's dad was a pathologist'

Serendipity and employer engagement in medical careers

Steven Jones, Anthony Mann, Elnaz Kashefpakdel and Rachael McKeown

Introduction

The broad problem that is addressed in this research is the social and economic imbalance of young people entering careers in the 'professions', and the role of employers and workers within a target profession in supporting fair access. While there is an agreed need for representation that better reflects the wider population (Sullivan, 2016), many elite professions remain stubbornly resistant to diversification (Macmillan et al. 2015). The focus of this study is the UK and on career paths within health care that are skilled-based and lead to a professional occupation and a good livelihood. The chapter forms part of a wider investigation (Jones, 2016) that addresses the difficulties faced by many UK secondary school students in securing meaningful workplace experience in a medical context and which specifically explores job shadowing as an option for resolving this problem.

Evidence that the medical profession is not representative of UK society comes from multiple sources. Almost half (49.9%) of entrants to UK undergraduate medical or dentistry degree courses are from society's highest socio-economic quintile, and only one in twenty-five (4.1%) are from the lowest socio-economic quintile (HEFCE, 2014). Eighty per cent of applicants to study medicine at university come from only 20% of UK secondary schools or colleges, and half of all schools and colleges do not provide any applicants at all (MSC, 2014). Furthermore, 22% of medical and dental undergraduates in the UK were educated privately, compared to 7% of the total population (Milburn, 2012). This context forms the backdrop for this chapter. Findings are of significance because the survey presented is among the largest of its kind, and was designed to allow key gaps in knowledge to be filled; specifically, the evidence reported exposes the real-world impediments to gaining meaningful experience and the less visible barriers that arise as a result of young people from different backgrounds conceptualising entry to the medical profession in different ways.

The nature of the problem

Unequal access to the professions is discussed extensively in policy discourses and scholarly literature. Research highlights the importance of exposure to authentic workplaces in helping young people to develop and pursue appropriate career aspirations, both in general terms (McDonald et al. 2007) and in specific healthcare contexts (Porter et al. 2009). Workplace experience is vital in tackling commonly-held stereotypical views of the medical profession (Greenhalgh et al. 2004), but students of lower socio-economic status attending schools situated in poorer geographic locations are severely limited in their access to suitable opportunities (Southgate et al. 2015). Less advantaged young people may also lack the wherewithal to navigate the processes required to gain experience, many of which are complex and disaffecting (Kamali et al. 2005).

Interventions have been shown to make a positive difference. Smith et al. (2013) took pupils from schools in areas of deprivation and paired them with mentors who were medical students. All were offered consultant-led workplace experience and guaranteed places at a student-led outreach conference. In terms of accessing medical courses at university, the students' success rate was ultimately similar to that of the general population. Neilson and McNally's (2010) interviews with 20 high-achieving school pupils in Scotland suggested that the UK lagged behind rival nations in providing suitable opportunities and reiterated the need for more authentic work experience. Using the same data set, the authors later examined the influence of 'significant others' on would-be nurses, noting that the advice given was not always appropriate (Neilson and McNally, 2013).

Other studies have focused on the progression challenges faced by young people applying to university degree programmes for which work experience is demanded or preferred. Rehill (2016) reviewed the entry requirements for courses in medicine offered by the UK's most research-intensive universities and found that in 86% workplace experience was listed as a desirable or essential requirement. In the UK, university candidates are also judged on a personal statement submitted through the Universities and Colleges Admissions Service (UCAS), the agency responsible for handling applications to Higher Education institutions, and a lack of relevant work experience is one of the main reasons given by selectors for rejecting medical applicants without interview (Turner and Nicholson, 2011). Again, however, interventions have been shown to make a positive difference. Kamali et al.'s project (2005) involved helping university applicants with their personal statement, a key point of inequity (Jones, 2013), and offered rates increased from 9% to 44% as a result.

More widely, attention is beginning to shift towards the benefits of diversity in professions, not only as an indicator of social mobility, but also as a practical measure to increase confidence among users (Panel on Fair Access to the Professions, 2009). Thacker (2005) focuses on the lack of diversity within the medical profession, arguing for a need to explicitly "target underrepresented population groups for recruitment and retention" (p. 62). Raffo and Reeves

(2000) contend that young people's actions and choices are not completely free, but rather "constrained by a practical knowledge and understanding of what is possible", while Jones at al. (2016) introduce a model of school-mediated employer engagement that emphasises the cyclical nature of social, cultural and human capital accumulation and shows how some young people can become progressively 'locked out'. The study that follows explores such barriers, notably the challenges presented in securing appropriate work experience placements, episodes of job shadowing or comparable work-based experiences of value in applications to university study.

Data and methods

The case study under discussion in this chapter relates to the National Health Service (NHS), the state-funded public health system in operation in the UK. The broad approach undertaken was to ask a large number of stakeholders to share their reflections on access to their profession. The project aimed to gain as wide-ranging a picture as possible, triangulating our surveys to include:

1   those responsible for advising young people and arranging their work experience;
2   those undergoing medical training and
3   those now working for the NHS.

Respondents were asked a mixed of 'closed' questions ("Did you undertake any work-based experience that allowed you to gain insights into what working for the NHS might be like?") and 'open' questions ("Please tell us about any barriers or difficulties that you encountered when considering a career in the NHS"). Similar approaches were taken by Watson (2009), Sheridan (2013) and Buddel (2017) in their use of personal testimonies to uncover individual identities, dispositions and values in relation to educational and career trajectories.

Written evidence from the three 'stakeholder' surveys is presented. First, the views of 707 members of staff at state schools in England were canvassed. In total, approximately one fifth of all English secondary schools and colleges are represented in this sample. Second, 1,074 medical students were surveyed, 89.8% of whom were under 30 years of age. Third, 317 NHS staff members were surveyed, 96.4% of whom were under 30 years of age.

The significance of interviewees being under the age of 30 is that their journey into the profession was recent and therefore of most immediate relevance. The distribution of NHS staff splits evenly between clinical and non-clinical professionals. Participation for all surveys was self-selecting, and results are not intended to be representative of the wider population. Quantitative evidence is used only to structure the qualitative analysis offered. Analytic methods utilised draw on phenomenographic approaches (Marton 1986) to offer multi-level explanatory narratives (Nash 2005). A 'concept mapping' approach to the

Table 8.1 Background characteristics of medical students and NHS professionals

Gender	
Male	62%
Female	38%
Age	
24 or younger	86%
25–30	11%
31 or older	3%
School type attended	
Non-selective state schools/FE colleges	51%
Selective state schools, grammar	14%
Independent schools	22%
A mixture of different school types	6%
Didn't go to school in the UK	6%
Other	1%

analysis of open-ended survey responses is discussed and advocated by Jackson and Trochim (2002), among others.

Thematic analysis

Based on the methods above, findings are presented under four subheadings, each corresponding to an emergent theme in the data. First, the importance of authenticity and trusted advice is established. Second, the role played by family connections in accessing workplace experience is considered. Third, perceived barriers around 'red tape' are explored. And fourth, the above is considered in relation to wider structural inequalities.

Authenticity and trusted advice – "the real thing, not a diluted experience for teenagers"

For NHS staff, the benefits of workplace experience emerged from showing would-be recruits "what it's really like, as often they have an unrealistic idea." Many picked up on the idea that experience was necessary to avoid perceptions being shaped by second-hand portrayals in popular culture: "It gives them a chance to see what the real job is about, not just what they've read or seen on TV". This was mirrored by the testimonies of medical students, one of whom wrote: "I'm embarrassed to say that my expectations on entering medical school came from episodes of *Casualty*." This reference to a long-running UK television drama, set in a hospital, was not the only one in the data and points to an understanding of the medical profession being shaped by the media in the absence of opportunities for genuine workplace experience.

More positively, some respondents talked about the moment when everything "clicked" and they realised that a medical career was the right one for them. One reflected that "medicine no longer felt like a distant aspiration that I had no chance of getting into," and many others reported reaching key career decisions during or immediately after workplace experience. Authenticity was crucial in this respect. Medical students frequently offered comments such as "it gave me a genuine insight into the realities of working within the NHS", "it allowed me to enter medical school with my eyes very much open, under no illusions that what I was about to get into was easy or glamorous", and "this made me think very seriously about pursuing a career within medicine and whether I was cut out for it emotionally and mentally".

Family connections – "Daddy knew someone who worked there"

Two of the stakeholders groups – NHS staff and current medical students – were asked to recall the single most helpful work-based activity that they undertook and reflect on how they came about it. Over one third of respondents reported arranging their most helpful work-related experience themselves, by directly approaching someone they did not know. A further 40% made use of family networks. On fewer than 13% of occasions were schools responsible for enabling access, although a further 7% of respondents indicated that arrangements were made personally with the help of school contacts.

Qualitative evidence suggests that the route to experience is haphazard for those without familial connections. One medical student talked about a fortuitous meeting with a progressively inclined consultant ("I did not know him at all prior to this chance conversation – he just believed that those from normal state schools should have the same opportunities as others") and an NHS staff member drew on a chance encounter with a medical professional ("My brother's football teammate's dad was a pathologist at the local hospital – he let me shadow him for the morning once").

For young people with 'insider' contacts, particularly within their family, workplace experience was less serendipitous. One NHS staff reported: "My aunt was a radiographer who arranged for me to spend time with other radiographers, a physiotherapist and an occupational therapist." Another highlighted the importance of family ties, even if they did not result directly in workplace experience: "I was fortunate to benefit from spending time with medical relatives during the school holidays." Such advantages in social capital did not pass unnoticed by other respondents, many of whom expressed frustration at a system that was felt to implicitly privilege such connections. One medical student wrote:

> As someone who had no friends or family working in the NHS and a first generation uni applicant, I found it incredibly difficult to secure a

placement. It was frustrating to see my school colleagues securing placements because their mum/uncle/godmother was a doctor, especially as a
lot of these people never had the grades to get into medical school.

From a different perspective, one NHS staff member reported that in her day-
to-day practice, "the children who manage to get workplace experience with
doctors seem to be 95% from private schools with a parent or a parent's friend
who is a doctor." Medical students had similar stories. One complained that
they were refused access because of unspecified confidentiality issues, despite
having friends who secured experience "because Daddy knew someone who
worked there." Another "tried to apply via [formal routes], but after nearly a
year of being told to wait, ended up asking family friends who managed to sort
experience out within a week."

Red tape and hospital regulations – "Too many forms to fill out"

When it came to procedural barriers, evidence from teachers and careers advisors was consistent with that of NHS staff and medical students. Many noted
that "the local hospitals are inundated with requests for work experience placements" and, as Figure One shows, nine out of ten reported that access to experience in the NHS was fairly or very difficult to secure.

Teachers were asked to expand on why access was so difficult, and responses
again pointed to a lack of family ties, with 31% citing this as the main reason.
However, many also noted how bureaucratic the process could be and how
young people struggled to navigate a system that was not designed with their
needs in mind. One teacher reported being "from pillar to post when trying

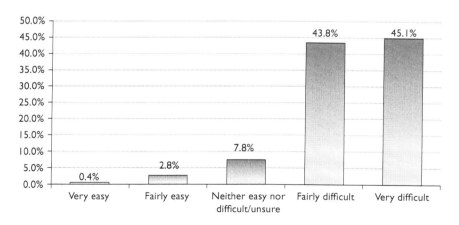

Figure 8.1 Teacher's perspective on the level of difficulty of access to experiences of jobs at the NHS (n = 669)

to contact someone regarding work experience," a frustration compounded by having pupils that were ideal for such placements: "I have amazing students who wish to go into nursing, biomedical science, paediatric nursing, social work, care etc., but it is too difficult to gain any experience." Some teachers also mentioned the tension between securing experience for their pupils and universities' demands of medical students: "The local hospital is (quite rightly) committed to providing work placements to university students and hence cannot accommodate ours." In addition to age-related access problems, a connection between high performance and access was also noted: "Hospitals' HR departments refuse to allow under 16's to do work experience and then over 16 only if they are A★ pupils." The problem was becoming more difficult according to some teachers: "We used to be assured of five placements in our local hospital, then it went down to two and now there are none."

Many teachers reported that different hospitals had different application processes and policies, while others made explicit the connection between social capital and the bureaucratic challenges of the procedure: "Students with less support tend to see it as too difficult a process." Another noted that "red tape within NHS trusts make it a difficult and lengthy process," a problem echoed by medical students, one of whom talked about "websites difficult to navigate . . . people [who] don't answer emails. . . [hospital] trusts restructured all the time!"

The data presented in Table Two is broken down according to respondents' school type, and the trend that emerges that may help to explain the lack of diversity in the medical profession. Of the 203 respondents from an independent school, 28.6% found it 'fairly easy' (and 8.4% 'very easy') to access work-based experience. However, of the 496 respondents from a non-selective state school, only 16.9% found it 'fairly easy' (and 2.0% 'very easy') to access work-based experience. More than three out of four found it difficult to source a placement.

Table 8.2 Level of difficulty to access work-based experiences by school type (NHS staff and medical students under the age of 30, n = 835)

N= (835)	Non-selective state schools	Selective state schools	Independent	Total
Very easy	2%	5.1%	8.4%	4.1%
Fairly easy	16.9%	26.5%	28.6%	21.3%
Not sure	2.4%	1.5%	4.4%	2.8%
Fairly difficult	39.9%	39.7%	33.5%	38.3%
Very difficult	38.3%	25.7%	24.6%	32.9%
Not applicable	0.4%	1.5%	0.5%	0.6%
Total	496	136	203	835

Structural Inequity – "I'd say my school was probably my biggest burden"

The school type differences reported above point to deeper and more structural inequalities. Many NHS staff acknowledged that the lack of interest in a medical career from peers within their educational cohort itself compounded difficulties: "Very few people applied for medicine," said one, adding that the school was therefore "not really prepared to support looking for work experience or other activities to help applications." Figure Two offers quantitative evidence of this, breaking down medical students' access to trusted advice by school type.

Medical students who were educated at independent schools were most likely to have talked to family or friends who work in the NHS (69.5%, compared to 60.3% for those at selective state schools and 53.6% for those at non-selective state schools). They were also most likely to have received trusted advice from more than one source (43%, compared to 31% vs. 26%). This reflected the perception of NHS staff, 71% of whom agreed that it was hard for state school pupils to secure NHS work-based experience and over half of whom had found it difficult to get NHS work-based experience themselves. Where NHS staff had secured workplace experience, they had tended to draw on personal networks (43%) or coldcalling (30%) rather than make use of their school's

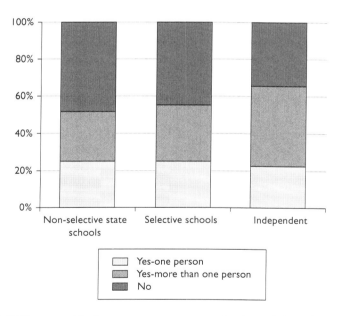

Figure 8.2 "When considering your own career aspirations, did you know anyone (friend or family) who worked in the NHS and was able to offer you trusted and useful advice?" (n = 835)

networks (21%). One bluntly told us that "the real barrier is hierarchy – people turn their nose up at the young."

Many of the participants reflected on where the responsibility lay for the barriers that they faced. For most, the issues were systemic – inadequate allocation of opportunities for workplace experience and the perception of 'red tape' – but others drew attention to more local and personal barriers. For example, one medical student reported that their state schoolteachers "never believed I would get the grades to get into medical school, so never gave me any advice." Another said that their school was "useless at work experience." More alarmingly, some reported direct discouragement: "When talking to a careers advice employee at my school I was told that being a female would put me at a disadvantage when applying to med school. Although I didn't believe her, I feel that it could have severely damaged other young women's motivation for completing their application."

Such responses are reflected by the broader trend captured in Figure Three. Here, the perceptions of teachers and careers advisers within schools are captured. School staff report on how confident they are that their pupils have access to sources of trusted and useful information. Responses are broken down according to the percentage of pupils in each school eligible for free school meals – a proxy for disadvantage in the UK (Holford, 2015). The data shows a clear downward trend: over 60% of teachers from schools at which fewer than 10% of pupils were eligible for free school meals reported their pupils were able to access trusted advice. But for young people attending schools at which over 40% of pupils were eligible for free school meals, this proportion fell to 28%.

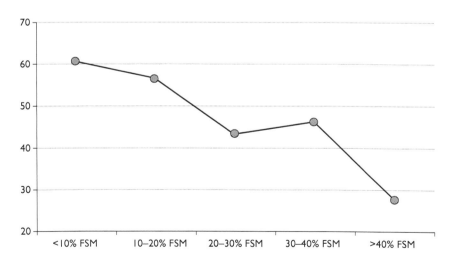

Figure 8.3 Access to 'extensive' or 'some' trusted advice by percentage of school's pupils eligible for free school meals

Differences in opportunity based on school type were freely noted. One NHS staff member recalled that a local hospital "refused my application for work experience claiming they didn't take students – however, my friend who attended the local private school was accepted the following week." Another NHS staff member, unconsciously channelling Bourdieu's (1990) descriptions of the unspoken 'laws' that shape practice within a field, said "the knowledge of 'how to play the game' was something unbeknown to everyone that I was in contact with at the time, so I had to figure it out for myself, and in this respect I was always a bit behind the curve."

Several respondents made direct connections between their workplace experience and their subsequent progress to Higher Education. One medical student reflected that "I found it easier I think to apply to medical school because my dad is a doctor so I know what kind of things I need to say on my personal statement because he read through it several times." An NHS staff member noted that "the opportunity to contribute and reflect on my experiences in my UCAS statement was useful", and a teacher talked about "getting [their students] an edge over other students when applying for highly competitive university places." On the other hand, teachers noted that one effect of fewer places being available was that "over the past couple of years we have had issues with students not getting on to courses due to lack of work experience."

Discussion

This study into workplace experience opportunities in the medical profession draws directly on the testimonies of those most affected and paints a picture of an employment destination that remains obstinately beyond the reach of many young people despite efforts to diversify the profession. In the UK, the evidence is clear that young people from state schools in general, and from more disadvantaged areas in particular, find access to relevant workplace experience most difficult to secure. Despite substantial effort and remarkable individual commitment, staff at those schools remain frustrated by structural barriers.

The study provides evidence which concurs with the view that trustworthy reciprocal social relations within individualized networks allow young people to "gain information, observe, ape and then confirm" (Raffo and Reeves, 2000, 89) key decisions. The problem arises when the 'constellation' of such networks is insufficient to gain the experiences deemed necessary for a particular career path. The ability to create and sustain social relations is not equally distributed (Beck, 1992). Weak ties (Granovetter, 1973) create opportunities for those who sit outside the cycle of capitals to amass experience in more idiosyncratic, entrepreneurial ways. However, occasional instances of young people overcoming the odds do not make a substantial difference to the demographic composition of large employers like the NHS.

In the medical profession, imbalance in the distribution of social capital is compounded by more structural educational inequality, such as universities offering places only to students with demonstrable workplace experience. Negative experiences can be off-putting, but having no experience is much more costly to those seeking employment in a specialist field. In the medical profession, becoming 'a fish in water' (Zukas, 2013) poses particular challenges. While progress continues to be made in understanding employer engagement generally, the main contribution of this article has been to show how social advantage continues to reproduce itself (Bourdieu & Passeron, 1977) within the medical profession.

Conclusion

Diversity is essential to providing high-quality care, and the importance of 'cultural competence' for health professionals in securing the trust of patients is now well established in the literature (Sullivan, 2016). However, testimonies from respondents who successfully navigated a path into the NHS from disadvantaged backgrounds repeatedly recall chance encounters with benevolent insiders, suggesting that their progression was heavily reliant on good fortune. Of course, the 'serendipity' reported in this data – and referred to in the title of this chapter – can be viewed through many lenses. In research examining non-traditional students in Higher Education, Lehmann (2009) moves beyond 'deficit models' to demonstrate how such young people deploy their flexibility and ingenuity to flourish in environments that are historically unfamiliar. And throughout the data, evidence is found of young people's "resistance, innovation, negotiation and accommodation to a range of socializing forces" (Raffo and Reeves, 2000, 149) as they seek to pursue career paths that are ostensibly open to them but do not, in practice, offer clear entry points or the support needed to access them. Clearly, when it comes to access to the medical profession, young people draw on an impressive array of individual resources to compensate for structural disadvantage: personal energy and creativity is mobilised, alternative paths to success are carved out and habitus does not always predetermine professional destiny.

However, exceptional individualised histories can mislead. Given that the medical students and NHS staff that were surveyed were successful in achieving their professional goals, one might expect their narratives to be self-regarding or triumphalist, with appeals to meritocratic discourses (Guinier, 2016). In fact, the opposite is found. Those who 'make it' into the medical profession rarely attribute their success to individual exceptionality. Rather, good fortune is routinely acknowledged, coupled with awareness of – and often resentment towards – structural barriers and other perceived inequities. These inequities are particularly evident around workplace experience, where anger was voiced by many participants about what they perceived as the systematic, albeit inadvertent, exclusion of young people from less advantaged backgrounds. As one NHS staff member put it: "The current system is grossly unfair – it should not be that hard."

A striking limitation of this research is that only the 'winners' have been canvassed. The study does not report on the experiences – or lack of them – of those young people for those whom a career in the medical profession was sought but never realised. This constituency is sizeable, and had the surveys included their testimonies, it is likely the evidence of inequity would be even more overwhelming.

This chapter has focused on the problem identified in the study: inequitable access to periods of work experience of value in progression to highly selective courses of study at elite universities. In so doing, it seeks to add to a growing literature exploring the issue of equity in employer engagement in education. It reveals a situation whereby links between secondary school students and employees within the NHS are numerous but are clearly patterned by social relationships which are rooted in social class. The chapter does not explore how greater levels of fairness can be introduced to provide access to these work placements – this is a question demanding further study. However, it does point towards employers within the NHS, and other comparable institutions, accepting the need for change if they are to ensure that they have access to all young talent, regardless of social circumstance.

Acknowledgements

The authors are grateful to Katie Adams and Claire Churchill of Health Education England for their clear support and guidance in production of this report. They also wish to thank the many individuals in schools and across the NHS who came forward to offer and support surveying and Work Taster pilots during the duration of the project.

References

Beck, U. (1992). *Risk society: Towards a new modernity (Vol. 17)*. London: Sage Publications.

Bourdieu, P. (1990). *The logic of practice*. Stanford: Stanford University Press.

Bourdieu, P. and Passeron, J. (1977). *Reproduction*. London: Sage Publications.

Buddel, N.A. (2017). Teaching the path towards university: Understanding student access through storied-futures and meritocratic grand narratives. *British Journal of Sociology of Education* 27: 1–16.

Granovetter, M.S. (1973). The strength of weak ties. *American Journal of Sociology* 78(6): 1360–1380.

Greenhalgh, T., Seyan, K. and Boynton, P. (2004). Learning in practice: "Not a university type": Focus group study of social class, ethnic, and sex differences in school pupils' perceptions about medical school. *British Medical Journal* 1–6.

Guinier, L. (2016). *The tyranny of the meritocracy: Democratizing higher education in America*. Uckfield: Beacon Press.

HEFCE. (2014). *Further information on POLAR3: An analysis of geography, disadvantage and entrants to higher education*. London: Higher Education Funding Council for England.

Holford, A. (2015). Take-up of free school meals: Price effects and peer effects. *Economica* 1:82(328): 976–93.

Jackson, K.M. and Trochim, W.M. (2002). Concept mapping as an alternative approach for the analysis of open-ended survey responses. *Organizational Research Methods* 5(4): 307–336.

Jones, S. (2013). Ensure that you stand out from the crowd: A corpus-based analysis of personal statements according to applicants' school type. *Comparative Education Review* 23;57(3): 397–423.

Jones, S. (2016). *How access to the medical profession is conceptualised by key stakeholders: Evidence from a case study of NHS 'work tasters'.* Paper given at the international conference on Employer Engagement in Education and Training held in London, July 2016.

Jones, S., Mann, A. and Morris, K. (2016). The 'Employer Engagement Cycle' in secondary education: Analysing the testimonies of young British adults. *Journal of Education and Work* 29(7): 834–856.

Kamali, A.W., Nicholson, S. and Wood, D.F. (2005). A model for widening access into medicine and dentistry: The SAMDA-BL project. *Medical Education* 39: 918–925.

Lehmann, W. (2009). Becoming middle class: How working-class university students draw and transgress moral class boundaries. *Sociology* 43(4): 631–647.

Macmillan, L., Tyler, C. and Vignoles, A. (2015). Who gets the top jobs? The role of family background and networks in recent graduates' access to high-status professions. *Journal of Social Policy* 44(3): 487–515.

Marton, F. (1986). Phenomenography – a research approach to investigating different understandings of reality. *Journal of Thought*: 28–49.

McDonald, S., Erickson, L.D., Johnson, M.K. and Elder, G.H. (2007). Informal mentoring and young adult employment. *Social Science Research* 36: 1328–1347.

Milburn, A. (2012). *Fair access to professional careers: A progress report by the independent reviewer on social mobility and child poverty.* London: Cabinet Office.

MSC. (2014). *Selecting for excellence: Help and hindrance in widening participation: Commissioned research report.* London: Medical Schools Council.

Nash, R. (2005). Explanation and quantification in educational research: The arguments of critical and scientific realism. *British Educational Research Journal* 31(2): 185–204.

Neilson, G.R. and McNally, J. (2010). Not choosing nursing: Work experience and career choice of high academic achieving school leavers. *Nurse Education Today* 30(1): 9–14.

Neilson, G.R. and McNally, J. (2013). The negative influence of significant others on high academic achieving school pupils' choice of nursing as a career. *Nurse Education Today* 33(3): 205–209.

Panel on Fair Access to the Professions. (2009). *Unleashing aspiration: The final report of the panel on fair access to the professions.* London: Cabinet Office.

Porter, G., Edwards, P.B. and Granger, B.B. (2009). Stagnant perceptions of nursing among high school students: Results of a shadowing intervention study. *Journal of Professional Nursing* 25(4): 227–233.

Raffo, C. and Reeves, M. (2000). Youth transitions and social exclusion: Developments in social capital theory. *Journal of Youth Studies* 3(2): 147–166.

Rehill, J. (2016). *The importance of experience of the world of work in admissions to health-based undergraduate courses at Russell group universities: A desktop review.* London: Education and Employers.

Sheridan, V. (2013). A risky mingling: Academic identity in relation to stories of the personal and professional self. *Reflective Practice* 14(4): 568–579.

Smith, S., Alexander, A., Dubb, S., Murphy, K. and Laycock, J. (2013). Opening doors and minds: A path for widening access. *The Clinical Teacher* 10: 124–128.

Southgate, E., Kelly, B. and Symonds, I. (2015). Disadvantage and the 'capacity to aspire' to medical school. *Medical Education* 49: 73–83.

Sullivan, L.W. (2016). Grasping at the moon: Enhancing access to careers in the health professions. *Health Affairs*. 1: 35(8):1532–1535.

Thacker, K. (2005). Academic-community partnerships: Opening the doors to a nursing career. *Journal of Transcultural Nursing* 16(1):57–63.

Turner, R. and Nicholson, S. (2011). Reasons selectors give for accepting and rejecting medical applicants before interview. *Medical Education* 45(3): 298–307.

Watson, T. (2009). Narrative, life story and manager identity: A case study in autobiographical identity work. *Human Relations* 62: 425–452.

Zukas, M. (2013). A Bourdieusian approach to understanding employability: Becoming a 'fish in water'. *Journal of Vocational Education and Training* 65(2): 208–216.

Chapter 9

Someone in your life who really believes in you

Evidence and practice in employer mentoring

Tristram Hooley and Jonathan Boys

Young people face a range of challenges with respect to their futures. They must navigate the education system and emerge with sufficient qualifications to serve as a passport to employment, make decisions about their career direction and make a successful transition to a first job. They must also consider how to translate the learning they have gathered from the education system into the skills needed for work and recognise that their first job is only the beginning of a lifetime of career development. Young people's ability to make this transition has enormous economic, social and psychological implications for their lives. It is also of considerable interest to employers and governments keen to ensure smooth flows of human capital and align them to the skills needed in the economy. Governments, moreover, have an interest in the social implications of career aspirations and transitions, variously emphasising policy goals such as social mobility, social inclusion and wellbeing.

The individual, organisational and societal interests in young people's career transitions have led to the development of a wide range of interventions of the kind discussed in this book and its predecessor (Mann et al. 2014). In policy terms, such interventions can be described as being part of a career guidance system (OECD, 2004). Career guidance interventions take many forms but generically offer "a purposeful learning opportunity which supports individuals and groups to consider and reconsider work, leisure and learning in the light of new information and experiences and to take both individual and collective action as a result of this" (Hooley et al. 2017).

A challenge for policymakers and practitioners in delivering an effective career guidance system is that there are gaps in the evidence base for this activity which makes comparison between interventions difficult (Hughes et al. 2016). The evidence that does exist emphasises the importance of programmatic combinations of interventions (Christensen and Søgaard; Larsen, 2011; Gatsby Charitable Foundation, 2014; Hooley et al. 2012) and the importance of maximising young people's connections to employers and working people (Kashefpakdel and Percy, 2016; Mann and Dawkins, 2014; Mann and Percy, 2013). Yet, this high-level evidence still leaves programme makers with decisions about which elements to include.

This chapter discusses one of the possible ingredients of a career guidance programme by focusing on career mentoring programmes which involve an employer or working person. This type of mentoring is utilised regularly in UK schools and has been identified by teachers and careers practitioners as helping to engage young people with the world of work (Mann, Dawkins and McKeown, 2017). It offers a straightforward way to bring a young person and a working adult together through a supportive series of conversations.

This chapter examines what mentoring is, how it works, the strength of the evidence supporting it and how it might be best organised within a wider programme of career support for young people. It will make use of an earlier rapid evidence review which drew together academic and 'grey' literature to explore the impacts associated with employer mentoring and propose a framework for evidence-based practice (Hooley, 2016). This review drew on 63 research papers including four meta-analyses (DuBois et al. 2002; Eby et al. 2008; Wheeler et al. 2010; and DuBois et al. 2011).

The chapter will also make use of application data submitted to the *Mentoring and Community Fund* by UK-based mentoring providers (The Careers and Enterprise Company, 2016) to ground the literature in recent practice. This fund was launched in January 2016 to support the growth of mentoring relationships between employers and working people and young people in school years 8, 9 and 10 (between the ages of 12 and 15) in England and attracted a diverse range of bids from 252 mentoring organisations across England. Of these, 39 bids (one for each Local Enterprise Partnership in England) were successful, and the total amount of money awarded was £4 million. The bids offer insights into how employer mentoring is articulated by mentoring providers and the models of delivery that are in use. An initial sift of the 252 bids was conducted to remove any proposals that did not use a similar definition of employer mentoring to the one used in this chapter. Following this a thematic analysis was conducted on the remaining proposals and included both successful and unsuccessful applications. Quantitative data was also collected and analysed from all bids.

What is mentoring?

Mentoring describes a relationship between individuals which is designed to support the mentee by providing them with access to the mentor's experience, knowledge, social and cultural capital and by creating a space for self-reflection and growth. Mentoring can variously involve professionals and amateurs or volunteers and can be employed to serve a range of purposes. Mentoring can take place between adults, between adults and young people or amongst young people and can be organised in one-to-one or group forms, face-to-face or at a distance. In this chapter we are focusing on relationships between employers/ working people and young people in schools, primarily for the purposes of career development.

Many young people find mentors organically through their family and community networks. Such informal mentoring is more likely to emerge when young people are embedded within dense and stable networks (Keller and Blakeslee, 2014). However, access to this kind of social network is unevenly distributed across the population and is often patterned in similar ways to other inequalities in capital (Stanton-Salazar, 2011). Access to a mentor therefore raises social justice issues, particularly as there are many observed benefits to informal mentoring (McDonald and Lambert, 2014; Stanton, Salazar and Spina, 2003; Timpe and Lunkenheimer, 2015). Given this, it is important to consider how young people from different backgrounds might be empowered to recruit informal mentors (Schwartz et al. 2016) and how such relationships could be integrated into career development programmes and systems (Schwartz and Rhodes, 2016).

The unequal distribution of informal mentoring and the difficulty of bringing it into being in a purposeful way has led to the development of interventions that seek to replicate the benefit of such mentoring relationships. Typically these interventions are employed in ways that make them available to all young people and particularly to those who are socially disadvantaged. There are limited comparative studies which look at the relative impacts of formal and informal mentoring with young people, but those that have compared the two interventions with adults often find that informal mentoring has stronger impacts (Ragins et al. 2000), although Desimone et al. (2014) also find that the two types of mentoring can be both complementary and compensatory.

There are some important differences between informal and formal mentoring on which it is worth reflecting. Informal mentoring emerges organically out of young people's social networks and provides young people with an extension to the normal benefits of social capital associated with participation in their network. So, a young person might routinely bump into an uncle at family parties and use these opportunities to participate in an informal mentoring relationship. When an attempt is made to recreate this kind of regular happenstance encounter, it becomes necessary to place some rules around the encounter to ensure that an appropriate match is made, that regular meetings take place, that the young people's parents are informed about this relationship and so on. Similarly, there is a need to provide formal mentoring relationships with clear ethical and practical boundaries and guidance that are not usual in informal mentoring relationships. Formal mentoring can be seen as an attempt to trap the lightning of informal mentoring in a bottle. Its purposeful and inorganic nature means that it requires the development of rules, regulations and standardised practices that do not require codification in informal mentoring.

Formal mentoring can take a variety of forms (Hooley, 2016), but this chapter will focus on *employer mentoring*, where the mentor is an adult volunteer who is usually drawn from the world of work. In this chapter we use the terminology 'employer mentoring', but it is important to recognise that this term masks a number of possible forms and motivations for mentoring. Such mentoring could include business owners working with young people, their employees participating in employer-sanctioned volunteering activities either in or outside of work time or working people giving up their own time without involving their employers in the mentoring arrangements. Within this chapter we refer to all of these forms of mentoring with the terminology of 'employer mentoring'. A distinctive feature of this form of mentoring is that it demands mentors who possess first-hand knowledge of the labour market which will ultimately be joined by mentees.

Such employer mentoring can vary in a range of ways, including the length, intensity and location of mentoring and be delivered through a variety of modes (face-to-face, telephone, online). It is also possible to organise mentoring on an individual or group basis and to deliver it as a stand-alone intervention or as an element within a larger career development programme. The applicants to the Mentoring Fund were able to seek funding for a range of different models of employer mentoring and demonstrated the variability of activities that currently exist under the banner of [employer] mentoring. While some offered one-to-one mentoring, most bids described group mentoring with some programmes combining both approaches. Most of the applicants' delivery models were face-to-face, but some blended this with online resources and/or interactions. The mentoring outlined by the applicants took place in a variety of locations including schools, workplaces or other community spaces with a popular option being to conduct mentoring in the school setting and to supplement this with some visits to the employer site. A minority of mentoring applications also embedded mentoring within a larger programme of personal or career development – for example, including activities such as sport, community volunteering or other kinds of projects and challenges alongside more conventional mentoring relationships.

The impacts of employer mentoring

Theories that seek to explain the value of employer engagement activities commonly emphasise the impact that they have in sharing social and cultural capital and providing young people with opportunities to build a bridge beyond their immediate educational and occupational habitus (Mann and Stanley Archer, 2014). Mentoring should be an ideal intervention for supporting the transmission of such social and cultural capital as it is based around a long term and substantial relationship between an adult and a young person. Other employer activities usually have a primary aim such as the provision of career information or the development of employability skills with the development of social capital existing as a secondary aim. Conversely in mentoring, the development of social and cultural capital is in many ways the primary aim of the intervention. It seeks to add a new individual to a young person's network who, by design, has different occupational experiences, and typically higher status, than those people who they already know.

The evidence on mentoring includes a wide range of studies, including some that have used control groups to isolate impacts (e.g. Grossman et al. 2012; Herrera et al. 2011) and benefits from several literature reviews and meta-analyses which have helped to move the evidence in this area towards some consensus (e.g. DuBois et al. 2011; Eby et al. 2013). There are also some important limitations to this evidence base, including the fact that it is strongly US-centric and would benefit from more large-scale evaluations; greater use of randomisation in the establishment of control groups; more information about the relative effects of different models of mentoring; more studies focused on e-mentoring and group mentoring; and more interventions and evaluations that are designed in ways that support their replication in different contexts (Hooley, 2016).

The evidence presented by Hooley (2016) finds that there are consistent positive effects associated with mentoring, albeit often with small effect sizes. Studies on the impact of mentoring include those that find that young people welcome the opportunity to be involved in mentoring and report on their experiences positively (Bruce and Bridgeland, 2014) and those that highlight positive impacts on young people's behaviour and on their engagement with education (Clarke, 2009; Collier and Kuo, 2014), on their educational attainment (Bayer, Grossman and DuBois, 2015; Miller, 1999) and, less clearly evidenced, on their educational and career aspirations, decision-making and progression (Bruce and Bridgeland, 2014; Phillips et al. 2015; Sowers et al. 2016). More recently, there have been some emergent findings which highlight wage premiums for young people who have participated in mentoring (Mann, Kashefpakdel, Rehill and Huddelston, 2017). Many of these findings have been confirmed by DuBois et al. (2011) meta-analysis of 73 independent studies which found a small effect size across behavioural, social, emotional and academic domains of young people's development. Similar impacts were also highlighted by Hughes et al. (2016) in their systematic review of careers interventions which reported that mentoring delivered economic, educational and social outcomes. Applicants to the Mentoring Fund reported a wide range of outcomes associated with their provision which broadly aligned with those highlighted in the literature. In addition they argued that mentoring could support young people to increase their employability skills and to provide them insights into specific industries, although these additional impacts have yet to be evidenced.

There are a minority of studies which identify negative impacts from mentoring or which do not find statistically significant impacts (Bernstein et al. 2009; Hickman and Garvey, 2006). Such studies, as well as many that report small effect sizes, often reflect on the quality and consistency of mentoring relationships, speculating that if mentoring was more effectively implemented, larger effect sizes might be observed. One finding that supports this is the existence of some research which highlights negative impacts that are associated with poor quality mentoring – for example, where mentors are unreliable, unhelpful or attempt to use the relationship for personal gain – and with mentoring relationships that terminate in less than six months (Bruce and Bridgeland, 2014; Grossman and Rhodes, 2002; MENTOR, 2015).

The broad range of outcomes associated with mentoring creates challenges for the emergence of a robust evidence base. As everyone is measuring different things, it can be difficult to be clear about the comparability of different interventions. The Fund applicants provide insights as to why there are so many outcomes being claimed and monitored. Each applicant emphasised different outcomes in part due to their organisational history and the way in which their programmes had been funded in the past. For example, organisations that had been funded by local government were often interested in labour market outcomes such as reducing the likelihood of young people being not in education, employment or training (NEET) after leaving education, whilst organisations funded by employer or sector bodies were interested in boosting aspirations for careers in that sector, and organisations funded by educational institutions or training providers were typically interested in progression and attainment outcomes. The interplay between funders, delivery organisations, the models and aims of mentoring and the evidence that supports it merits further discussion in the future. Such complexity reminds us that mentoring follows political and organisational agendas at least as much as it follows the evidence.

This is not to say that there is no interest in evidence-based interventions. A minority of applicants to the Mentoring Fund made overt reference to the existing evidence base in support of their mentoring models, and most applicants were able to articulate an approach to the evaluation of future provision. The level of sophistication of evaluation approach outlined varies from limited forms of measurement of participant satisfaction to some organisations with more developed approaches using validated measurements and investing in systems to support detailed tracking and analysis of administrative data (often in partnership with schools and local authorities). Some of the larger national programmes were also able to cite independent or external evaluations that had been conducted on their programmes. Research by Behavioural Insights Team (2016), a research organisation, undertaken for the Careers & Enterprise Company to support the Mentoring and Community Fund, highlighted the challenges of effective evaluation in this field. It found that providers were keen to contribute to the evidence base, but also raised concerns about tensions between the desire to use evaluation formatively to learn and develop interventions and the need to use it summative to justify funding.

Theorising the impacts of mentoring

While mentoring is associated with a range of benefits for individuals, it is less clear why this is so. Is it, as is hoped, that the well-documented benefits of informal mentoring can be forced into being through formal mentoring programmes? Rhodes (2005) theorises the impact of formal mentoring by arguing that it provides a context for young people to reflect on themselves. Mentoring conversations foster social-emotional, cognitive and identity development. Such self-work relies on the capacity of the mentor and the mentee to forge a relationship based on mutuality, trust and empathy, which in turn places a demand on the mentoring programme to ensure that the relationship is framed in ways that support this through forms of training and role clarification.

Mentors offer young people the space to think and encourage them to act and to reflect on their experiences. They offer mentees feedback in both direct and implicit ways that enhance their self-image and steer them to develop themselves in pro-social directions. Keller (2010) builds on this psycho-social explanation by highlighting the way in which mentoring works as an educative intervention. The mentor uses their own experience and resources, as well as those provided by the mentoring programme, to create a social learning space where mentees can build their skills and knowledge.

Keller (2010) also highlights the way in which the mentor brokers their mentee's access to wider social capital. McDonald et al. (2007) argue that the benefits of increased social capital in mentoring are consistent with Granovetter's (1973) 'weak ties' thesis and with the transmission of non-redundant information about the opportunity structure. In addition to information with direct instrumental usefulness (e.g. information about recruitment processes), such information may include a variety of forms of cultural capital that facilitate individual's integration into unfamiliar social milieu. Hamilton et al. (2016) build on this social capital theory and note other benefits associated with enhanced social capital such as direct connections to key gatekeepers or 'institutional agents' associated with entry to particular employment routes.

Consequently, a three-stranded explanation of the impact of mentoring can be observed. Employer mentoring (1) supports psycho-social self-work, (2) fosters learning and the development of personal competence and (3) enables the development of social and cultural capital.

What makes mentoring most effective?

The literature suggests that poorly organised and low quality formal mentoring programmes are unlikely to deliver observable impacts and may even be detrimental to those participating in them (Hooley, 2016). At the heart of these questions of quality is the recruitment of an appropriate mentor, who can relate to a young person and provide consistent and useful mentoring over an extended period. Questions of quality, therefore, relate to both dyadic questions about the mentoring relationship and to programmatic questions about how the mentoring programme is organised (Deutsch and Spencer, 2009).

There are considerable challenges in recruiting and retaining sufficient volunteers to participate in mentoring programmes. Mentoring is a demanding intervention that requires volunteers to commit to regular activity over an extended period of time. Such problems become more acute for those programmes that are seeking to increase the diversity of mentors. The challenges of recruitment were highlighted by Fund applicants who noted that the recruitment of mentors can be a stumbling block to programme success and constitutes a significant part of their operations. This echoes findings from the literature (Hooley, 2016) which particularly notes challenges in recruiting some demographic groups.

The literature also provides insights into what kinds of mentors lead to the best outcomes. It suggests that gender (Kanchewa et al. 2014) and ethnicity (DuBois et al. 2011) are not associated with more successful mentoring relationships and that it is more important to match on shared educational and occupational interests. Fund applicants also highlighted the importance of geographical proximity and historical connections between the mentor and the area in which they are mentoring as they argued that these forms of secondary connection facilitate greater engagement from mentors and results in stronger mentoring relationships. Raposa et al.'s (2016) study of mentoring at-risk youth suggests that mentors who have greater self-efficacy and experience of working with young people have a greater ability to sustain successful mentoring relationships. Taken together the evidence on mentor characteristics suggest that what mentors do within the mentoring relationship is probably more important than their background and that while careful attention to matching is important, this cannot be done in a simplistic way based solely on external characteristics.

As well as challenges with finding sufficient and suitable mentors, there are also challenges in engaging young people in mentoring. The literature suggests that formal mentoring benefits young people who are in need of academic support (Miller, 1999), have behavioural issues (DuBois, 2011) or experience various forms of socio-economic disadvantage (Collier and Kuo, 2014). However, the literature also suggests that young people need to have the motivation to participate (Mtika and Payne, 2014) and the ability to manage and sustain social relationships (Bayer et al. 2015). Such findings remind us that mentoring is, at its heart, a human relationship which inevitably suffers from all of the challenges that other human relationships suffer from. Mentors and mentees may not get on, may find it difficult to work together and inevitably some adults and young people are likely to find this kind of intervention aligns with their personality better than others. Bayer et al. (2015) argue that these relationship factors and the ability to build emotional closeness and a good relationship are critical to effective mentoring relationships.

In addition to the dyadic elements of quality discussed so far, there are also important programmatic or organisational factors. Successfully engaging young people in mentoring typically requires the involvement of an intermediary body to facilitate access. This is usually a school, often supported by an external third party, but schools commonly find extended and regular delivery of mentoring challenging (Karcher, 2008). Mtika and Payne (2014) argue that mentoring programmes need to be well integrated into schools if they are going to be effective, and Miller (2002: 187–188) raises the importance of developing 'whole school approaches' by developing in-school leadership and structures for planning and managing mentoring activities.

The need to view mentoring programmatically is a key learning point for those seeking to make mentoring relationships work effectively (Miller, 2002). Hooley's (2016) literature review identifies six elements of effective mentoring programmes: (1) programmatic design; (2) recruitment and screening; (3) matching; (4) orientation, guidance and training; (5) support and supervision; and (6) closure. All of these features of formal mentoring require a purposeful element of design and management which are beyond the mentoring dyad and often beyond the organisational capability of a single school. In many cases this programmatic input is provided by a specialist organisation which takes responsibility for the brokerage of the relationships, the pedagogic design of the mentoring and on-going support, monitoring and quality assurance.

The need to organise mentoring programmatically and to embed it within strong organisational structures both within and without the school is an important finding of the evidence about effective practice (Hooley, 2016; Miller et al. 2013; Mtika and Payne, 2014). In addition to creating a need for programme management, the codification of effective mentoring suggested by the evidence base also emphasises the importance of clearly articulated roles and boundaries for mentors and mentees and that mentors are provided with guidance and training. There is evidence that suggests that mentor training is positively associated with mentor satisfaction (Martin and Sifers, 2012) and the efficacy of the mentoring intervention (Miller et al. 2013). Both mentor and mentee need to understand that the mentoring dyad is supplementary and complementary to family roles and to professional roles such as teacher, therapist and career guidance professional (Keller, 2005; Sandford, Armour and Stanton, 2010). Training and orientation, therefore, needs to focus on both how mentors can work with the young person's wider support network as well as encouraging the development of the skills to support psycho-social self-work, the development of personal competence and the transmission of social and cultural capital. Analysis of Fund applications showed that, in practice, the nature and length of mentor training is variable in length (ranging from 2 hours to 2 days) and that it variously addresses safeguarding, understanding of the education system and understanding young people and the challenges that they face. Most applicants described how on-going support and training is usually built into mentoring programmes, and the importance of on-going support is also highlighted in the literature (Clarke, 2009; Miller, 1999).

Conclusions

Mentoring has long been considered to be an important part of the career guidance or education/employer engagement mix (Miller, 2002). In England, there is a well-developed body of practice and a wide range of organisations delivering mentoring. The analysis of data from Applicants to 2016

Mentoring Fund offers a snapshot of the current provision which aligns well with the findings from the largely US-based evidence base. However, it also highlights the range of different approaches and interventions which nest under the term 'mentoring'. In addition to the diverse delivery models, there are no standard agreed-upon outcomes of what mentoring should achieve and a seemingly endless list of outcomes that organisations claim mentoring can achieve. It would be valuable if the impacts associated with mentoring could be more focused, clearly articulated and underpinned with viable theories of change.

This chapter argues that mentoring supports psycho-social self-work, fosters learning and the development of personal competence and enables the development of social and cultural capital. This framework provides a useful way to understand how observable outcomes around behaviour, engagement, attainment and educational and career aspiration, decision-making and progression are brought about.

The impacts associated with mentoring require careful attention to be given to ensuring and assuring quality. Research suggests that interventions involving young people and employers typically provide cumulative benefits (Percy and Mann, 2014). However, the mentoring literature also suggests that programmes should be just as focused on quality as they are on quantity. Such quality needs to be understood at both the level of the dyadic relationship and at the level of the programmatic organisation of mentoring.

Some of the findings of the literature on mentoring pull against the reasons why mentoring is attractive to policy makers. While employer mentoring is comparatively cheap in relation to interventions that require extensive contact time with an educational professional, the use of volunteers does not mean that there are no costs involved. The need for programmatic structures, training and support for mentors means that there is a need for appropriate levels of resourcing. The application data suggests an average cost around £11.50 per mentor hour, but costs can differ markedly between programmes depending on how they are organised. Alongside some of the issues raised already about the need to create an evidence base that allows for comparison between different models of mentoring, it is also important to pay attention to costs as a vital element of considering the relative return on investment.

Not all the challenges associated with running effective mentoring programmes are related to resources. Wider schools' policy has reduced, as of 2017, the time available for substantial career-focused interventions such as mentoring. While the solution to this is not entirely divorced from resourcing questions, simply throwing more money at the problem will not solve it. Similarly, if demand for mentors outstrips recruitment, this may be associated with geographical and local economic issues which reduce the availability of employers and working people. Mentoring organisations are seeking creative solutions to this through experiments with innovative but less well-evidenced approaches to mentoring such as group and online mentoring. There would be real value in investing in further evaluation of diverse forms of mentoring to support access to mentoring across a wide range of local labour market settings.

There is much to be positive about in the evidence for employer mentoring. While there is a need to continue to develop and refine the evidence base, there is also substantial evidence that suggests that employer mentoring can have impacts across a range of domains. This article has proposed a theoretical explanation for these impacts, arguing that employer mentoring (1) supports psycho-social self-work, (2) fosters learning and the development of personal competence and (3) enables the development of social and cultural capital evidence base. It is hoped that this theory can provide some useful structure for future research and evaluation and help to increase the coherence of research on mentoring.

Mentoring, like the other interventions in this book, does not offer a magical solution to all of society's ills. Mentoring needs to be done carefully and employed critically with considerable attention paid to the quality of what happens within the mentoring programme. Where this happens it can make a real difference to young people's life, education and career. Thankfully the existing evidence gives us some strong clues about what 'quality mentoring' looks like, and our application data suggests that this is understood and acted on by many of the providers in the field. As ever, there is much we don't know and much that we would like to see happen, but there is also cause for hope and optimism that we are walking down the right road.

References

Bayer, A., Grossman, J.B. and DuBois, D.L. (2015). Using volunteer mentors to improve the academic outcomes of underserved students: The role of relationships. *Journal of Community Psychology* 43(4): 408–429.

The Behavioural Insights Team. (2016). *Levers for change*. London: The Careers & Enterprise Company.

Bernstein, L., Dun Rappaport, C., Olsho, L., Hunt, D. and Levin, M. (2009). *Impact evaluation of the U.S. Department of Education's student mentoring program*. Washington, DC: USA Department of Education.

Bruce, M. and Bridgeland, J. (2014). *The mentoring effect: Young people's perspectives on the outcomes and availability of mentoring*. Washington, DC: MENTOR.

The Careers and Enterprise Company. (2016). *Mentoring fund and campaign*. London: The Careers & Enterprise Company.

Christensen, G. and Søgaard Larsen, M. (2011). *Evidence on guidance and counselling*. Aarhus: Danish Clearinghouse for Educational Research.

Clarke, L.O. (2009). *Effects of a school-based adult mentoring intervention on low income, urban high school freshman judged to be at risk for drop-out: A replication and extension, doctoral dissertation*. New Brunswick, New Jersey: State University of New Jersey.

Collier, R.J. and Kuo, A.A. (2014). Youth development through mentorship: A Los Angeles school-based mentorship programme among Latino children. *Journal of Community Health* 39: 316–321.

Desimone, L.M., Hochberg, E.D., Porter, A.C., Polikoff, M.S., Schwartz, R. and Johnson, L.J. (2014). Formal and informal mentoring: Complementary, compensatory, or consistent? *Journal of Teacher Education* 65(2): 88–110.

Deutsch, N.L. and Spencer, R. (2009). Capturing the magic: Assessing the quality of youth mentoring relationships. *New Directions for Student Leadership* (121): 47–70.

DuBois, D.L., Holloway, B.E., Valentine, J.C. and Cooper, H. (2002). Effectiveness of mentoring programs for youth: A meta-analytical review. *American Journal of Community Psychology* 30(2): 157–197.

DuBois, D.L., Portillo, N., Rhodes, J.E., Silverthorn, N. and Valentine, J.C. (2011). How effective are mentoring programs for youth? A systematic assessment of the evidence. *Psychological Science in the Public Interest* 12(2): 57–91.

Eby, L.T. d.T., Allen, T.D., Hoffman, B.J., Baranik, L.E., Sauer, J.B., Baldwin, S. and Evans, S.C. (2013). An interdisciplinary meta-analysis of the potential antecedents, correlates, and consequences of protégé perceptions of mentoring. *Psychological Bulletin* 139(2): 441–476.

Eby, L.T., Allen, T.D., Evans, S.C., Ng, T. and DuBois, D.L. (2008). Does mentoring matter? A multidisciplinary meta-analysis comparing mentored and non-mentored individuals. *Journal of Vocational Behaviour* 72(2): 254–267.

Gatsby Charitable Foundation. (2014). *Good career guidance*. London: Gatsby Charitable Foundation.

Granovetter, M.S. (1973). The strength of weak ties. *American Journal of Sociology* 78: 1360–1380.

Grossman, J.B., Chan, C.S., Schwartz, S.E. and Rhodes, J.E. (2012). The test of time in school-based mentoring: The role of relationship duration and re-matching on academic outcomes. *American Journal of Community Psychology* 49(1–2): 43–54.

Grossman, J.B. and Rhodes, J.E. (2002). The test of time: Predictors and effects of duration in youth mentoring relationships. *American Journal of Community Psychology* 30(2): 199–219.

Hamilton, S.F., Hamilton, M.A., DuBois, D.L., Martínez, M.L., Cumsille, P., Brady, B., Dolan, P., Núñez Rodriguez, S. and Sellers, D.E. (2016). Youth-adult relationships as assets for youth: Promoting positive development in stressful times, in Petersen, A., Koller, S. H., Verma, S. and Motti, F. (eds.), *Positive youth development in global contexts of social and economic change*. New York, NY: Taylor & Francis.

Herrera, C., Grossman, J.B., Kauh, T.J. and McMaken, J. (2011). Mentoring in schools: An impact study of big brothers big sisters school-based mentoring. *Child Development* 82: 346–361.

Hickman, G.P. and Garvey, I.J. (2006). An analysis of academic achievement and school behavior problems as indices of program effectiveness among adolescents enrolled in a youth-based mentoring program. *Journal of at-Risk Issues* 12(1): 1–10.

Hooley, T. (2016). *Effective employer mentoring: Lessons from the evidence*. London: The Careers & Enterprise Company.

Hooley, T., Marriott, J., Watts, A.G. and Coiffait, L. (2012). *Careers 2020: Options for future careers work in English schools*. London: Pearson.

Hooley, T., Sultana, R. and Thomsen, R. (2017). The neoliberal challenge to career guidance – mobilising research, policy and practice around social justice, in Hooley, T., Sultana, R. and Thomsen, R. (eds.), *Career guidance and the struggle for social justice in a neoliberal world*. London: Routledge.

Hughes, D., Mann, A., Barnes, S-A., Baldauf, B. and McKeown, R. (2016). *Careers education: international literature review*. London: Education Endowment Foundation.

Kanchewa, S.S., Rhodes, J.E., Schwartz, S.E.O. and Olsho, L.E.W. (2014). An investigation of same- versus cross-gender matching for boys in formal school-based mentoring programmes. *Applied Developmental Science* 18(1): 31–45.

Karcher, M.J. (2008). The study of mentoring in the learning environment (SMILE): A randomized evaluation of the effectiveness of school-based mentoring. *Prevention Science* 9: 99–113.

Kashefpakdel, E.T. and Percy, C. (2016). Career education that works: An economic analysis using the British cohort study. *Journal of Education and Work* 30(3): 217–234.

Keller, T.E. (2005). A systematic model of the youth mentoring intervention. *Journal of Primary Prevention* 26(2): 169–188.

Keller, T.E. (2010). Youth mentoring: Theoretical and methodological issues, in Allen, T.D. and Eby, L.T. (eds.), *The Blackwell handbook of mentoring: A multiple perspectives approach*. Oxford: Wiley-Blackwell.

Keller, T.E. and Blakeslee, J.E. (2014). Social networks and mentoring, in Dubois, D.L. and Karcher, M.J. (eds.), *Handbook of youth mentoring*. Los Angeles: Sage Publications: 129–142.

Mann, A. and Dawkins, J. (2014). *Employer engagement in education: Literature review*. Reading: CfBT.

Mann, A., Dawkins, J. and McKeown, R. (2017). *Towards an employer engagement toolkit: British teachers' perspectives on the comparative efficacy of work-related learning activities*. London: Education & Employers.

Mann, A., Kashefpakdel, E.T., Rehill, J. and Huddleston, P. (2017). *Contemporary transitions. young Britons reflect on life after secondary school and college*. London: Education and Employers.

Mann, A. and Percy, C. (2013). Employer engagement in British secondary education: Wage earning outcomes experienced by young adults. *Journal of Education and Work* 27(5): 496–523.

Mann, A., Stanley, J. and Archer, L. (eds.). (2014). *Understanding employer engagement in education*. London: Routledge.

Martin, S.M. and Sifers, S.K. (2012). An evaluation of factors leading to mentor satisfaction with the mentoring relationship. *Children and Youth Services Review* 34(5): 940–945.

McDonald, S., Erickson, L.D., Johnson, M.K. and Elder, G.H. (2007). Informal mentoring and young adult employment. *Social Science Research* 36(4): 1328–1347.

McDonald, S. and Lambert, J. (2014). The long arm of mentoring: A counterfactual analysis of natural youth mentoring and employment outcomes in early careers. *American Journal of Community Psychology* 54(3–4): 262–273.

MENTOR. (2015). *Elements of effective practice for mentoring*. Boston: MENTOR.

Miller, A. (1999). Business mentoring in schools: Does it raise attainment? *Education & Training* 41(1): 73–78.

Miller, A. (2002). *Mentoring students and young people: A handbook of effective practice*. London: Kogan Page.

Miller, J.M., Barnes, J.C., Miller, H.V. and McKinnon, L. (2013). Exploring the link between mentoring program structure & success rates: Results from a national survey. *American Journal of Criminal Justice* 38(3): 439–456.

Mtika, P. and Payne, F. (2014). Student – adult mentoring relationships: Experiences from a Scottish school-based programme. *Educational Research* 56(4): 436–452.

Organisation for Economic Cooperation and Development (OECD). (2004). *Career guidance and public policy: Bridging the gap*. Paris: OECD.

Percy, C. and Mann, A. (2014). School-mediated employer engagement and labour market outcomes for young adults: Wage premia, NEET outcomes and career confidence, in

Mann, A., Stanley, J. and Archer, L (eds.), *Understanding employer engagement in education: Theories and evidence*. London: Routledge.

Phillips, L.A., Powers, L.E., Geenen, S., Schmidt, J., Winges-Yanez, N., McNeely, I.C., Merritt, L., Williamson, C., Turner, S., Zweben, H. and Bodner, C. (2015). Better futures: A validated model for increasing postsecondary preparation and participation of youth in foster care with mental health challenges. *Children and Youth Services Review* 57: 50–59.

Ragins, B.R., Cotton, J.L. and Miller, J.S. (2000). Marginal mentoring: The effects of type of mentor, quality of relationship, and program design on work and career attitudes. *Academy of Management Journal* 43(6): 1177–1194.

Raposa, E.B., Rhodes, J.E. and Herrera, C. (2016). The impact of youth risk on mentoring relationship quality: Do mentor characteristics matter? *American Journal of Community Psychology* 57(3–4): 320–329.

Rhodes, J.E. (2005). A model of youth mentoring, in Dubois, D.L. and Karcher, M.J. (eds.), *Handbook of youth mentoring*. Thousand Oaks, CA: Sage Publications.

Sandford, R.A., Armour, K.M. and Stanton, D.J. (2010). Volunteer mentors as informal educators in a youth physical activity program. *Mentoring & Tutoring: Partnership in Learning* 18(2): 135–153.

Schwartz, S.E., Kanchewa, S.S., Rhodes, J.E., Cutler, E. and Cunningham, J.L. (2016). I didn't know you could just ask: Empowering underrepresented college-bound students to recruit academic and career mentors. *Children and Youth Services Review* 64: 51–59.

Schwartz, S.E. and Rhodes, J.E. (2016). From treatment to empowerment: New approaches to youth mentoring. *American Journal of Community Psychology* 58(1–2): 150–157.

Sowers, J.A., Powers, L., Schmidt, J., Keller, T.E., Turner, A., Salazar, A. and Swank, P.R. (2016). A randomized trial of a science, technology, engineering, and mathematics mentoring program. *Career Development and Transition for Exceptional Individuals*. online first.

Stanton-Salazar, R.D. and Spina, S.U. (2003). Informal mentors and role models in the lives of urban Mexican-origin adolescents. *Anthropology & Education Quarterly* 34(3): 231–254.

Stanton-Salazar, R.D. (2011). A social capital framework for the study of institutional agents and their role in the empowerment of low-status students and youth. *Youth & Society* 43(3): 1066–1109.

Timpe, Z.C. and Lunkenheimer, E. (2015). The long-term economic benefits of natural mentoring relationships for youth. *American Journal of Community Psychology* 56(1–2): 12–24.

Wheeler, M.E., Keller, T.E. and Dubois, D.L. (2010). Review of the three recent randomized trials of school-based mentoring. *Social Policy Report* 24(3): 3–21.

Chapter 10

Aligning school to work

Assessing the impact of employer engagement in young people's transitions from education to work

Terence Hogarth and Lynn Gambin

Introduction

Young people face a daunting prospect in making the transition from school to work in the UK. Youth unemployment and NEET (Not in Employment, Education or Training) rates remain relatively high following the financial crisis in 2007–2008 when they rapidly increased to levels from which they are only slowly recovering. One way in which young people can insure themselves against the vagaries of the economic cycle is by investing in education and training. It is well-established that the chance of being unemployed and/ or being dependent upon benefits is lower for the relatively highly qualified (Buscha and Urwin, 2013). But young people from disadvantaged backgrounds often face more formidable barriers in gaining access to further and higher education and, subsequently, to secure employment. Schools can be of critical importance here, especially so in providing the advice and guidance that will help students to align their activities in school with their aspirations in the labour market. Education-business partnerships can be of importance here. Over the years there have been, and continue to be, manifold programmes that have sought to bring schools and businesses together to help prepare young people for the world of work (Chaplain and Gray, 2000; Huddleston, 2012). These can be of vital importance in providing the support and guidance, via employers, that students need if they are to more efficiently and effectively make the transition from school into sustainable, rewarding employment.

In order to demonstrate how education-business partnerships can assist students, especially socially disadvantaged ones, evidence is provided from the evaluation of Business Class (Gambin et al. 2015). Business Class is a partnership between schools and employers designed to assist young people, often from disadvantaged backgrounds, to acquire inside knowledge about what employers are really looking for when they recruit for those types of jobs in which the students are interested. Evidence is provided about how Business Class – and by implication the wider range of similar programmes available – helps young people to align their activities in school with their job market aspirations.

Business-education partnerships allow messages about what employers are look-ing for in would-be recruits to be conveyed to students directly by employers. This potentially lends greater credence to the message than if it were delivered by their teachers such that students will be more likely to act upon the advice and information received.

Education-business partnerships such as Business Class are supply-side initia-tives. It helps ensure that students' activities in school are consistent with what they want to do when they exit compulsory education. These types of pro-grammes are designed to increase alignment between the students' activities in school with what the student wants do after school. Alignment, in its broadest sense, can be seen as the student acquiring some of the skills – technical and generic – and behaviours that employers, of potential interest to the student, expect to see in their would-be recruits. It is readily apparent that young people face increasing competition – with one another and with older people – to gain entry into what might be loosely termed good quality employment. Mak-ing young people aware, at an early stage, of the competition they are likely to face and how they might prepare themselves to secure the type of job they would like to do is clearly of some importance. But if the gains from these types of programmes are to be fully realised, there needs to be concomitant developments on the demand side, too. Whilst increasing alignment might have a positive impact on the quality of skills supply, one has to be sceptical about its capacity to affect the demand-side; in other words, the willingness of employers to recruit young people. There need to be the opportunities – via programmes such as apprenticeship – which will allow students to capitalise on the work they undertake in programmes such as Business Class. Without measures that will increase employer demand to recruit young people, the danger is that ini-tiatives that are designed to make students more work-ready or more aligned will come to nought or deliver less than their potential suggests. For evidence of this, one only has to look at conditions in the youth labour market.

The youth labour market: employer demand and skills policy

As noted above, the labour market for young people has been, and continues to be, relatively weak. Youth unemployment and the percentage of young people not in employment, education or training (NEET) is relatively high compared with those countries that have relatively well developed vocational education and training (VET) systems, such as Germany, and in comparison with the average in the European Union (see Figures 10.1 and 10.2). In fact, compared with most west European countries, the NEET rate in the UK is high (see Fig-ure 10.3). Clearly, the economic crisis in 2007–2008 had a calamitous impact on the youth labour market. Faced with a surplus of relatively well-skilled people, employers had relatively little demand for new trainees (Hogarth et al. 2009). This seems to have persisted in the period since the crisis because, in

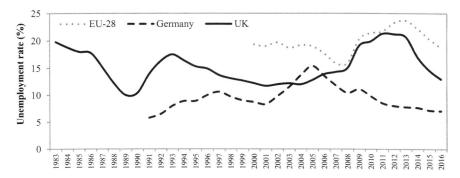

Figure 10.1 Youth unemployment rates in the UK

Source: Eurostat Unemployment rates [reference file – une_rt_a]

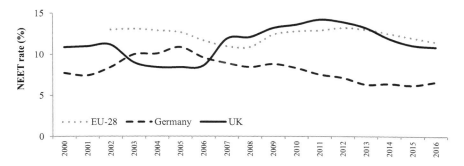

Figure 10.2 NEET rates in the UK

Source: Eurostat NEET rates [reference file – edat_lfse_20]

part, it reflects a deeper malaise in the youth labour market than one simply explained away by the economic cycle. Policy has responded principally by trying to better align the skills system (especially in relation to initial VET) with the demands of the labour market in an effort to stimulate employer investment in skills and thereby the employment of young people.

Policy makers over recent decades have sought to reorient the skills system so that it is more demand-led; that is, making it more focused on meeting the near term skill demands of employers (Gambin and Hogarth, 2017). In 2006, the Leitch Review laid bare the extent to which the skills system delivered courses and programmes that met the needs of the training provider rather more than those of the labour market and, thereby, of learners. But it needs to be borne in mind that much of the skills debate, from the 1970s onwards at least, was

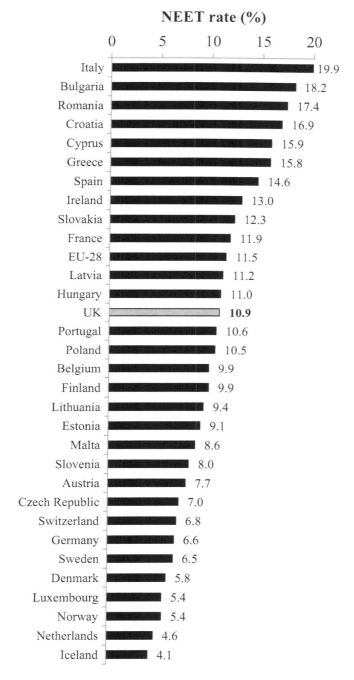

Figure 10.3 A comparison of NEET rates in the UK and in Europe

Source: Eurostat NEET rates [reference file – edat_lfse_20]

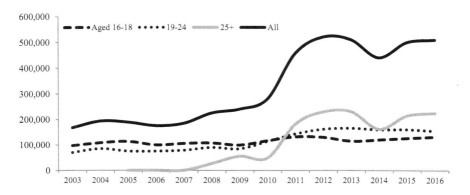

Figure 10.4 Apprenticeship starts in England, 2003–2016

Source: FE Data Library – Apprenticeship Programme Starts 2002/03 to 2016/17

focused on finding the means to increase the volume of training undertaken by young people in the period immediately after leaving compulsory schooling (Gospel, 1995). Policy makers from the 1970s onwards can perhaps be forgiven for trying to establish a critical mass of activity in the first instance – especially so given the hitherto rather paltry provision of further education and training to young people – before fine-tuning the skills system to better match labour market demand. Despite efforts to increase participation in post-compulsory education and training, the problem of increasing participation in work-based VET has never really gone away. Even the most cursory glance at the number of apprenticeship starts over recent years reveals that demand for this kind of training, from employers at least, has remained relatively modest (see Figure 10.4).

Apprenticeship warrants special mention because successive governments have promoted it as a particularly effective means of bringing about the transition from school-to-work. Even if the overall number of apprentices has increased over time, most of this growth has been accounted for by older apprentices (25 years and older), many of whom were already employees of the company providing the apprenticeship such that, for many, an apprenticeship constituted a form of continuing, rather than initial vocational, education and training (Gambin and Hogarth, 2017). This has not necessarily been good news for those young people looking for apprenticeships on leaving compulsory education.

Facilitating the transition from school to work

The figures and discussion above have highlighted the relative weakness of the youth labour market in the UK. In a weak labour market, the young person making the transition from school to work is likely to face stiff competition for the better jobs. While a basic tenet of the argument pursued in this chapter is that more needs to be done to boost the labour demand for young people, if the most is to be made of activities carried out in education-business partnerships, it is also the case that in a relatively weak labour market there is an even greater need for interventions such as Business Class to enable young people to compete for, and gain access to, the good quality jobs that are available.

Most of the evidence demonstrates that young people's understanding of the labour market is weak (Mann et al. 2013). Moreover, where young people are unrealistic, indecisive, or confused about their future careers, they can encounter considerable labour market penalties later on (Mann and Dawkins, 2014). The work of Yates and his colleagues is instructive in this regard in that it shows where young people's career choices are poorly matched to their educational plans, and it can result in an increased risk of becoming NEET (Yates et al. 2011). Reviewing much of the literature in this area, Mann and Dawkins (2014) identified the importance of activities that address the confusion, indecisiveness, and misalignment that some young people on the cusp of entering the labour market experience. They made the following observation:

> Studies using British longitudinal datasets which have explored the long-term implications of uncertain or 'misaligned' teenage career aspirations – where young people at age 16 misestimate the educational requirements needed for specific occupations – have found that there are significant consequences linked to underestimates of qualifications required for preferred career ambitions. Young people from more disadvantaged backgrounds are systematically more likely to fall into this category and consequently are more likely to be able to benefit from reliable interventions.
>
> (Mann and Dawkins, p. 16)

The research literature is clear that a reliable intervention requires employer engagement. A review of what constitutes good career guidance in schools sets as two of its eight benchmarks: encounters with employers and employees and experience of workplaces (Holman, 2014). In relation to the former it states:

> Every pupil should have multiple opportunities to learn from employers about work, employment and the skills that are valued in the workplace. This can be through a range of enrichment activities including visiting speakers, mentoring, and enterprise schemes.
>
> (p. 7)

This draws attention to the type of employer-school engagement that might effectively provide young people with encounters with employers and employees (Grant, 2010). This is where programmes based on business-education partnerships can potentially have an important role to play by providing students with an opportunity to learn from employers about the world of work and what they are looking for, or value, when they recruit young people. How this can be delivered and how young people respond to it is outlined below.

The impact of education-business partnership programmes

Many schools develop partnerships with local employers to help develop the employability of their students. Indeed, partnerships between businesses and schools have been in and out of fashion, under various guises, over many years. It has always been in the interests of employers to have some role in determining what qualities and skills are of value in prospective employees (Chaplain and Gray, 2000). A number of initiatives over the years have attempted to develop links between businesses and education with expansion of such activity in the 1990s and partnerships developed at local and national levels. For instance, Education Business Partnerships (EBPs) were established in 1990 with funding from the then Department of Employment, but from 2011 were no longer government funded, perhaps reflecting public policy's loss of interest in this type of initiative. It is interesting, by way of an aside, to note that the proposed introduction of T levels in post-16 education will require substantial work placements to be provided to students (Department for Education, 2017). This may well reignite policy interest in education-business partnerships.

To illustrate the impact education-business partnerships have on student's preparedness to enter the labour market, evidence is drawn from a particular programme – Business Class. It is run by Business in the Community (BITC) to create school-business partnerships designed to be long-term and driven by the needs of the school. The programme focuses on schools that have an above average number of students eligible for free school meals, are located in the most deprived areas of the country according to the Income Deprivation Affecting Children Index,[1] and/or are not achieving national average GCSE results. In Business Class, partnerships are developed between schools and employers with their work concentrated in four areas: (1) leadership and governance, (2) curriculum, (3) enterprise, and (4) employability and wider issues. Under the programme, schools will work in partnership with a single employer; but it will be the school that is in the driving seat when it comes to identifying the support it needs from its business partner. Each school-business partnership is nestled within a local area cluster. Within the cluster schools and employers are brought together on a regular basis to share best practice, identify common challenges, and accelerate improvements. It is anticipated that the partnership between school and employer will last for a minimum of three years. At the start of the partnership, a detailed assessment process is undertaken where the school and employer evaluate the needs of the school, after which BITC supports the partnerships to deliver outputs of mutual benefit to school and employer. The particular focus of the study which provides the evidence for this paper was upon enterprise and employability. In practice, employers engaged in a number of different projects – with differing levels of intensity – designed to improve the enterprise and employability skills of the schools' students. It was volunteers from the employers' workforces who undertook the activities with the schools (for many of the volunteers it was seen as contributing to their own career development).

The evaluation of Business Class was based on collecting data from students through questionnaire surveys and semi-structured interviews conducted in the secondary schools participating in the initiative as a consequence of public funding made available by the then UK Commission for Employment and Skills. The study was designed so that it was possible to compare students participating in Business Class with those who had not yet participated in it (but might do so at some point in the future). In all schools, only selected students were chosen to participate in Business Class. These students were selected by the schools. The fieldwork was conducted between 2013 and 2016.

As noted above, much is already known about effectiveness of business-education partnerships (for example, see Mann and Dawkins, 2014; Mann, 2012). It is nevertheless timely, drawing on more recent data from Business Class, to revisit how education–business partnerships are preparing people to enter the labour market. The evidence provided below will demonstrate the extent to which schools, working in collaboration with employers, ensure their students are ready to enter the labour market even in the most disadvantaged areas.

Assisting young people enter the labour market

The principal benefit of education-business programmes such as Business Class is that it engages young people in a range of activities designed to open their eyes to the world of work. Table 10.1 below provides an indication of the types of activity in which participants were engaged. The evidence indicates that the programme increased the likelihood that a person would participate in an activity designed to improve their readiness for employment and the range of activities in which they engaged. Multivariate analysis undertaken to determine

Table 10.1 Percentage of students taking part in particular activities with employers

	Non-Business class	Business class	All
Work experience	74%	70%	72%
Enterprise	20%	40%	33%
Employer talk	64%	74%	70%
Mock interview	45%	68%	59%
Visit to employer	44%	54%	50%
Business project	30%	46%	40%
Mentoring	23%	29%	27%
Average number of activities	8.4	10.5	9.8
Base	*349*	*601*	*950*

Source: Business Class Evaluation – Survey of all students (n=950)

Note: Multiple responses permitted (column percentages do not sum to 100%)

the extent to which Business Class increased the participation of students in various activities, while controlling for their educational and socio-economic characteristics, demonstrated that Business Class had a positive impact. Other things being equal, a student who was in Business Class had, on average, taken part in two more activities when compared with those students not in the programme. The evidence also points to participants being more likely to engage in more intensive activities. By more intensive activities is meant those that take up much of the employer volunteers' time – including mock job interviews, enterprise activities, and business projects.

Volume is not everything. It is also important that the various types of activity proved to be of some use to students. Figure 10.5 summarises the students' views of the usefulness of activities in which they engaged. It is readily apparent that engagement with employers made students think about the skills needed to obtain a job (or the type of job they wanted) and made them think about what they wanted to do after school. So it had the impact of focusing students' minds on the labour market.

Those participating in the Business Class engaged in a range of other activities in addition to those outlined in Table 10.1 which constituted the core elements of the programme. These included:

- going to careers fairs (56 per cent of students in Business Class);
- having careers interviews (44 per cent);
- going to presentations from employers (41 per cent);
- going on visits to local business (39 per cent).

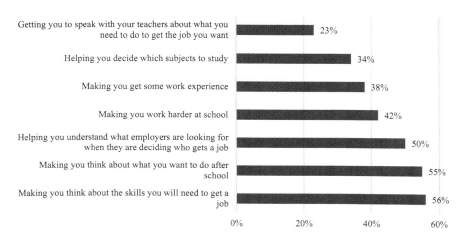

Figure 10.5 Percentage of all students reporting that a Business Class was useful in particular ways

Source: Business Class Evaluation – Survey of students in intensive activities(n = 133)
Note: Multiple responses permitted

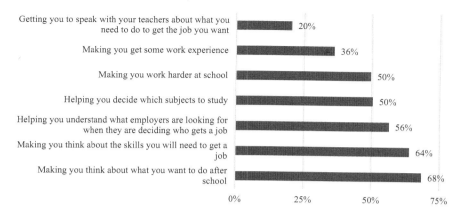

Figure 10.6 Percentage of all students reporting that another activity was useful in particular ways

Source: Business Class Evaluation – Survey of students in intensive activities (n = 133)

Note: Multiple responses permitted

When asked about the usefulness of these activities, the responses from students were similar to the responses relating to the core activities undertaken in Business Class with students reporting a number of positive impacts (see Figure 10.6). More than half of students felt that the activities had been useful in making them think about what they wanted to do after school (68 per cent); making them think about the skills they need to get a job (64 per cent); and helping them understand what employers are looking for when they are hiring (56 per cent). If employers are looking for a good fit between a person and a job when they are recruiting, then the more students are attuned to the qualities that employers are looking for, the better able they will be to not only get any job, but a job that goes some way towards meeting their career aspirations.

The importance of work experience

Work experience was particularly highly valued by students. When asked to select only one of the activities in which they had taken part as part of Business Class, work experience came out top of the list (mentioned by nearly a quarter of students). Prior to going on the work experience placement, more than half of students had at least some definite ideas about their future career (some had discussed these with others whilst most did not know much about the job they were considering). Most work experience placements involved the student being in the workplace for five consecutive days whilst others had spent more than five days in the workplace – for some these were consecutive days whilst for others they had been spread out over a number of weeks. As a result of going on the placement, many students felt that they had gained or been able to practice various skills and had gained better understanding of work-related issues. Amongst the most common answers here were that after the placement, students knew what personal qualities employers think are important and they understood better the skills employers look for in their workers.

Figure 10.7 summarises how students felt their work experience placement had affected their thinking about their futures in terms of careers and school. The most commonly agreed upon effect was that students intended to work hard in their lessons and coursework at school (90 per cent of students agreed or strongly agreed with this statement). And just under three-quarters of students agreed or strongly agreed that after their placement they were clearer about what they wanted to do in their future education and career (73 per cent), and that they had a good chance of getting a part-time job with their placement employer (71 per cent).

The benefits of work experience are well known (see, for example, Huddleston, 2012, Mann and Dawkins, 2014). What is perhaps of interest is that in this particular case students were slightly more likely to engage in work

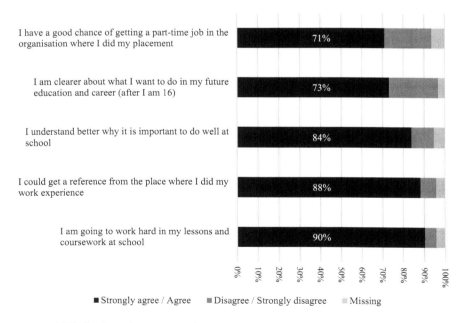

Figure 10.7 Students' views on how work experience through Business Class affected their thoughts about future careers and school

Source: Business Class Evaluation – Survey of students on work experience (n = 93)

Note: Multiple responses permitted

experience if they had not participated in Business Class. This may well suggest that it is the school, rather than the education-business partnership, that drives provision of work experience. So the conclusion here is the value derived from work experience is not necessarily one that is dependent upon an education-business partnership. But there is an important caveat. It is known, for example, that many work experiences are often found by young people themselves, often through their family and social networks (Natcen/SQW, 2017). Where students do not have the requisite family and social networks, the existence of an education-business partnership such as Business Class may well facilitate their access to work experience.

The importance of intensive, work-related activities

In exploring further, through semi-structured interviews with students in Years 8 and 9, the types of activity which they thought benefited them most, a number of key findings emerged. These included:

- the value attached to enterprise days – which were much enjoyed by students – were there was role playing with respect to running a business, or engaging in Dragon's Den type activities where the students need to persuade people to invest in their ideas;
- attending careers fairs which students thought useful, though some students said they were pitched at too general a level such that it was difficult to get much from them that might be of use;
- the importance of hearing messages conveyed by employers about the jobs market and how to develop careers. In particular, students valued hearing about how employees themselves had developed their careers and how it might be possible for the students to gain entry to that line of work.

To some extent, the types of activity mentioned above involve light touch involvement by the volunteers from the schools' partner employers. Where the students were particularly enthusiastic was with reference to more intensive employer engagement. In particular, the following were considered important:

- visits to employers were very much welcomed. For some students this was a real eye – opener in that it demonstrated the range of jobs that might be available. For example, a large employer near one school invited students to visit its headquarters and the students were struck by two things:
  1 the attractiveness of working in a modern corporate workplace that was on their doorstep immediately struck home. They previously had little knowledge that the office complex was near their homes, or if they did, that it might be a possible job destination for them. As the

next point demonstrates, it immediately became apparent that there might well be a place for them;

2   the range of jobs available in that workplace was also much wider than students had initially expected such that they could see that there might be a place for them in such a workplace despite the fact that they wanted to work in engineering or hospitality rather than administration and finance, because jobs in the former were available in the corporate HQ. This latter point was also in evidence where one group of students had visited a large hospital. Whereas previously they thought most NHS jobs were clinical ones (doctors and nurses), they were made aware of the wide variety of jobs available in the NHS, many of which were of interest to those who had little interest in clinical roles;

- as a consequence of the above, some students said that they had reconsidered what they might want to do after finishing education such that it had contributed to broadening their career horizons;
- students also valued highly their one-to-one engagement with employee volunteers. Mock job interviews were particularly valued because of the feedback that the student received from the employee volunteer. This was the type of information students valued because it told them exactly what they needed to know if they were to successfully negotiate the interview stage when applying for a job;
- students also were able to see how employers dealt with issues such as lateness and use of bad language. They could see that such behaviour might not be as acceptable as they had previously thought.

The above suggests that where education-business partnerships work best is where they deliver intensive activities to students. Overall, students seemed to derive much from their involvement in Business Class, but it was the closer, more intensive contact with the employer and their employee volunteers that students most valued. It was this type of engagement that seemed to have most influence over how they viewed the labour market.

Increasing student alignment with the needs of the jobs market

The evidence provided above indicates that students experienced a variety of effects from taking part in an education-business partnership of a type that Business Class exemplifies. The experiences of students revealed that the activities they engaged in will affect, in all likelihood, their later experiences in the labour market. Students were provided with access to opportunities to engage with employers and in employability-related activities that they would have been unlikely to have encountered – with the exception of work experience – without an education-business partnership such as Business Class being in place. Across the more intensive types of activities in which students participated, there was a high degree of agreement from students that their participation in these had made them think more about the job they would like to do once they had completed school and the skills and behaviours employers valued when comparing applicants for jobs. These results suggest that various intensive activities had had an impact on students' thinking about their future careers. The importance of engagement between students and employers being intensive and individualised is evident in all of the various data collected in the evaluation of Business Class.

The concept of alignment is sometimes defined narrowly with respect to pursuing education appropriate to the broad entry qualifications required to gain access to certain occupations. In practice, the labour market tends to be more flexible than such a model permits. In many respects, the concept of alignment needs to be broader so that more importance is placed on considering how students can be better informed about the types of skills upon which employers place value. For certain occupations, this will mean acquiring qualifications at a certain level in specific subjects, but for many jobs this will not be necessary. Arguably, just as important is the process of opening students' eyes to the opportunities that exist in their local labour markets and how they might acquire jobs within it. It was very much apparent in the semi-structured interviews with students that they placed a particularly high value on hearing messages about how to get into a certain line of work and what to expect from it from people either filling those jobs currently, or who worked for organisations where those jobs were to be found. This is where programmes such as Business Class can add much value. So if one takes a relatively broad view of alignment that focuses more on attuning students to the opportunities available in the local jobs market and what is required to obtain those jobs, then education-business partnerships such as Business Class can be particularly effective in bringing about alignment.

Conclusions

The evidence provided above indicates the way in which education-business partnerships, such as Business Class, can support young people to develop the skills – in the widest sense of the term – to make an efficient and effective transition into the labour market. This would appear to work best where more intensive, individualised support is provided to the student. In many respects the supply-side is doing its bit. But the demand side remains weak. This means that programmes which connect schools, students, and employers become even more important as they provide the wherewithal for students to help them find the job they want to do in a relatively tough labour market. But it also indicates the limits of such programmes. They can improve, other things being equal, the employability and enterprise skills of young people, but it is difficult to see how this alone can increase overall aggregate demand for labour in the youth jobs market. There need to be other stimuli to bring this about. Similarly, improving the capacity of the VET system to meet employers' current and future skill needs will improve the matching of young people's skills to the jobs available, but again it is not clear how this will affect overall aggregate labour demand in the youth jobs market. Important here, of course, is the introduction of the Apprenticeship Levy (Gambin et al. 2016). This has the capacity to substantially increase employer demand for apprentices, but there is no guarantee that it will be for young people if employers choose to train existing employees – many of whom are aged 24 years of over – rather than recruit young people as apprentices. Only time will tell what impact it will have on the training and employment of young people.

For now, it is apparent that there are education-business partnerships in place, such as Business Class, that have the impact of shaping and aligning the activities of students in school in a way that ensures that they possess the critical employability skills that employers say they need. And employers have played a role, too, in improving skills supply through their engagement with schools. The evidence points to the supply-side – via education-business partnerships such as Business Class – being flexible and responsive to the demands side (i.e. by suitably preparing students for the world of work). So in this respect the education and training system – certainly for the 14–19 age group – has significantly contributed to the long cherished public policy goal of creating a demand-led skills system. But demand in the youth labour market is weak. Without demand side policies that will boost employer demand for the skills and attributes young people bring to the workplace, then it is apparent that the returns from programmes such as Business Class will be sub-optimal. So in conclusion, one may say that the supply side would appear to be willing and able to do its bit, but the demand side needs to step up to the mark, too. The youth labour market is sorely lacking a demand-side stimulus that will increase the number of good quality job openings for young people. On of the basis of the evidence provided here, schools via education-business partnerships are equipping their students with skills to fill those jobs should they become available.

Note

1 The Income Deprivation Affecting Children Index (IDACI) measures the proportion of all children aged 0 to 15 living in income deprived families. Available from: www.gov.uk/government/statistics/english-indices-of-deprivation-2015. [accessed January 10, 2018]

References

Buscha, F. and Urwin, P.J. (2013). *Estimating the labour market returns to qualifications gained in English further education using the Individualised Learner Record (ILR)*. London: Department for Business, Innovation and Skills.

Chaplain, R. and Gray, J. (2000). Young people's perceptions of themselves and their futures: Do education business partnerships make a difference? *Journal of Vocational Education & Training* 52(3): 349–371.

Department for Education. (2017). *Post-16 educational reforms: T level action plan.* London: Department for Education.

Gambin, L. et al. (2015). *Evaluation of Business Class.* Report to Business in the Community.

Gambin, L. and Hogarth, T. (2017).*Employers and apprenticeships in England: Costs, risks and policy reforms.* Empirical Research in Vocational Education and Training.

Gambin, L., Hogarth, T., Winterbotham, M., Huntley-Hewitt, J., Eastwood, L. and Vivian, D. (2016). *The apprenticeship levy: How will employers respond?* DfE Research Report, DFE-RR612. London: Department for Education.

Gospel, H. (1995). The decline of apprenticeship training in Britain. *Industrial Relations* 26(1): 32–44.

Grant, P. (2010). *Business class: An evaluation.* London: Cass Business School and BITC.

Hogarth, T., Owen, D., Gambin, L., Hasluck, C., Lyonette, C. and Casey, B. (2009). *The equality impacts of the current recession.* Equality and Human Rights Commission Research Report No.47.

Holman, J. (2014). *Good careers guidance.* London: Gatsby Trust.

Huddleston, P. (2012). Pupil work experience, in Huddleston, P. and Stanley, J. (eds.), *Work-related teaching and learning a guide for teachers and practitioners.* Abingdon: Routledge.

Leitch, S. (2006). *Prosperity for all in the global economy – world class skills.* London: HM Treasury.

Mann, A. (2012). *It's who you meet: Why employer contacts at school make a difference to the employment prospects of young adults.* London: Education and Employers Taskforce.

Mann, A. and Dawkins, J. (2014). *Employer engagement in education: Literature review.* London: Education and Employers Taskforce/CfBT Trust.

Mann, A., Massey, D., Glover, P., Kashefpakdel, E. T. and Dawkins, J. (2013).*Nothing in common: The career ambitions of young people mapped against projected labour market demand (2010–2020).*

Natcen/SQW. (2017). *Work experience and related activities in schools and colleges.* London: Department for Education Research Report.

Yates, S., Harris, A., Sabates, R., and Staff, J. (2011). Early occupational aspirations and fractured transitions: A study of entry into 'NEET' status in the UK. *Journal of Social Policy* 40(3): 513–534.

Chapter 11

Ethnographies of work and possible futures

New ways for young people to learn about work and choose a meaningful first career

Nancy Hoffman with Tobie Baker Wright and Mary Gatta

This chapter describes a new approach to helping young people develop the knowledge and experiences that will increase their access to good jobs. Adopting an investigative approach, *Ethnographies of Work* as pioneered by a U.S. institution of higher education, Guttman Community College, and *Possible Futures*, a curriculum for 11 to 15-year-olds developed by Jobs for the Future, a Non-Governmental Organization, present the modern workplace as a field of enquiry and experience for students. The programmes engage working people directly as informants about various careers and equip students with deep knowledge about employer expectations and behaviours so that they will be better job seekers, able to cast a critical eye on potential workplaces as they make sense of their career options. They also introduce students to the idea that social networks and connections (forms of social capital) matter in entering the labour market. This chapter reviews the rationale, design and potential impact of these pilot programs. The example of practice is located within the research literature on ethnographic methods, social and cultural capital, employability skills, college and career readiness and adolescent development.

In the United States, a career pathways movement is growing. The term "career pathways," used here, is defined as: public education experiences that serve young people between age 11 and the early 20s and include not only strong academic provision, but also a sequence of opportunities to learn about work, to learn to work, and, under the best circumstances, to choose and prepare for a first career. The ideal sequence of experiences as defined by career pathways developed starts with career awareness in the middle grades (ages 11–13), followed by career exploration and career preparation in the high school grades (ages 14–18), and career training (at the early tertiary or later upper secondary level) leading to a smooth transition into the labour market[1] (Hoffman and Schwartz, 2017).

A non-U.S. reader might ask: why now and what is the cause of this new emphasis on career preparation in the United States? Isn't all education designed to lead to a career? Are vocational education systems not intended for this purpose specifically? While the U.S. has a vocational education system (called "career and technical education" or CTE), it serves only about 20% of young people and still carries a stigma based on a history of serving students whom teachers judged "not fit" for college.[2] Such students were predominantly low income, youth of colour and from weaker high schools (Symonds, Schwartz and Ferguson, 2011; Oates and Saunders, 2008). They often had few choices about their tertiary pathways. Students channelled into vocational education, therefore, fit a pattern of racial and economic discrimination, but this is not the only reason that vocational education went out of style.

Since the 1990s, when the U.S. discovered that it was below the middle of the pack in international comparisons of student achievement, with incentives from the federal government, the fifty states, private philanthropies and the business community set their sights on raising the academic achievement of the nation's school children. Education reform moved far in the direction of rigorous academics with the career preparation that once existed in many high schools overshadowed by instruction and high stakes testing devoted to mathematics, science, reading and writing so that all students would graduate from high school ready for college. The goal of many educators and policy makers was and still remains "college for all."

The career pathways movement is solving several problems. First, only 36% of 25 to 29 year olds in the U.S. now have a four-year tertiary degree, so like many aspirational policies in the U.S., "college for all" has proved to be an unrealistic expectation (Institute of Education Sciences,, 2016). Second, while the returns to the four-year degree far outpace the returns for those who enter the labour market with only a high school diploma, even students with a bachelor's degree swirl in the labour market, often reaching their late 20s before settling into a career because they lack appropriate work experience and training. Third, while the U.S. is almost at full employment, low-income youth are still unemployed at rates out of proportion to their numbers (Kroeger et al. 2016). And finally, employers complain that they cannot fill entry level positions because the skills, experience and behaviours that recent college graduates bring to the labour market are out of alignment with employer needs and requirements (Deming, 2015).

Their complaints point to a disconnect between educators' views of the ends of education and that of employers. This disconnect was pointed out in an influential 2011 report from the Harvard Graduate School of Education, *Pathways to Prosperity*, which argued that the "American system for preparing young people to lead productive and prosperous lives as adults is clearly badly broken. Failure to aggressively overcome this challenge will surely erode the fabric of our society" (Symonds, Schwartz and Ferguson, 2011).

While there are many solutions to the career problem, few address the issues that *Ethnographies of Work* (EOW) and *Possible Futures* (PF) take on, the former with a target audience of first-year community college students, the second focused on students aged 11 through 15 years old. EOW is a year-long course designed to give students tools for understanding and addressing the challenges and opportunities they face in the labour market; it does so in both a theoretical and applied context by putting the subject of "work" at the centre of learning. PF is a school career awareness and exploration curriculum that, through projects, simulations and career and college visits, helps students come to see themselves as "young professionals."[3]

These new initiatives recognize that certain groups of young people are particularly disadvantaged entering working life. They are ill informed about the labour market, how careers are developed and not linked to the networks that might help them on their way (Hoffman and Schwartz, 2017). Schools do not routinely teach about the role of work in human lives or how the labour market operates, nor do they address race, class and gender barriers to employment, let alone help young people understand that even with a degree they will need to activate informal social networks to find a first job. Few schools collaborate with employers to help students get in the door for internships, summer jobs or job shadowing. In his recent book, *Our Kids*, the political scientist Robert Putnam, decries the disappearance of vocational education from most American high schools, and advocates for more programs that offer "a curriculum that mixes academic coursework with hands-on technical courses designed to build work skills" (Putnam, 2015, 255). He contrasts the situation of low income youth entering the job market with only a high school diploma and no job skills with that of affluent young people whose parents make up for this lack by spending on "music lessons, summer camp, travel, school supplies, books, computers, extracurricular activities, recreation, and leisure," all of which introduce youth to the adult world, including the world of careers (Putnam 2015, 125).

EOW and PF tackle the central questions of this chapter: how do educators better prepare the nation's young people for the world of work – not just with technical skills or so called "soft skills," but more broadly and holistically – with the kind of knowledge about the working world that youth learn in families of means? Can schools provide disadvantaged youth with the social and cultural capital that makes them adept at the "rules of the game" so they can navigate transitions into satisfying employment? (Archer et al. 2010) The approaches embodied in EOW and PF emphasize not only understanding the world of work, but a critical consideration of it, trying out careers with full knowledge of opportunities as well as of barriers that make it harder to break in to arenas where there is little class, race or ethnic diversity.

Ethnographies of work[4]

Guttman Community College, a two-year college in the City University of New York higher education system, opened in 2012 with the aim of introducing students to the integral connection between intellectual exploration, acquisition of concrete skills and knowledge and career development (Evenbeck and

Merians, 2016; Bailey et al. 2015). Guttman students attend full-time and enrol on the understanding that the college will prepare them for a limited number of career areas linked to jobs in high and growing demand in New York City. Students come from all boroughs of New York. In the autumn of 2016, 73% of the student body was 19 or younger and 60% Hispanic, 27% African American, and 8% white. Just over 50% of students are women; 73% receive financial aid from the federal government based on their family's income.[5]

Guttman has an innovative approach to the first-year experience, which aims to empower students to approach career choice critically. Students take only three courses in Year I: *Statistics*, *City Seminar* (about New York City with topics including sustainability, food, housing, gentrification and immigration), and *Ethnographies of Work* (EOW). EOW builds upon an explicit theory of action: students who understand the meaning of work in human lives, the sociology of the professions and who have some professional work experience will have greater agency in entering the labour market than those who believe only a credential is needed. In addition, students who understand the challenges that being different impose in the professional world – being working class, dark skinned, speaking with an accent – will, armed with that knowledge, enter the job market alert to the meanings of these aspects of identity. In EOW, students interview and observe people doing jobs of interest to them, some that are completely new to them and some familiar from their communities and the media. They also read ethnographic studies on the nature of work, including *Gig: Americans Talk About Their Jobs* (Bowe, J, Bowe, M. and Streeter, S.. 2001) and selections from theorists such as Karl Marx.

EOW is a two-sequence, year-long course. In EOW I, the students master ethnographic methods (research design, observation, mapping and interviewing) and use workplaces as research sites to refine their ethnographic skills. The signature course assignment is a semester-long ethnographic investigation of a career or workplace that the student has an interest in pursuing. In EOW II, having mastered the research methodology and developed confidence as researchers in workplaces, the focus is on critical analysis of the workplace using a social science lens (approaches from history, anthropology and sociology).

Students also use their ethnographic skills to conduct original research and investigate a research question associated with the worlds of work. They work in research teams (akin to consulting groups) to explore workplace problems such as the challenges faced by women in senior information technology positions; how professionals in the financial services industry balance work and family; or the experiences of workers in on-demand gig jobs like Uber driver or management consultancy. In addition to three hours a week in EOW, students spend ninety minutes a week in a group class, *Learning About Being a Successful Student (LaBSS)*, where they engage in a skill-based curriculum associated with work and career readiness. Facilitated by a college advisor, students conduct an analysis of their strengths, weaknesses, opportunities and threats (SWOT), reflect on career and academic major research, create résumés and vision boards, and practice networking and interviewing.

Within the EOW curriculum, reflection on the character of work from an individualized perspective is infused into the academic curriculum, rather than seen as a separate endeavour. Since EOW is a social science course, students interact with workplaces in distinctive ways. Rather than entering a workplace as an intern, they enter as observers, able to spend a significant amount of time uncovering the dynamics that will help inform their career decisions and future work experiences. For example, students will often first read an academic ethnographic text of a particular workplace dynamic – such as hierarchical leadership structures. They then will visit selected workplaces to replicate the ethnographic study. In doing so, they are able to use theory and methods to gain critical cultural knowledge of workplaces.

Episodes of employer engagement are often viewed within research literature as developing forms of social and cultural capital, because students are accessing new sources of information and meeting people who influence their thinking about their prospective future selves. Such analysis draws heavily on Stanford University sociologist Mark Granovetter's conception of the strength of weak ties to describe social interactions which lead to the generation of "non-redundant trusted information" of ultimate economic relevance (Jones Mann and Morris, 2015; Mann Stanley and Archer, 2014; Granovetter, 1973). EOW students increase their social networks gaining new access to people who are useful to them, possessing information which can raise, broaden, and challenge occupational aspirations. Such new connections are particularly important for CUNY students since many are without expansive social networks. Because students interact with employers in professional settings as researchers, this is a low-key way for employers to meet young people about whom they may have preconceived notions. Over the years, these observations have led to trusted social relationships of demonstrable value to both student and employer as witnessed in internship placements and job opportunities.

The EOW experience is distinct from the traditional way students learn about careers in U.S. colleges and universities. In general, information about careers and entry to the labour market is handled through career service offices separated from the main academic endeavours. Students can complete their studies having never paid a visit to such an office. With their limited funding and staffing, such offices often struggle to keep up with demand. In addition, educators tend to signal that college is about the intellectual endeavour itself, and that, with a degree in hand, career choice will take care of itself. Consequently, students can learn too late what they should have done to be better prepared (Young, 2016).

Possible futures: Filling the middle years' gap in career awareness[6]

Research identifies adolescence as a unique developmental window for youth to explore and create a college and career-focused identity (Hinton et al. 2012;

Halpern, 2013; Nagaoka et al. 2015), and this is the terrain on which Possible Futures (PF) operates. Through projects, simulations and career and college visits, 11 to 15-year-old PF participants become "young professionals." As they complete challenges based on real-world, work-related problems, they build the foundation for critical thinking, collaboration and innovation. While this is not workplace learning, it sets the stage in an age-appropriate way for students to begin to understand and experience the world of work and to anticipate what employers might ask of them as older teens. By better understanding themselves and their future possibilities, students develop a future-ready mindset with a skill set to match (Lee and Oyserman, 2009).

Three interlinked concepts undergird the program's design: self, society and security. While the first two are familiar educator themes, security is a new and powerful additional concept. The notion of "security" emerged from discussions with employers and knowledge of and research about the challenges facing students who are first in their families to enter tertiary education (Pascarella et al. 2004; Savitz-Romer and Bouffard, 2012). The discussion of security veers from the usual upper middle-class advice to youth – "follow your passion" – which, important as it is, omits the lived realities of young people who must consider early how to support themselves economically, contribute to their family's income and pay for tertiary education. In the U.S., students complete a bachelor's degree with debt that averages $28,000, and low-income students typically borrow more than that from banks and the government. Such students often end up in low-paying career paths because they have neither the confidence nor connections (cultural and social capital) needed to aspire to and attain well-paying and satisfying careers (Patten, 2016). To compound the challenge of living on low wages, they must pay off their college debts, and many end up defaulting. The three "S"s framework honours individual passions, but also acknowledges the more practical demands shaping the choices of young people who do not have a social or familial safety net.

Middle school is a time when young people often disconnect from and foreclose on STEM identities, so rich, engaging opportunities to maintain and deepen STEM connections, both in school and beyond, are particularly important (National Research Council, 2011). Possible Futures' career modules focus on three STEM fields: health sciences, IT and engineering. Students hone their twenty-first century skills as they apply design thinking to create solutions to problems contextualized in the world of work. Whether becoming young coders and designing apps to solve a community problem or supporting patient recovery as allied health workers, young participants experience STEM activities tuned to the STEM careers that shape our world

For some youth, exploring the world of college and careers holds an additional complexity – they may discover environments where they feel they do not belong. This especially impacts young women and underrepresented students interested in many STEM fields (U.S. Department of Education, 2016). Through Possible Futures, students not only see diverse images of STEM professionals, but also explore how they can make powerful contributions to their communities within STEM fields. For example, youth attending the East Bay Academy in San Francisco conducted water quality research in their East Oakland community; they discovered pollution in a local creek, a danger to their community that they reported to the Public Works Department which closed off the sewage link causing the problem (East Bay Academy for Young Scientists, 2017).

While this approach does not mitigate gaps in STEM representation which is majority white and male in the U.S., it does begin to change the narrative of who belongs in STEM fields and how STEM can be used in service of diverse communities. Archer et al. (2015) developed the useful concept of "science capital," a twenty-first century complement or corrective to the heavily cultural focus of Bourdieu. Updating the notion of class and race inequality in relation to science, Archer notes that students with "low science capital" tended to be female and from low income families. The same groups also have low cultural capital. With this recognition, PF can address the issue directly.

In addition to enriching the curriculum of middle school, PF helps to mitigate the absence of training in career counselling of school guidance counsellors. The ratio of guidance counsellors to students is extremely high in most schools, and in challenging school environments, guidance counsellors must prioritize crises that are daily occurrences so have little time to set up job shadows or to explore options for workplace visits (Seaton, 2017). The Lenses on the Future module uses *self, society* and *security* to support families and educators as they offer informal guidance to students. Possible Futures pilots school-to-home connections – inviting contributions from families as young people explore and grow clearer about their own values and future options. Possible Futures encourages schools to re-evaluate the notion that education occurs before – and separate from – careers, and instead, to ground academic challenges in real-world contexts. By working with families and helping them understand the economic returns to STEM careers as well as the intellectual satisfactions that often go with science, PF addresses and builds community social capital.

The research context for these two courses

As with many innovations, long-term impact data will not be available until EOW and PF are well established; however, both of these approaches are underpinned by research assembled from diverse resources. In the final section of this essay, we review some of that research. We also note that additional research is required to better understand how students and their future employers view each other.[7]

Social capital and cultural capital

As suggested above, an understudied but critical aspect of finding a career is the quotient of social and cultural capital of the job seeker. Beyond schools attended and degrees earned, social capital is a powerful engine of differentiation. The Organization for Economic Cooperation and Development defines social capital as "networks together with shared norms, values and understandings that facilitate cooperation within or among groups" (OECD Insight, 2007, 103). The OECD breaks the definition into "bonds, bridges and links," with the connections between each moving from bonds between family and close friends, to bridges to distant friends and colleagues, to links to those further up or down the social ladder. The greater the quotient of social capital, the more likely a credentialed young person is to move beyond family and community bonds to activate promising connections to the labour market. Cultural capital works as an aid and reinforcement of social capital. Though the definitions overlap, cultural capital refers to the symbolic elements that enable a person to be recognized as belonging to a network or social group – how they dress, speak, where they live, and what entertainment they consume. In the STEM arena, as in other professions, cultural capital reflects the subtle norms and expectations, understanding of which enable confident engagement and progression within a working culture (Archer et al. 2010).

Elites (and the organisations which they sponsor) work hard to ensure that their children develop social capital. For example, professional parents take care to have their children meet young people of similar background, their parents and colleagues. In the U.S. such parents invest in their children's cultural capital by enrolling their children in after school enrichment activities such as music and language programs and summer internship or academic programs where they interact with professionals in fields of interest (Lareau, 2002, 2011). Such parents reach out to "helping professionals" when they see signs of anxiety, stress or non-compliance with the social norms of their reference groups. Mutually reinforced at school and at home, constructed social and cultural experiences produce young people who make appropriate small talk with adults and take advantage of social networks.

Lareau (2002, 2011) has documented what many sense intuitively – that privilege increases privilege. In *Unequal Childhoods: Class, Race, and Family Life*, she studied what she called "the cultural logic" of parenting styles as they impact home, afterschool and school lives of working class and middle-class youth. She documented the reasons for the higher achievement and success rates of more privileged young people describing the "concerted cultivation" of children (Lareau, 2002, 30). Middle-class parents work to "develop" children in ways that fit the standards of mainstream institutions and that benefit their children later in the working world. Such families are adept at cultivating social capital. In contrast, Lareau characterizes working-class children's parenting style as privileging "natural growth." Children have long periods of unstructured time. Play is child initiated without the mediating parental proviso that it be a learning experience. Clear boundaries exist between children and adults, so children are less likely to meet their parents' friends and work colleagues.

Reconnecting in 2011 with the children she studied in 2002, Lareau shows that the "intensity of middle-class and upper middle-class parents in building their children's social capital only increases as children grow into young adults. Middle-class parents continued the process of gathering information and intervening in their children's lives . . . even when the children had moved hundreds of miles from home" (Lareau, 2011, 29). As young adults turned to their parents for guidance, the parents guided them, in key ways, as children. In working-class and poor families, the parents saw the young adults as "grown," a view shared by the young adults themselves. The working-class parents loved their children very much, but they did not have the means or tendency to intervene. Thus, trajectories which began when the children were 10 continued to unfold into adulthood. The middle-class kids generally achieved greater educational success than the working-class and poor kids. Since education is the foundation for shaping labour market chances, the career prospects of the middle-class young adults were much brighter than those of their less privileged counterparts.

Social skills

Current research suggests that in decades ahead, two kinds of knowledge will be the best predictors of workforce success: technical skills and social skills. An extensive economic literature documents the return to technical skills (Acemoglu and Autor, 2010), but scholars have paid less attention to the returns for social skills. Social skills are a subset or result of having social capital, and according to numerous researchers, over the last generation have been increasingly linked to wage premiums (Deming, 2015; Acemoglu and Autor, 2010). The change is not just from manual work to "thinking for a living," but to a labour market that rewards skills that robots cannot easily replace like empathy and collaboration. James Heckman earlier documented such trends showing that occupations that combine technical and interpersonal expertise can be expected to resist automation and thus to have high value. To Heckman, non-cognitive skills like "persistence, motivation, and self-esteem" are as important as cognitive achievement" (Heckman, 2006, 29).

Both PF and EOW attend to social skills: EOW, through readings on such topics as "emotional labour" or observations that illuminate power dynamics and other nuances in the workplaces. PF builds social skills through the *Skills for Success* and *Lenses on the Future* modules, as well as through teamwork and creativity required in PF projects.

Adolescent development

The challenge for educators, consequently, is to better prepare all young people with "school knowledge," and with the experiences that will help them to navigate the social worlds of mainstream institutions. PF is deeply grounded in research on adolescent development, particularly the middle years. Two syntheses from the University of Chicago Consortium on School Research were particularly helpful in the PF design: Teaching Adolescents to Become Learners (Farrington et al. 2012) and Foundations for Young Adult Success (Nagaoka et al. 2015). In general, this research confirms that by the time students are in middle school, regularity of school attendance, beliefs about how the world works, behaviour and commitment to course completion are already consequential and correlate with future success. Additionally, the middle years are a pivotal time when students may either disengage from or begin to truly connect to the STEM subjects' key to today's most promising professional opportunities.

Stanford Professor Carol Dweck's work has been particularly important in counteracting the belief of so many youth that they cannot succeed in science and math because they were born without talent for these subjects. Dweck is the originator of the concept of "growth mindset" (2006) which she opposes to "fixed mindset." Dweck's research has a had a major influence on teachers who now help their students to understand intelligence is not fixed and immutable, an unchangeable quality, but rather that purpose and effort supported by strategies focused on how to learn can make you a more successful student; a growth mindset can help overcome the fixed and destructive idea that you are born unable to do math or become a scientist (Dweck, 2006).

This chapter ends by rephrasing a pivotal question: how do youth gain a sense of what their lives will be as adults in the labour force? How will they know what Robert Halpern calls their future' "vocational selves" (2008)? Yes, students take interest inventories and observe some professions in the media, but that is different from trying out skills and knowledge used in a workplace or observing workplaces with a rigorous methodology – experiences that EOW and PF put into place. Almost a lone voice researching this topic, Halpern argues for the value of learning in workplaces: "the most interesting and compelling value of vocationally-oriented learning is personal. It fosters maturity, nurtures a sense of personal competence and of having a place in the world. . . " (2012, 87).

From the employer's perspective, hesitation to hire young people is grounded in a reality. Without an understanding of the workplace, and with little experience of translating school knowledge to the workplace, many young people have difficulty adapting. But it is likely that those young people who have higher levels of social skills can adapt more easily and quickly. Such skills do not emerge at birth. They are not hereditary but are grown in families, but also in internships, summer jobs and episodes of employer engagement which develop "hard and soft professional skills, networking opportunities, reduced risk of negative socioeconomic outcomes," as a recent Massachusetts report on youth unemployment concludes (Borella, 2016, 1). Too often low-income young people receive the message "Get a college degree, and you'll be just fine," but academic achievement alone does not guarantee success. Experience in work settings scaffolded by teaching and learning about work addresses this need. The two innovative approaches described in this chapter share the ambitious goal of compensating for privileges emerging from family backgrounds. Both make explicit what is usually obscure – how "the working world is pitched as never before in favour of the well-connected, the socially knowledgeable and the rich" (Russell, 2017).

Notes

1 In the U.S., high school culminates at grade 12; students are around 18 when they complete their required studies. Upper secondary vocational education generally goes one year beyond U.S. high schools and includes much more intensive career training. We use the term high school in this article to distinguish the U.S. version from upper secondary.
2 In the U.S., "college" means a four-year bachelor's degree granting institution; university means a tertiary education institution with substantial post bachelor's degree granting authority.
3 PF was developed as an initiative of the Pathways to Prosperity Network, a collaboration between Jobs for the Future and the Harvard Graduate School of Education, which Hoffman co-founded. The goal of the Pathways Network is to create career-focused pathways from at least ninth grade through at least an industry recognized credential or an associate's degree in a technical field in demand in the labor market.
4 This summary draws in part from Hoffman, N. (2016). Guttman Community College Puts 'Work' at the Center of Learning: An Approach to Student Economic Mobility. *Change: The Magazine of Higher Learning* 48(4) (2016): 14–23.
5 Latest data available via Guttman Center for College Effectiveness. Available from: https://guttman-cuny.digication.com/idea/about [accessed January 10, 2018]
6 See Tobie Baker-Wright, "Career Pathways: Preparing Youth for STEM Futures," STEM Ready America, Available from: http://stemreadyamerica.org/article-career-pathways [accessed January 10th 2018].
7 Some content of this section is drawn from Hoffman, N. (2017). The Power of Work-based Learning. *Rethinking Readiness: Deeper Learning for College, Work, and Life*. Eds. Rafael Heller, Rebecca E. Wolfe, and Adria Steinberg. Harvard: Harvard Education Press and Hoffman, N. and Schwartz, R. (2017). *Learning for Careers: The Pathways to Prosperity Network*. Harvard: Harvard Education Press.

References

Acemoglu, D. and Autor, D. (2010). *Skills, tasks and technologies: Implications for employment and earnings*. Cambridge, MA: NBER.

Archer, L., Dawson, E., DeWitt, J., Seakins, A. and Wong, B. (2015). "Science capital": A conceptual, methodological, and empirical argument for extending Bourdieusian notions of capital beyond the arts. *Journal of Research in Science Teaching* 52(7): 922–948.

Archer, L., Hollingworth, S. and Mendick, H. (2010). *Urban youth and schooling*. Berkshire: Open University Press.

Bailey, T., Smith Jaggars, S. and Jenkins, D. (2015). *Redesigning America's community colleges: A clearer path to student success*. Cambridge, MA: Harvard University Press.

Borella, N., Jurek, C. and Martin, L. (2016). *The young adult labor force in Massachusetts*. Hadley, MA: UMass Donahue Institute, Economic & Public Policy Research.

Bowe, J., Bowe, M. and Streeter, S. (eds.). (2001). *Gig: Americans talk about their jobs*. New York, NY: Three Rivers Press.

Deming, D. (2015). *The growing importance of social skills in the labor market*. Cambridge, MA: NBER.

Dweck, C.S. (2006). *Mindset: The new psychology of success*. New York, NY: Random House.

The East Bay Academy for Young Scientists. (2017). *In your community*. Lawrence Hall of Science. Available from: www.lawrencehallofscience.org/do_science_now/in_your_community [accessed June 20th 2017].

Evenbeck, S. and Merians, L. (2016). After the doors opened: Asking why at a new community college, in Misangyi Watts, M. (ed.), *Finding the why: Personalizing learning in higher education*. New York, NY: New Directions: 67–76.

Farrington, C.A., Roderick, M., Allensworth, E., Nagaoka, J., Keyes, T.S., Johnson, D.W. and Beechum, N.O. (2012). *Teaching adolescents to become learners: The role of noncognitive factors in shaping school performance: A critical literature review*. Chicago: University of Chicago Consortium: Chicago School Research.

Granovetter, M. (1973). The strength of weak ties. *American Journal of Sociology* 78(6): 1360–1380.

Halpern, R. (2008). *The means to grow up: Reinventing apprenticeship as a developmental support in adolescence* (Critical Youth Studies). London: Routledge.

Halpern, R. (2012). Supporting vocationally oriented learning in the high school years: Rationale, tasks, challenges. *New Directions for Youth Development* 134: 85–106.

Halpern. R. (2013). *Youth, education, and the role of society: Rethinking learning in the high school years*. Cambridge, MA: Harvard Education Press.

Heckman, J., Stixrud, J. and Urzua, S. (2006). *The effects of cognitive and noncognitive abilities on labor market outcomes and social behavior*. Cambridge, MA: NBER.

Hinton, C., Fischer, K.W. and Glennon, C. (2012). *Mind, brain, and education: Students at the Center Series*. Boston, MA: Jobs for the Future.

Hoffman, N. (2016). Guttman community college puts 'work' at the center of learning: An approach to student economic mobility. *Change: The Magazine of Higher Learning*, 48(4): 14–23.

Hoffman, N. (2017). The power of work-based learning, in Heller, R., Wolfe, R. and Steinberg, A. (eds.), *Rethinking readiness: Deeper learning for college, work, and life*. Cambridge, MA: Harvard Education Press.

Hoffman, N. and Schwartz, R. (2017). *Learning for careers: The pathways to prosperity network*. Cambridge, MA: Harvard Education Press.

Institute of Education Sciences. (2016). *Digest of education statistics*. Washington, DC: National Center for Education Statistics.

Jones, S., Mann, A. and Morris, K. (2015). The "Employer Engagement Cycle" in secondary education: Analysing the testimonies of young British adults. *Journal of Education and Work* 29(7): 834–856.

Kroeger, T., Cooke, T. and Gould, E. (2016). *The class of 2016*. Washington, DC: Economic Policy Institute.

Lareau, A. (2002, 2011). *Unequal childhoods: Class, race, and family life*. 1st and 2nd ed. Oakland: University of California Press.

Lee, S.J. and Oyserman, D. (2009). Possible selves theory, in Anderman, E. and Anderman, L. (eds.), *Psychology of classroom learning: An encyclopedia*. Detroit, MI: Palgrave Macmillan.

Mann, A., Stanley, J. and Archer, L. (2014). *Understanding employer engagement in education: Theories and evidence*. London: Routledge.

Nagaoka, J., Farrington, C., Ehrlich, S. and Heath, R. (2015). *Foundations for young adult success: Developmental framework*. Consortium on Chicago School Research. Chicago: University of Chicago.

National Research Council. (2011). *Successful K-12 STEM education: Identifying effective approaches in science, technology, engineering, and mathematics*. Washington, DC: National Academies Press.

Oates, J. and Saunders, M. (2008). *Beyond tracking: Multiple pathways to college, career, and civic participation*. Cambridge, MA: Harvard Education Press.

OECD. (2007). *OECD insights:* Human *capital*. Paris: Organisation for Economic Co-Operation and Development.

Pascarella, Ernest, T., Pierson, Christopher, T., Wolniak, G. and Terenzini, P. (2004). First-generation college students: Additional evidence on college experiences and outcomes. *Journal of Higher Education* 75(3): 249.

Patten, E. (2016). *Racial, gender wage gaps persist in U.S. despite some progress*. Washington, DC: Pew Research Center.

Putnam, R.D. (2015). *Our kids*. New York, NY: Simon & Schuster.

Russell, J. (2017). *Britain's broken ladder of social mobility*. New York Times, June 27, 2017. Available from: www.nytimes.com/2017/06/27/opinion/britains-broken-ladder-of-social-mobility.html?_r=0 [Accessed June 27th 2017].

Savitz-Romer, M. and Bouffard, S. (2012). *Reading willing and able: A developmental approach to college access and success*. Cambridge, MA: Harvard Education Press.

Seaton, G. (2017). *Supporting postsecondary success in Delaware: A landscape analysis of student opportunities, jobs for the future*. Available from: www.jff.org/sites/default/files/publications/materials/DE_Landscape_Analysis_Full_Report.pdf [Accessed June 27th 2017].

Symonds, W., Schwartz, R. and Ferguson, R. (2011). *Pathways to prosperity; Meeting the challenge of preparing young Americans for the 21st century*. Cambridge, MA: Harvard Graduate School for Education.

U.S. Department of Education. (2016). *STEM 2026: A vision for STEM education*. Washington, DC: U.S. Department of Education.

Young, J. (2016). Reinventing the career center. *The Chronicle of Higher Education* 63(9).

Chapter 12

What impact can employer engagement have on student attitudes towards school and their academic achievement?

An analysis of OECD PISA data

Elnaz Kashefpakdel, Jordan Rehill and Matteo Schleicher

In recent years, organisations such as the Organisation for Economic Co-operation and Development (OECD) have advocated greater engagement of employers in education to support the progression of young people into an increasingly challenging labour market (OECD, 2010; Musset and Kurekova, 2018). Interviewed in 2014, the OECD's Director of Education and Skills, Andreas Schleicher, argued that not only might positive impacts from employer-enriched provision be expected in the economic outcomes of young people as they transition into the labour market, but also be seen in the classroom in increased student motivation. Employer engagement, he maintained, offered young people a new perspective on the value of education and qualifications being undertaken.

> As well as thinking anew about the curriculum and the preparations for modern working life that schooling provides, greater attention needs to be focused on improving signalling of the different pathways available to young people. This is why exposure to the workplace is so important within education. It not only provides excellent opportunities for experiential learning across the curriculum, but also underpins effective careers education and the decision-making of young people. Work experience and other forms of employer engagement demonstrate to young people the links between what they do in the classroom and how those skills ultimately will be used in the labour market. For young people, and for their teachers, that is a great motivator.
> (Andreas Schleicher cited in Mann and Huddleston, 2015, 28)

This chapter explores the evidence surrounding Schleicher's contention that episodes of employer engagement can impact on the academic motivation of teenagers by using the unique dataset on student attitudes and academic proficiency: the OECD's own Programme International Student Attainment (PISA).

Context: the link between school-mediated employer engagement and student academic achievement

While policy and research discourses surrounding the effects of school-mediated teenage participation episodes of employer engagement has largely been driven by economic policy imperatives (Stanley and Mann, 2014; Mann et al. 2018), a strong emphasis within what is a limited research literature has focused on academic impacts of engagement. In Mann et al.'s 2018 Education Endowment Foundation (EEF) review of international research literature undertaken using experimental and quasi-experimental methodologies (largely Randomised Controlled Trials and longitudinal studies), 17 studies (six from the UK) testing the relationship between participation in employer engagement activities and educational attainment were identified. Of these, six were assessed as identifying largely positive outcomes, eleven mixed outcomes and none negative outcomes. Where positive outcomes were identified, the scale of impact was typically modest with impacts assumed to vary by student type and quality of delivery (p. 15).

The study built on an earlier EEF literature review (Hughes et al. 2016) of Careers Education which identified 67 different interventions covering both employer engagement activities aimed at enhancing careers thinking as well as professional careers advice and guidance which provided reliable assessments on the educational achievement of young people. Of these, 60% provided largely positive findings evidencing improvements in educational outcomes, one study reported negative results and the remainder, mixed outcomes. Again, educational boosts were largely seen as modest. This chapter looks at the impact of both commonplace careers guidance activities and engagement with employers to further investigate the character of such relationships.

If the literature exploring the relationships between employer engagement and academic achievement is limited, evidence-based explorations of the causal character contained within such relationships is still more constrained. Both Hughes et al. (2016) and Mann et al. (2018) have sought to make sense of evidence of improved educational outcomes and in so doing have enabled the creation of a logic model which is tested in this chapter.

The work of Stanley and Mann (2014) provides both with a helpful starting point for understanding how employer engagement can be used as a tool by teaching professionals. They argue that, from an educational context, the resource provided by employers can be understood in one of three ways. It can be:

Supplementary – wherein employer engagement activities are intended to directly support conventional teaching and learning processes by offering additional resource. For example, number partners and reading support programmes.

Complementary – Employer engagement activities designed to offer alternative processes that are intended to achieve established learning outcomes as recognised by qualifications. For example, mentoring programmes. As discussed by Stanley and Mann (2014), employee mentors helped pupils to improve attainment.

Additional – Employer engagement activities designed achieve learning outcomes in addition to conventional learning outcomes as recognised by qualifications. Interventions that aim to develop employability skills or entrepreneurial capability are examples of this additionally. Although these kinds of outcomes are not usually recognised by qualifications, they may nevertheless be of value to young people, employers or policymakers. (Stanley and Mann, 2014: 38–39)

Of the three approaches, it is the *complementary* assessment which is found to resonate particularly strongly across the literature relevant to both careers guidance and employer engagement in terms of educational outcomes. Hughes et al. (2016) and Hooley et al. (2014), for example, draw on the work of Killeen and colleagues (1999) who argue that career guidance can help improve attainment because of its capacity to:

- . . . understand the relationship between educational goals and access to occupational goals;
- clarify valued outcomes;
- set attainable educational goals; and
- understand the relationship between current educational effort and performance to the achievement of educational and career goals

(Killeen et al. 1999, 18).

In this admirably simple manner, Killeen et al. (1999) suggest that the career guidance activities have the capacity to change the thinking of young people by exposing them to new information about the relationship between educational and economic outcomes. In a complementary approach to traditional teaching and learning, young people are presented with new reasons, from new sources, to drive their motivation.

This theory of change resonates with other more impressionistic data from other sources. Survey evidence supports the case that any positive impact on attainment largely stems from such attitudinal change – an enhanced regard for the value of education and qualifications improving motivation. Surveys of teaching staff have routinely recorded majorities agreeing that pupils taking part in career development activities return more mature, more motivated at school and with greater confidence (Hillage et al. 2001, 110; Eddy Adams, 2008, 37; see also Kashefpakdel et al. 2016a, 2016b, 2017), a view endorsed by pupil surveys (National Support Group for Work Experience, 2008, 20).

This chapter seeks to build on the existing literature by specifically investigating two hypotheses, exploring whether relationships can be drawn between participation in what the OECD describes as career development activities and both more positive attitudes towards education and improved academic achievement. In doing so, the analysis makes use of a unique dataset collated and made publically available for analysis by the OECD. This chapter draws upon this data in order to:

1 Investigate whether statistically significant relationships can be drawn between participation in selected career development activities and more positive attitudes towards the value of education as witnessed in responses to four attitudinal questions.
2 Investigate whether participation in selected career development activities is associated with higher PISA mathematics scores (a proxy for academic achievement at school).

Methodology

The OECD's PISA is a unique study both in scale and that it develops tests for young people which are not directly linked to the school curriculum. The tests, rather, are designed to assess the extent to which students, as they reach the end typically of their period of compulsory education, are able to apply their knowledge to real-life situations in preparation for full entry to society as adults. Every three years, dozens of countries and regions from around the world work with the OECD to randomly select students, aged 15, to take part in the tests which measure capability in reading, mathematics, science, problem-solving and financial literacy. The PISA test takes a young person about two hours to complete and involves students responding to open ended and multiple-choice questions. In total, nearly 400 questions are asked and include explorations of the social background and family life of students. Participating schools also return data on the broader school system and learning environment and some parents are also asked to complete returns.

Collecting a rich set of data about the family and social backgrounds of the 15-year-old survey participants and their schools, PISA allows analysts to control for the characteristics which commonly drive academic performance to isolate and analyse the impacts of distinctive interventions. Over 500,000 students from 65 countries and regions took part in the 2012 PISA surveys which asked a number of questions about participation across a series of career development activities including a number commonly organised by schools, some involving engagement with local employers (e.g., attendance at job fairs, job shadowing, internships). Only a minority of participating countries, however, opted into this series of questions (Sweet et al. 2014). In the analysis that follows, statistical analysis is initially presented exploring relationships between activity participation and evidence of student engagement with learning and academic motivation.

Careers development activities

The Educational Career Questionnaire within PISA 2012 asked student respondents: "Have you done any of the following to find out about future study or types of work?" Respondents were able to answer either "yes" or "no, never" to four questions which explored the extent to which young people had come into direct contact with workplaces or careers professionals through the agency of their school.[1]

- I did an internship
- I attended job shadowing or work-site visits
- I visited a job fair
- I spoke to a career advisor at my school

Participating countries

Only a minority of countries and regions undertaking PISA in 2012 chose to opt into these questions about career development activities. Twenty-two countries arranged for young people to be asked three or more of the four questions about career development activities. Of these, results from six countries are considered: Australia, Belgium, Canada, Denmark, Finland and Ireland.

Control variables

As is routine within statistical analysis of such a database within the social sciences, it is important for researchers to understand and control for key background characteristics which might distort findings. These control variables are used within analysis to determine whether any detected impacts related to career development activities as interventions are, in reality, a mask for some deeper variation in the experience of student participants. The control variables used in the analysis which follows drew on those applied within the OECD's own analyses of the performance of students in the problem-solving assessment:

- Gender.
- Socio-economic status. Measured by the PISA Index of Economic, Social and Cultural Status – an index including parental occupation, parental education and home possessions.
- School type. The school type control variable includes details of school location, drop-out rates, class size, staff/student ratios and private/public status.
- Immigrant background. The control variable includes immigrant status (native/first generation/second generation) and language spoken at home.
- Motivational factors. Control variable includes truancy factors (missing whole school days and classes within a school day).
- Cognitive potential. The variable includes responses to questions on whether respondents have been required to repeat a year of study.

Measuring student motivation

Within the long list of questions asked of young people, four focused on pupils' perceptions of the utility of schooling to their own economic futures as adults.

"Do you think that school...

... does little to prepare you for life?
... is a waste of time?
... is useful for jobs?
... helps you to get a job?"

Students were given four choices in responding:

• Strongly Agree
• Agree
• Disagree
• Strongly disagree.

Student participation in career development activities

In Table 12.1 descriptive statistics are presented illustrating the variation in student participation across the four career development activities managed through schools and engaging local employers by country.

Measuring student attainment in mathematics

PISA measures the students' "capacity to formulate, employ, and interpret mathematics in a variety of contexts. It includes reasoning mathematically and using mathematical concepts, procedures, facts and tools to describe, explain and predict phenomena" (OECD, 2013, 25). Students are presented with a series of questions with points allocated against on their responses. In 2012, 65 countries/regions participated in the PISA tests. Average scores against the

Table 12.1 Students reporting participation in four career development activities by country

	Internship	Job shadowing or work-site visit	Taken part in a job fair	Spoken to a careers adviser at my school
Australia	49%	30%	52%	66%
Belgium	11%	20%	15%	30%
Canada	9%	34%	40%	40%
Denmark	69%	52%	25%	94%
Finland	62%	43%	38%	84%
Ireland	7%	39%	11%	52%

assessments were published for each country/region. The six countries under consideration within this chapter were among the higher performers. On a scale running from 368 (Peru) to 613 (Shanghai), all six countries featured in the highest third of performers with the following average mathematics scores:

Australia   504 points
Belgium   515 points
Canada   518 points
Denmark   500 points
Finland   519 points
Ireland   501 points

These averages, however, disguise considerable variation within countries with highest and lowest performers separated by up to 300 points (OECD, 2014). The assessment of numeracy is of particular interest given the strong relationship between numeric proficiency and adult economic outcomes (Hanushek et al. 2013).

Results

Motivation and attitudes

In the first analysis, statistical regressions explored the relationship between participation in career development activities and attitudes towards schooling. Using controls to account for demographic characteristics and social background, the study asked whether students who had taken part in activities with careers professionals and employers through their schools exhibited more positive attitudes towards schooling that would have otherwise been expected. Table 12.2 sets out the results of a first analysis looking at the propensity to agree or disagree with the statement that "school does little to prepare you for life." In Australia, for example, young people who spoke with a careers advisor in school are 20% less likely to agree with the statement than comparable peers and the relationship is statistically significant at 5% meaning there is a 95% or better chance that the relationship is not coincidental. The relationship between taking part in certain activities and more positive attitudes towards school is statistically significant in all six countries. In every country, seeing a careers advisor at school is associated with a more positive perception of the lifelong value of schooling. The highest effect size is seen in Denmark and Belgium for people who received career advice at school.

Similar patterns are found when analysing responses to the statement "School is a waste of time" (see Table 12.3). Statistically significant relationships are found between participation in career development activities and lower levels of agreement with the statement with the exception of results from Belgium (which did not take part in this set of questions). Again, speaking with a careers

Table 12.2 Analysis: relationship between participation in career development activities and student disagreement/agreement with the statement: "School does little to prepare you for life"

Country	Activity	Odds ratio
Australia	Job fair	−14%*
	Career advisor at school	−20%*
Belgium	Job shadowing	−30%*
	Career advisor at school	−10%**
Canada	Job shadowing	−7%**
	Career advisor at school	−23%*
Denmark	Career advisor at school	−33%*
Finland	Internship	−16%*
	Career advisor at school	−26%*
Ireland	Career advisor at school	−18%*

* Statistically significant at 5%
** Statistically significant at 10%

Note: The negative sign means respondents are less likely to agree with the statement.

Table 12.3 Analysis: relationship between participation in career development activities and student disagreement/agreement with the statement: "School is a waste of time"

Country	Activity	Odds ratio
Australia	Job fair	−20%*
	Career advisor at school	−12%*
Canada	Job shadowing	−7%*
	Job fair	−6%*
	Career advisor at school	−18%
Denmark	Career advisor at school	−35%**
Finland	Internship	−24%*
	Job fair	−25%*
	Career advisor at school	−48%*
Ireland	Internship	−66%*
	Job shadowing	−16%*
	Job fair	−30%*
	Career advice at school	−41%

* Statistically significant at 5%
** Statistically significant at 10%

Note: The negative sign means respondents are less likely to agree with the statement.

advisor is valued most highly with visits to job fairs also strongly related to more positive perspectives. The highest levels of positive relationship are found in Ireland, Finland and Canada. Irish teenagers who took part in an internship are 66% less likely to agree that school is a waste of time than their peers.

Table 12.4 illustrates strong relationships between taking part in the four career development activities and more positive responses to the statement

Table 12.4 Analysis: relationship between participation in career development activities and student disagreement/agreement with the statement: "School is useful for jobs"

Country	Activity	Odds ratio
Australia	Job shadowing	16%*
	Job fair	6%*
	Career advisor at school	20%*
Belgium	Job shadowing	9%**
	Career advisor at school	11%*
	Internship	13%*
Canada	Job fair	16%*
	Career advisor at school	47%*
Denmark	Job shadowing	35%*
	Career advisor at school	2.53 x more likely*
Finland	Internship	80%*
	Job shadowing	35%*
	Job fair	30%*
	Career advisor at school	2.15 x more likely*
Ireland	Job shadowing	19%*
	Job fair	2.47 x more likely*
	Career advisor at school	39%*

* Statistically significant at 5%
** Statistically significant at 10%
Note: Results show respondents being more likely to agree with the statement.

"School is useful for jobs." On a number of occasions, respondents taking part in activities are more than twice as likely to agree with the statement than their comparable peers who did not take part in the activity. For example, Irish teenagers who took part in job fairs are nearly two and a half times more likely to agree that their schooling is useful for the working world than peers who missed out on the activity.

In Table 12.5, positive relationships are also found between participation in one or more of the four career development activities and a greater willingness to agree with the statement that "School helps to get a job" in all countries with the exception of Belgium. In Australia, for example, young people attending job fairs are 28% more likely to agree with the statement than peers who did not attend. And in Ireland, they are more than twice as likely to agree with the statement. Across the four statements, impact sizes are often sizable.

In Table 12.6, the results are summarised. Across the career development activities, it is speaking with a careers advisor which stands out – in 91% of occasions across the six countries, there is a statistically significant more positive response to the four attitudinal questions. In a majority of cases, more positive responses are also associated with attendance at a job fair (57%) and participation in job shadowing or workplace visits (52%). In 30% of occasions, participation in internships is associated with more positive attitudes towards schooling.

Table 12.5 Analysis: relationship between participation in career development activities and student agreement with the statement: "School helps to get a job"

Country	Activity	Odds ratio
Australia	Job fair	28%*
Canada	Job shadowing	6%*
	Job fair	11%*
	Career advisor at school	24%*
Denmark	Internship	17%*
	Job shadowing	2.08 x more likely*
	Career advisor at school	2.03 x more likely*
Finland	Internship	18%*
	Job shadowing	45%*
	Job fair	22%*
	Career advisor at school	63%*
Ireland	Job fair	2.21 x more likely*
	Career advisor at school	56%*

* Statistically significant at 5%

Note: Results show respondents being more likely to agree with the statement.

Table 12.6 Summary of statistically significant positive responses to four attitudinal statements by career development activity and country

	Australia	Belgium	Canada	Denmark	Finland	Ireland
School does little to prepare you for life						
• Internship					x	
• Job shadowing		x	x			
• Job fair	x					
• Career advisor	x	x	x	x	x	x
School is a waste of time						
• Internship		NA			x	x
• Job shadowing		NA	x			x
• Job fair	x	NA	x		x	x
• Career advisor	x	NA	x	x	x	x
School useful for jobs						
• Internship			x		x	
• Job shadowing	x	x		x	x	x
• Job fair	x		x		x	x
• Career advisor	x	x	x	x	x	x
School helps to get a job						
• Internship				x	x	
• Job shadowing		x		x	x	
• Job fair	x	x			x	x
• Career advisor		x		x	x	x

In terms of national performance, it is Finland where positive attitudes are most commonly associated with participation in career development activities (81% of potential occasions), followed by Ireland (63%), Belgium (58%), Australia (50%), Canada (44%) and Denmark (44%).

Attainment

In the analysis which follows, linear regression is used to assess whether participation in each of the four career development activities under consideration can be associated with higher student achievement in the PISA mathematics assessment, after taking account of the control variables. The analysis compares young people with peers in their own countries. Results are expressed as coefficients, which represent a number of points obtained in the mathematics tests. Only relationships with statistical significance of 1% or better are included. This means that there can be a 99% or better confidence that the relationships observed are not coincidental and neither mask for a variation in social background detected by use of the control variables. When it comes to judging the strength of the relationship, the lower the level of statistical significance, the better.

Tables 12.7 and 12.8 show the statistically significant results found in the data. It is learners in Finland who have taken part in career related and employer engagement activities who experienced the most consistent improvements in their PISA mathematics scores compared to their peers. Across the six countries, participation in internships is associated with higher mathematics scores only in Finland. The highest improvements in the PISA mathematics scores are found in Denmark (12.2 points), Finland (17.6 points) and Ireland (8.7 points) all in relation to speaking with a career advisor in school. In four of the six countries analysed, career advice at school had a strong positive associated with student achievement. In Canada, no positive relationships were identified.

Table 12.7 Analysis: relationship between participation in internship and student achievement

Activity	Country	Coefficient
Internship	Finland	2.045*
Job shadowing	Finland	2.379*
	Ireland	4.048*
Job fairs	Finland	5.004*
	Australia	4.048*
Career advice	Belgium	3.035*
	Denmark	12.188*
	Finland	17.544*
	Ireland	8.686*

* Statistically significant at 1%

Table 12.8 Summary of statistically significant positive relationships between career development activities and higher scores in PISA mathematics tests, by activity and country

	Australia	Belgium	Canada	Denmark	Finland	Ireland
Internship					x	
Job shadowing					x	x
Job fair	x				x	
Career advisor		x		x	x	x

The increase in PISA mathematics score points is moderate but significant. Students participating in selected career development activities recorded scores 2 to 17 points higher than would otherwise be expected. While the spectrum of points separating the highest and lowest PISA performers in 2012 was considerable – the difference between the average score in Shanghai and Peru was 245 points – the average Mathematics scores associated with the six countries which are the subject of this study are clustered more narrowly. Only 19 points separate the performance of Finland and Denmark. In this context, while the scale of assumed impact is modest, it is still meaningful.

Discussion

This chapter has tested the hypothesis that greater teenage engagement in career development activities organised by schools and including elements of direct exposure to the contemporary working world will be associated with more positive attitudes towards schooling, as well as improved academic achievement. The hypothesis originated from a 2014 interview with the OECD's Director of Education and Skills and makes use of a unique OECD dataset to test it. Within the 2012 Programme for International Student Assessment (PISA), a series of questions explored teenage participation in career development activities and attitudes towards schooling. In this analysis, four activities have been isolated (participation in internships, job fairs, job shadowing and speaking with a careers advisor in school). Only a minority of countries taking part in PISA 2012 opted into these questions, and of these, six were selected for analysis (Australia, Belgium, Canada, Denmark, Finland and Ireland). Drawing on existing OECD analytical practice, a series of control variables were applied to the analysis, enabling account to be taken of the typical social and demographic factors which can determine student engagement and success in education. Important within these variables was school type. In a number of countries, young people are channelled at age 14 or younger into either vocationally or academically focused educational institutions. Controlling for attendance at such institutions is particularly important as they can be indicators for very different school environments and curricula and very different types of student, particularly by attainment level. Put simply, in presenting this analysis, there is confidence that it is not the type of school or college attended which drives the impact of career development activities undertaken.

In this chapter, statistically significant associations between participation in the career development activities and more positive attitudes towards the utility of schools in preparing teenagers for adulthood are often, but not always, found. Of the four activities, it is speaking with a careers advisor within school which is most consistently associated with more positive responses, followed by participation in a job fair, taking part in job shadowing and then internships. Of the six countries, it is teenagers in Finland and Ireland who demonstrate the greatest levels of responsiveness to participation in career activities.

Similar relationships were found between activities and attainment, but the results were much more moderate. The results given here suggest that participation in these activities appear to have a reasonable association with higher academic proficiency, in this case the PISA mathematics score. Again, of the four activities, it is speaking with a careers advisor in school which is most consistently associated with more positive responses, followed by participation in a job fair, taking part in job shadowing and internships.

The findings presented in this chapter fit within the wider literature on employer engagement and academic achievement. The data can be seen as broadly supporting the hypothesis put forward by Hughes et al (2016) and Hooley et al. (2014) that employer engagement activities and careers guidance sessions often help young people to better understand the relationship between educational goals and occupational outcomes. It is a resource that can help young people to change their perceptions of school and to understand the importance of studying hard and applying oneself if they wish to excel in both school and their future careers. It is perhaps unsurprising that results linked to academic achievement are comparatively modest. It is not unreasonable to assume that students in many countries engage with career development activities only as teenagers approaching key decision points. While experiences may well increase motivation to engage in academic subjects by providing new (and persuasive) information about the labour market value of educational success, mathematical proficiency represents the sum of engagement over a preceding decade of schooling. This may explain why the most significant impacts can be seen when assessing the attitudes of young people towards school, whereas the impact on academic attainment is more modest. Even so, the data suggest that schools would be well advised to set aside time to engage students particularly with careers advisors and at job fairs. Both activities represent a likely highly efficient means of influencing more positive outcomes for young people. Further research may consider more closely the delivery patterns in higher performing countries. For example, research may explore precisely how schools and colleges in Finland are delivering employer engagement and careers provision. The data presented in this chapter is a window on the world of Finnish practice and calls for greater consideration in order to ensure that lessons can be fully learned for policy and practice elsewhere.

Note

1 For more information about PISA, visit www.oecd.org/pisa/.

References

Eddy Adams Consultants. (2008). *Work experience in Scotland*. Edinburgh: The Scottish Government.

Hanushek, E., Schwedt, G., Wiederhold, S. and Woessman, L. (2013). *Returns to skills around the world: Evidence from PIAAC*. Paris: Organisation for Economic Co-operation and Development.

Hillage, J., Kodz, J. and Pike, G. (2001). *Pre-16 work experience practice in England: An evaluation*. London: Department for Education and Employment.

Hooley, T., Matheson, J. and Watts, A.G. (2014). *Advancing ambitions: The role of career guidance in supporting social mobility*. London: Sutton Trust.

Hughes, D., Mann, A., Barnes, S-A., Baldauf, B. and McKeown, R. (2016). *Careers education: International literature review*. London: Education Endowment Foundation.

Kashefpakdel, E.T., Mann, A. and Schleicher, M. (2016a). *The impact of career development activities on PISA mathematics tests: An analysis of data from the Organisation for Economic Co-Operation and Development (OECD)*. London: Education and Employers.

Kashefpakdel, E.T., Mann, A. and Schleicher, M. (2016b). *The impact of career development activities on student attitudes towards school utility: An analysis of data from the Organisation for Economic Co-Operation and Development's Programme for International Student Assessment (PISA)*. London: Education and Employers.

Kashefpakdel, E.T., Rehill, J. and Mann, A. (2017). *Making the grade: Does involvement in activities with employers impact the academic achievement of young people? Research Summary*. London: Education and Employers.

Killeen, J., Sammons, S. and Watts, A.G. (1999). *The effects of careers education and guidance on attainment and associated behaviour*. Cambridge, MA: NICEC/University of Hertfordshire/ULIE.

Mann, A. and Huddleston, P. (2015). *How should our schools respond to the changing demands of the twenty first century labour market? Eight perspectives*. London: Education and Employers.

Mann, A., Rehill, J. and Kashefpakdel, E. (2018). *Employer engagement in education: Insights from international evidence for effective practice and research*. London: Education Endowment Foundation.

Musset, P. and Kurekova, L. (2018). *Career guidance and employer engagement: A review of the evidence*. Paris: Organisation for Economic Co-operation and Development.

National Support Group for Work Experience. (2008). *Students' perceptions of work experience*. London: Department for Children, Schools and Families and NEBPN.

OECD. (2010). *Learning for jobs*. Paris: Organisation for Economic Co-operation and Development.

OECD. (2013). *PISA 2012 assessment and analytical framework: Mathematics, reading, science, problem solving and financial literacy*. Paris: Organisation for Economic Co-operation and Development.

OECD. (2014). *PISA 2012 results in focus. What 15-year-olds know and what they can do with what they know*. Paris: Organisation for Economic Co-operation and Development.

Stanley, J. and Mann, A. (2014). A theoretical framework for employer engagement, in Mann, A., Stanley, J. and Archer, L. (eds.), *Understanding employer engagement in education: Theories and research*. London: Routledge.

Sweet, R., Nissinen, K. and Vuorinen, R. (2014). *An Analysis of the career development items in PISA 2012 and their relationships to the characteristics of countries, schools, students and families*. European Lifelong Guidance Policy Network Research Paper No. 1.

Chapter 13

Young people in the labour market

How teenage employer engagement makes a difference to adult outcomes[1]

Elnaz Kashefpakdel, Anthony Mann, Rachael McKeown and Jordan Rehill

Introduction

Employer engagement has become a commonplace aspect of schooling in Britain (Stanley et al. 2014). Through the encouragement of such activities as short periods of work experience, careers talks, mock interviews, CV workshops and workplace visits, governments have sought to close the gap between the classroom and the workplace (Mann et al. 2018; Stanley et al. 2014). In December 2017, for example, the English Department for Education (DfE) released its Careers Strategy highlighting the importance of employer engagement:

> Employers are integral to great careers advice. We need employers of all sizes, and from all sectors, to provide encounters that inspire people and give them the opportunity to learn about what work is like and what it takes to be successful in the workforce . . . There is a compelling case for increasing the opportunities for young people to meet employers.
>
> (DfE, 2017, 10)

Although the over-arching aim of such initiatives has commonly been to increase the employment and wage-earning potential among participants, this hypothesis has been robustly tested comparatively rarely. In 2011, researchers at Education and Employers[2] undertook an evaluation of whether these employer engagement interventions had served to meet their objective in improving the actual labour market prospects of young people as they transitioned from school to work. Based on an initial sample of nearly 1,000 young Britons aged 19 to 24, the study questioned in detail 169 respondents reporting full-time annual salaries, plotting those against a scale of remembered employer contacts whilst in school. Having controlled for age, highest level of attainment, school type attended and other available personal characteristics, the comparison found a significant relationship with each contact with an employer enabled through a secondary school on a scale of 0 to 4+ relating, on average, to a wage premium of 4.5% or £900 in young adulthood. Young adults recalling four or more contacts could be expected to earn £3,600 more than a comparable peer who remembered no such activities (Mann and Percy, 2014).

Analysis of the 2011 dataset also revealed statistically significant relationships between greater levels of contact with employers through school or college and a decreasing likelihood of respondents reporting being NEET (Not in Education Employment or Training) at the time of the survey. A similar positive relationship was observed, moreover, in terms of the confidence that young adults showed about their economic prospects (Percy and Mann, 2014). In addition, Jones et al. (2015) made use of the 2011 data to explore the character of positive impacts described by young adults, using textual analysis of write-in answers to argue that benefits were driven more through accumulations of social and especially cultural capital than of human capital.

Since the publication of analyses from the 2011 YouGov sample, evidence of the economic value of careers education, work-related learning and employer engagement in education has grown.

A recent review (Mann et al. 2018) commissioned by the UK Education Endowment Foundation (EEF) has explored the research literature on employer engagement in greater detail. It considered studies using experimental or quasi-experimental designs to test employer engagement interventions to ascertain how employers can best support schools to improve educational and economic outcomes for pupils. In total, 42 individual publications were identified, mostly US or UK studies focusing overwhelmingly on secondary education. They included 75 distinct assessments of different types of employer engagement in education related to career events, work-related learning, mentoring, work experience, enterprise activities, job shadowing, reading partners, recruitment skills, recruitment assistance, and workplace visits. Of these, 35 were found to provide evidence of largely positive outcomes for young people, 40 were found to provide evidence of mixed outcomes, and none offered evidence of largely negative outcomes (Mann et al. 2018). Reviewing the literature, the authors argue that positive outcomes cannot be taken for granted, but can be most effectively understood through the lens of social capital theory with episodes of employer engagement providing young people with *potentially* valuable insights into the operation of the labour market. To Mann and colleagues, effective school-mediated employer engagement must be authentic, recurrent, valued by young people and varied in character. It must be, moreover, contextualised within professional careers advice, personalised to the needs of individual young people and begun at a young age (Mann et al. 2018, 71–72).

One important and illustrative study highlighted by the 2018 EEF literature reviews is Kashefpakdel and Percy's, 2016 assessment of long-term economic impacts related to teenage career talks. The study examined the circumstances under which school-based careers talks could be linked to effects on future wages, controlling for a broad range of background factors and using a large dataset (the British Cohort Study) that tracked individuals born in 1970 into adulthood. The study explored specifically the relationship between participation of teenagers in career talks with 'someone from outside of school' at ages 14 to 16 and their later earnings, aged 26, if in full-time work. Results revealed that for each career talk young people reported participating in at ages 14–15, average earnings at age 26 were 0.8% higher. Using a rich array of control measures for social background and academic ability, the study reported results which were statistically significant at 5%, meaning that there is a 95% certainty the correlation did not occur by chance. A statistically significant relationship was not found for those aged 15–16, which implies that career talks had a greater value for the younger cohort. Analysis also found a significant relationship between student perceptions of the career talks that they had experienced and later earnings. Teenagers who reported that their career talks had been 'very helpful' to them at age 14–15 were compared with those who found careers talks 'not at all helpful/not very helpful'. Findings demonstrated students aged 14–15 who found career talks 'very helpful' witnessed a 1.6% increase in earnings at age 26 per career talk attended. Statistically significant wage premiums were also found in relation to young people who had found career talks participated in at ages 15–16 'very helpful' (Kashefpakdel and Percy, 2016).

The contemporary views of young adults

This chapter builds on earlier studies and presents results from a survey of some 1,700 young adults undertaken by the polling firm YouGov in the summer of 2016. The survey, undertaken by the Education and Employers team responsible for the 2011 study considered by Mann and Percy (2014), mimics the survey design of the earlier study to allow for comparisons to be made between the experiences of a first cohort who were engaged in secondary education between 2001 and 2011 and a second cohort, the subject of this chapter, who did so between 2006 and 2016. In reviewing the experiences of these young people, the chapter addresses three specific themes. It looks at young adults' recollection of school and college action to prepare them for the working world and, using regression analyses, explores what schools did to help young adults succeed in the adult working world. In addressing these questions, a number of recurring themes and questions emerge. How does socio-economic background, whether captured through school type attended or parental background, shape experiences and perspectives? Does gender, ethnicity, geographic location or academic achievement make a difference to results? How does the quantity and perceived quality of employer engagement impact on adult outcomes? By using statistical analysis, this study is able to take account of those elements of social background which commonly drive inequalities in the world of work. In so doing, it allows specific interventions in the lives of young people provided by their schools and colleges to be isolated in order to ask the question: did they make a difference to adult lives?

Methodology

This chapter considers the responses of 1,744 young British adults who completed a survey created by the Education and Employers Research team working with Prue Huddleston (University of Warwick). The fieldwork was undertaken in May 2016. Respondents were drawn from the YouGov panel consisting of many tens of thousands of individuals. Respondents were drawn equally from the genders and, reflecting population figures, the three nations composing Great Britain and the nine English regions. Similar numbers of respondents were sampled in each year band across the ages from 19 to 24.

In analyses of this type, it is important that data are gathered concerning those elements of young people's lives which might drive their employment outcomes as young adults. As well as their age, gender and ethnicity, consequently the survey collected information on the highest level of qualification possessed by the respondents, the type of school or college they attended between the ages of 14 and 16 (and, if relevant, between 16 and 18), whether the respondent recalled receiving Free School Meals at any point in their education (an indicator of childhood poverty) and whether their parents or carers had attended university. Highest parental educational achievement is a widely used indicator for the social background of young people, with parental experience of higher education serving as an indicator for middle class or higher social status (Marks, 1999; Erola, et al. 2016). Nineteen per cent of the sample stated that they had received Free School Meals, and just over half of the respondents reported that neither of their parents or carers had attended university. Such control variables are essential within statistical regressions. They allow analysts to ensure that any relationships found, for example, between participation in a particular type of activity and an economic outcome cannot be dismissed as a mask for social privilege.

Young adults' recollection of school and college action to prepare them for the working world

The survey began by asking respondents to describe the types of employer engagement activities in which they took part whilst in secondary education between the ages of 14 and 18. Respondents were asked about a range of activities commonly arranged by schools and colleges alongside participation in paid part-time employment during full-time secondary education.

The first part of the analysis shows that former students of independent and grammar schools recall greater levels of engagement than former pupils of comprehensive schools, but the gap is closing. As set out in Table 13.1 below, in 2011 young adults who had attended non-selective state (comprehensive) schools between the ages of 14 and 16 recalled, on average, 1.23 engagements with employers through their schools, 23% fewer engagements than former pupils of independent schools. Five years on, the numbers of recalled engagements

Table 13.1 Average number of recalled employer engagements by school type attended age 14–16, 2011 and 2016

	Comprehensive	Grammar	Independent
Average number of recalled activities 2016	1.54	1.92	1.74
Average number of recalled activities 2011	1.23	1.38	1.51

of former pupils of comprehensive, independent and grammar schools had all increased and the gap between former comprehensive and independent school pupils closing to 13%. The biggest leap in participation between the two surveys was seen in the engagements of former grammar school pupils, increasing by 39% to become the highest level of all groups reaching nearly two recalled engagements, on average, by 2016. The gap between students attending selective and non-selective state schools had widened from 12% in 2011 to 25% in 2016.

In the 2016 survey a series of questions was asked about the backgrounds of the young adults. Cross-tabulating the levels of recalled participation in employer engagement activities and recalled receipt of Free School Meals during schooling shows a 9% variation in average engagement levels with young adults from wealthier backgrounds recalling a higher average level of engagement whilst in secondary education. Whereas the average young adult recalled 1.6 engagements, young adults who had received Free School Meals remembered 1.5 occasions on which they were connected with employers. A similar pattern is revealed when comparing young adults' recollections of employer engagement activities and the educational status of their parents. Respondents whose parents were without university experience recalled an average of 1.55 engagements as opposed to 1.71 for the offspring of at least one graduate – a variation of 10%.

One of the most significant patterns identified in the 2016 sample was in the relationship between highest level of qualification and volume of recalled employer engagement. The analysis found that young adults possessing two or more A levels (or equivalent) and higher qualifications recalled significantly greater numbers of engagements with employers than peers whose highest level of qualification was at GCSE level (or equivalent) or lower. Of all subcategories of respondents, it is the young adults in the survey whose highest qualification was less than five GCSEs or equivalent who recalled the very lowest levels of employer engagement from their school days – an average of just 0.7 engagements. Their peers who achieved at least five GCSEs as a highest qualification reported higher engagement, recalling an average of 1.1 activities. By contrast, those who stayed on and achieved two or more A levels or university qualifications (or equivalent) recalled 1.6 and 1.8 engagements respectively. While such results can be explained, in part, by the likely failure of the first two groups holding lower level qualifications to stay on in full-time education after the age of 16 and so missing out on opportunities to take part in activities post-16 with employers, the strong indication remains that lower achieving children of poorer backgrounds have systematically accessed lower levels of school-mediated employer engagements than their more advantaged peers. While such results can be explained, in part, by the likely failure of the first two groups holding qualifications at Level 1 and 2 to stay on in full-time education after the age of 16 and so missing out on opportunities to take part in activities post-16 with employers, the strong indication remains that lower achieving children of poorer backgrounds have systematically accessed lower levels of school-mediated employer engagements than their more advantaged peers.

Young adults' perceptions of how well their schools and colleges prepared them for adult working life

A series of questions explored the perceptions of the respondents about how well their schools had prepared them for adult working life in general, but also to judge their perceptions of the helpfulness of the employer engagement activities which they had undertaken through their educational institutions.

The analysis found that most young people educated in the state sector think that their schools generally prepared them poorly for adult working life. Respondents to the survey were asked, "Looking back, how well do you feel that your school/college prepared you for adult working life?"; the majority of all respondents (53%) felt that they had been poorly prepared as did 56% of participants who attended non-selective state schools between the ages of 14 and 16. Former pupils, however, attending both grammar schools and fee-paying schools at the same ages countered the trend with majorities (58% and 61%, respectively) reporting that they felt well prepared by their schools for adult working life. Only one young adult in twenty-five who attended a non-selective state school felt that they had been 'very well' prepared by their secondary schooling for adult working life. One in eight felt that their school had prepared them 'very poorly'.

Similar results are observed when a comparison is made of young adults' perceptions of how well their educational institutions had prepared them for adult working life by attendance at different types of school and college at age 16–18. Across the sample, 52% of respondents argued that they had been poorly prepared. As set out in Table 13.2 below, this average hides some significant variations. Whereas 70% of former pupils of Independent schools felt that they had been well prepared, only 41% of peers who attended Further Education Colleges felt the same way.

Exploring the potential value of school-mediated employer engagement activities in enhancing progression into the early labour market, the analysis shows young adults who recalled a greater volume of employer contacts through their schools felt better prepared for adult working life. A consistent pattern emerges from the analysis. As set out in Table 13.3, whereas approximately two-thirds of young adults who recalled zero or one engagement felt poorly prepared by their schools, the proportions reverse when considering respondents who recalled three and four or more interactions with employers with two-thirds arguing that they had been well prepared by their schools.

Table 13.2 Respondent perception of how well schools and colleges had pre-pared them for adult working life by school/college type attended at age 16–18

School or college type attended at 16–18	"Looking back, how well do you feel that your school/college prepared you for adult working life?"	
	Very well/quite well	Very poorly/quite poorly
Non-selective state school, i.e. comprehensive school	49% (199)	51% (205)
Grammar/selective state school	60% (123)	40% (81)
Sixth Form College	43% (274)	57% (361)
Further Education College	41% (113)	59% (165)
Independent school/fee paying school or college	70% (89)	31% (39)

Table 13.3 Respondent perception of how well schools/colleges had prepared them for adult working life by volume of employer engagement activities recalled

"Between the ages of 14 and 19, did your school or college ever arrange for you to take part in any activities which involved employers/local business people? If so, on how many different occasions (more or less) did it happen?"	"Looking back, how well do you feel that your school/college prepared you for adult working life?"	
	Very well/quite well	Very poorly/quite poorly
Never	34% (113)	66% (221)
Once	40% (254)	60% (382)
Twice	52% (211)	48% (194)
Three times	65% (100)	35% (53)
Four times or more	68% (154)	32% (73)

Whilst some of the pattern detected here will potentially reflect the fact that the former students of grammar and Independent schools recalled, on average, higher volumes of employer engagements and felt more positive about their schooling, the limited number of respondents from such backgrounds means that this alone cannot explain the strength of the pattern observed.

Respondents were also asked to judge, from the perspective of young adult-hood, whether the employer engagement activities in which they had taken part through their schools and colleges had proved to be useful in three of the key staging posts along the school to work transition journey: decision-making at 16, and, if applicable, getting into a university and getting a job. The results illustrate a widespread feeling that activities had been often relatively unhelpful, particularly for the former students of non-selective state schools. However, attitudes again are seen to change in relation to the volume of employer engagement activities recalled. Consistently, young adults recalling higher volumes of engagements found the activities undertaken to have proved to have been more considerably helpful to them.

In the case of making decisions at 16, most young people testified that employer engagement activities were not helpful to them – unless they had recalled participating in four or more activities with employers between the ages of 14 and 18. One of the most common uses of employer engagement in British education is to help young people come to informed decisions about their choices at age 16, the end point of compulsory full-time education in the U.K (although young people are expected to participate in some form of education or training, but not necessarily full-time, to the age of 18). Across the sample, 31% of respondents felt the employer engagement activities which they had undertaken through school to have been helpful in making decisions. Those young people who found their employer engagement helpful took part, on average in 40% more activities than those who found them unhelpful (1.48 engagements against 1.06). Whereas one-quarter, or fewer, respondents who took part in just one employer engagement between the ages of 14 and 18 through school found the engagement to be helpful, the proportion rises to half for those who recalled taking part in three or more activities.

A slightly higher proportion of all respondents (who had actually applied for university at some point) reported that the employer engagement which they had experienced at school or college had proved to be helpful within an application. Again, when considered against the volume of recalled school-mediated engagements, a clear pattern is observable. The more activities a young person recalled, the more helpful they felt their employer engagement had been. Those who found episodes of employer engagement to have been helpful had undertaken an average of 1.99 activities, 31% more than the 1.52 engagements recalled by peers who had found the activities unhelpful in university applications.

In addition, most employer engagement was not felt to have been helpful in applying for a full-time job, but participation in 3+ activities made a big difference. Perhaps surprisingly, given the fact that employer engagement activities are often presented within education as approaches to improve the employability of young people (Mann et al. 2018), just 27% of respondents (who had ever applied for a full-time job) agreed that the engagement which they had experienced had been helpful to them when applying for jobs. Young people who recalled participating in higher volumes of activities stand out as being much more likely to agree that their employer engagement had proved helpful to them in applying for a full-time job. The typical young adult who found, with hindsight, that their employer engagement had proved helpful in getting a job experienced 31% more activities than peers who, looking back, felt that

Table 13.4 Respondents perception of helpfulness of school-mediated employer engagements in applying for university, decision making at 16, applying for a job(s) by volume of employer engagement at 14–19

"Between the ages of 14 and 19, did your school or college ever arrange for you to take part in any activities which involved employers/local business people? E.g. work experience, mentoring, enterprise competitions, careers advice, CV or interview workshops, workplace visits. If so, on how many different occasions (more or less) did it happen?"	Was the involvement you had with employers whist at school helpful to you when...		
	Applying for a job(s)? (% of sample who had ever applied for a full-time job agreeing)	Applying for university? (% of sample who had ever applied to enter university agreeing)	Decision making at 16 (e.g. whether to stay on, what and where to study, whether to try and get a job) (% of sample agreeing)
Once	21%	33%	25%
Twice	32%	38%	31%
Three times	42%	47%	49%
Four times or more	48%	53%	51%

their experience had not been helpful. For comparison, 44% of young people who experienced 4+ activities while in school said they were helpful to them when applying for jobs, whereas only 23% of young people who experienced one activity said they were helpful in applying for a job.

What schools did to help young adults succeed in the adult working world

In the final part of the analysis, logistic regression was used to explore relationships between recalled participation in school-mediated employer engagement activities and subsequent economic outcomes. A first analysis focused on the likelihood of respondents reporting being NEET on the day of the survey. Using demographic (age, gender, ethnicity, region, highest qualification achieved, school type attended) and socio-economic factors (whether the respondent recalled receiving Free School Meals at any point in their education and whether their parents or carers had attended university) as control variables, the analysis showed that the higher the volume of recalled engagement with employers, the lower the likelihood respondents reported of being NEET on the day of the survey. The analysis found that young people who recalled:

- one employer engagement activity were 44% less likely to report being NEET compared with those who did zero activities
- two activities were 56% less likely compared with those who did zero activities
- three activities were 85% less likely compared with those who did zero activities
- four activities were 86% less likely compared with those who did zero activities

Respondents recalling three or more school-mediated activities with employers between the ages of 14 and 18 were nearly twice more likely to be in education, employment or training as comparable peers who recalled no such interactions.

Further investigation into individual activities also identified relationships between respondents who declared themselves NEET and their teenage participation across specific employer engagement activities. As set out in Table 13.5 below, young adults who recalled taking part in career talks, enterprise competitions and work experience with employers at both pre- and post-16 were significantly less likely to report being NEET than comparable peers who had missed out on the activities whilst in school. No statistically significant associations were identified with regard to other employer engagement activities.

The second part of the analysis of economic outcomes examined whether correlations could be found between teenage participation in employer engagement activities and adult wage premiums. Using young adults' reported income when they were in full time employment, statistical analysis revealed

Table 13.5 Incidence of NEET by participation in employer engagement activities (regression analysis)

At 14–16 . . .	
Career talks with employers	81% less likely to be NEET than peers who did not do the activity
Enterprise competition with employers	75% less likely to be NEET than peers who did not do the activity
Work experience	45% less likely to be NEET than peers who did not do the activity
At 16–18 . . .	
Career talks with employers	78% less likely to be NEET than peers who did not do the activity
Enterprise competition with employers	80% less likely to be NEET than peers who did not do the activity
Work experience	44% less likely to be NEET than peers who did not do the activity

similar relationships with the quantity of engagement activities as reported in the 2011 analysis (see Mann and Percy, 2013). However, the association was not as straightforward. Echoing the findings of Kashefpakdel and Percy (2016), the perceived quality of activities young people recalled attending appears to play a much more significant role in 2016.

The survey asked a number of questions concerning the perceived quality of school experiences relevant to preparation for the working world (as seen above). As reported above, three questions asked respondents to reflect on the specific value of employer engagement activities in enabling progression through, and transition from, education. A fourth question asked, more generally, whether the young adults felt that their school and/or college had prepared them well for adult working life. As set out in Table 13.6 below, with the exception of participation in job shadowing at age 14–16, which was simply related to a wage premium of 11%, all other wage premiums identified combined participation in one or more employer engagement activities and value judgements on the utility of the provision. Young adults, for example, who recalled more than four activities and found their school-mediated employer engagement activities 'helpful in getting a job', earned up to 16.4% more than peers who did not take part in any activities. For each such school-mediated employer engagement activity undertaken between the ages of 14 and 18, young adults could expect to earn between 3.7% and 4.1% more than peers who recalled no such experience. Where young adults argued, furthermore, that their teenage employer engagement activities had been 'helpful in applications to university', the premium was higher reaching 22% (5.5% for each recalled activity on the scale of 1 to 4+) based on regressions against demographic control variables and socio-economic control variables. Respondents in full-time employment reported an average gross salary of £15,813. Regression analysis identified a range of

Table 13.6 Statistically significant wage premiums expressed in percentage and cash terms

Employer engagement activity	Average premium (expressed in percentage terms)	Average premium (expressed in cash terms)
Job Shadowing at 14–16	11%	£1,739
	3.7%	£585
Volume of engagements where engagement in general found to be useful in getting a job – *one engagement* (school type control, 14–16)		
Volume of engagements where engagement in general found to be useful in getting a job – *four plus engagements* (school type control, 14–16)	14.8%	£2,340
Volume of engagements where engagement in general found to be useful in getting a job – *one engagement* (school type control, 16–18)	4.1%	£648
Volume of engagements where engagement in general found to be useful in getting a job – *four plus engagements* (school type control, 16–18)	16.4%	£2,592
Volume of engagements where engagement in general found to be useful in getting into university – *one engagement* (school type control, 16–18)	5.5%	£869
Volume of engagements where engagement in general found to be useful in getting into university – *four plus engagements* (school type control, 16–18)	22%	£3,476
Enterprise competition at 14–16 where respondent felt school had prepared them well for adult working life	11%	£1,739
Mentoring at 14–16 where respondent felt school had prepared them well for adult working life	19%	£3,004
Mentoring at 16–18 where respondent felt school had prepared them well for adult working life	18%	£2,846

wage premiums expressed in percentage terms. By relating these to the average salaries reported, it is possible to describe premiums in cash terms. As set out in Table 13.6 below, premiums range from £585 (the average premium related to participation in a single recalled employer engagement activity where respondents found school-mediated engagement with employers to have been useful in getting a job) to £3,476 (the average premium related to participation in four or more recalled employer engagement activities where respondents found school-mediated engagement with employers to have been generally useful in getting into university).

Discussion and conclusions

This chapter outlined the results from a 2016 survey of 1,744 young British adults aged 19–24. Respondents were, at the time of the survey, in the midst of transitions between youth and adulthood, between full-time education and full labour market participation. The survey explored the extent to which they had engaged with employers as part of their educational experiences; whether they believed these engagements, and their schools in general, had been useful to them in preparing for adult life; and whether the interventions they had received had made an *actual* difference to their adult economic outcomes. Using statistical analysis, insights for policy and practice emerge. These relate to three specific themes highlighted in recent literature on the delivery of employer engagement in education: quantity of school-mediated contacts; its quality as perceived by young people; and equity in access.

Quantity matters: greater volume of school-mediated employer engagement is associated with better economic outcomes

Building on previous analyses, the study concludes by demonstrating relationships between the number of school-mediated teenage engagements with employers recalled by young adults and improved economic outcomes, including significantly reduced incidence of being NEET. The finding is consistent with strong relationships observed in the data between teenage participation in higher volumes of engagements with employers and the belief that schools had done a good job in preparing them for adult working life, providing experiences of genuine utility for later life. The findings support the view that in terms of employer engagement, greater engagement leads to better outcomes.

The analysis presented here finds evidence of improved economic outcomes related to each of four different employer engagement activities tested for work experience, job shadowing, enterprise competitions and mentoring. The strongest results are found with regard to job shadowing undertaken at 14–16 which is linked to premiums of 11% in full-time earnings. This activity was undertaken by fewer than 10% of respondents, and it is a further insight from

this work that young people in general are engaging with employers insuffi-
ciently. Engagement levels have increased since 2011, but only marginally, and
the typical young adult still recalls fewer than two engagements. The findings
presented here demonstrate that schools and colleges should aim to at least
double their interventions and engage students with four or more interactions
as a minimum – and, of course, that employers need to be in a position to
respond to such demand.

Quality matters: more highly regarded employer engagement is associated with better economic outcomes

One of the aims of this analysis was to test the insight, provided by Kashefpakdel and Percy (2016), that student perceptions of the quality of the provision
encountered is important – and that greater economic outcomes will be related
to more positive views of teenage experiences. In this survey, respondents were
asked to look back on their school-mediated provision and assess whether, with
hindsight, the activities which they had undertaken had proved to be helpful to
them in making decisions at 16, in getting into university or in getting a job. In
addition, they were asked whether they felt that their school(s) and/or college(s)
had, in general terms, prepared them well for adult working life. Analysis presented here shows a consistent relationship between higher regard for school-
mediated provision and better adult economic outcomes. It suggests that the
instincts of young adults were right: that the schools had prepared them better
than comparable peers. Wage premiums in excess of 20% are found linked to
higher volumes of employer engagement activities described, in general terms,
as having been helpful. There is a relationship, moreover, between quantity and
quality. It is young people who recalled higher levels of teenage engagements
(3 or more) who hold a higher regard for the quality of the preparation they
received from their schools for adult working life. The finding is consistent with
Kashefpakdel and Percy (2016) that young people's perceptions of the quality of
their school-based experiences engaging with employers matters, and this can
be witnessed in statistical outcomes.

Equity matters: access to school-mediated employer engagement is not fairly distributed

This new analysis began with a review of the volume of employer engagement activities recalled by young adults and found that it is patterned by
social background. Young adults who had experienced the greatest volume of
school-mediated employer engagement activities came, on average, from more
privileged backgrounds. They were more likely to have attended independent schools or grammar schools and to have achieved higher ultimate levels
of qualification. At the opposite end of the spectrum were respondents who
had received Free School Meals, whose parents had not attended university

and whose highest qualifications were GCSEs (or equivalent) or lower. Arguably those with greatest need for employer engagement within education have received it least.

Notes

1 The authors would like to express their gratitude to LifeSkills created by Barclays, which kindly sponsored the original research upon which this chapter is based. Go to www.educationandemployers.org/research/contemporary-transitions-young-britons-reflect-on-life-after-secondary-school-and-college/.
2 www.educationandemployers.org

References

DfE. (2017). *Careers strategy: Making the most of everyone's skills and talents*. London: Department for Education.

Erola, J., Jalonen, S. and Lehti, H. (2016). Parental education, class and income over early life course and children's achievement. *Research in social stratification and Mobility* (44): 33–43.

Jones, S., Mann, A. and Morris, K. (2015). The 'Employer Engagement Cycle' in secondary education: Analysing the testimonies of young British adults. *Journal of Education and Work* 29(7): 834–856.

Kashefpakdel, E.T. and Percy, C. (2016). Career education that works: An economic analysis using the British cohort study. *Journal of Education and Work*. Available from: http://dx.doi.org/10.1080/13639080.2016.1177636.

Mann, A. and Percy, C. (2013). Employer engagement in British secondary education: Wage earning outcomes experienced by young adults. *Journal of Education and Work* 27(5): 496–523.

Mann, A., Rehill, J. and Kashefpakdel, E.T. (2018). *Employer engagement in education: Insights from international evidence for effective practice and future research*. Education Endowment Foundation and Education and Employers.

Marks, G.N. (1999). The measurement of socioeconomic status and social class in the LSAY project technical paper No. 14. London: LSAY.

Percy, C. and Mann, A. (2014). School-mediated employer engagement and labour market outcomes for young adults: Wage premia, NEET outcomes and career confidence, in Mann, A., Stanley, J. and Archer, L. (eds.), *Understanding employer engagement in education: Theories and evidence*. London: Routledge.

Stanley, J., Mann, A. and Archer, L. (2014). Introduction, in Mann, A., Stanley, J. and Archer, L. (eds.), *Understanding employer engagement in education*. London: Routledge.

Chapter 14

Insiders or outsiders, who do you trust?

Engaging employers in
school-based career activities

Christian Percy and Elnaz Kashefpakdel

> *[I] trusted the word of someone in the working world [as opposed] to a careers advisor or teacher "telling" you what to do.*
>
> (23-year-old mixed-race man, in full-time employment, reflecting in a 2011 YouGov survey on his rich experiences of employer engagement during his independent school education)

Introduction

This chapter explores careers talks in schools to build on earlier work by the authors (Kashefpakdel and Percy, 2016) in light of new assessments of the impacts of careers activities on the economic outcomes of young people (Hughes et al. 2016) and how these activities can be best delivered (Rehill et al. 2017). The purpose is to improve our understanding of the link between careers activities presented primarily by outside speakers ("externally-supported careers activities") and the activities that are organised and delivered entirely by schools staff ("school-led careers activities"). This chapter first recaps Kashefpakdel and Percy (2016), which uses the same longitudinal database and core analytical approach, before explaining how insights from Jones et al. (2015), Hughes et al. (2016) and Rehill et al. (2017) suggest firstly that outside speakers are able to add value beyond what schools staff can deliver but clarify secondly that the school environment will be an important factor in determining how much of an impact outside speakers might have. The contribution of this paper is to affirm these two ideas in a quantitative setting focused on long-term labour market impacts, supplementing the practitioner insight, theoretical frameworks, student testimony and opinion survey data used elsewhere.

Literature context

Kashefpakdel and Percy (2016) exploited quantitative data from the 1970 British Cohort Study, a longitudinal dataset which follows the lives of thousands of Britons from their birth in 1970 to adulthood. Crucially, the survey participants were at secondary school in the mid-1980s during a period of curriculum experimentation that often sought to engage employers in school activities, including in careers advice. The wide variation in experiences caused by this period of experimentation and the limited control that individual students had over their participation, controlling in part for personal agency, makes it an ideal dataset for exploring the impact of employer-supported activities on students' later career outcomes.

The analysis, published in the *Journal of Education and Work*, revealed that each extra career talk by an outside speaker experienced at age 14–15 was associated with, on average, a 0.8% increase in wages at age 26. The analysis only compared students who were similar to other students in terms of key factors that influence wage, such as gender, highest qualifications, parental socio-economic status, home-learning environment and the local unemployment rate. As is usually the case, it is likely that the average value disguises variation along various axes. One key axis is whether young people described the talks when completing the survey at age 16, as "very helpful." Those who did so saw a wage premium 0.7 percentage points higher than those who described them as unhelpful. For talks experienced at age 15–16, there was a sizeable positive average effect if the talks were described as "very helpful" (0.9%), but only negligible benefits otherwise (0.2%). It is also noteworthy that very little benefit was identifiable from just 1, 2 or 3 careers talks in a single year – it takes a larger number before the average effect becomes visible statistically.

Kashefpakdel and Percy (2016) were inspired by, among others, Jones et al. (2015) which examines the reflections of 380 young adults on their school-mediated employer engagement experiences, finding that the clearest benefit lies in Cultural Capital, followed by Social Capital and then by Human Capital. Important to these benefits is the distinction between outside speakers or volunteers and other sources, notably schools staff. The paper argues that "common to young people of all educational backgrounds is a perception that workplace staff communicate more directly and truthfully about labour market realities than other sources" (Jones et al. 2015). It is possible, given this comparison, that more benefits might be expected from externally-supported careers activities than school-led ones.

While Kashefpakdel and Percy (2016) focused only on the wage premium associated with "outside speakers," two studies since have referenced it in the context of a broader set of careers-related activities in schools. The first study highlighted evidence that careers provision, both with and without employer involvement, can be positively associated with better outcomes – educational, economic and social – for young people (Hughes et al. 2016). This literature review of experimental or quasi-experimental studies from OECD countries, published in English since 1996, identified 96 in-depth studies exploring outcomes linked to different aspects of careers provision and teenage workplace exposure. Two-thirds (67%) of analyses presented in 27 studies which explicitly explored economic outcomes in terms of enhanced earnings and employment found evidence of generally positive outcomes for young people. While the literature review covered a range of activities, from careers provision and work-related learning through to work experience and mentoring, few studies looked at the interaction between these careers-led and externally-led activities.

The second study (Rehill et al. 2017) asks whether schools can act in ways to optimise the outcomes of careers talks. This study drew on 15 academic articles, evidence from a survey of 256 students (12–18-year-old) and the informed opinions of 38 experienced practitioners. One key finding of the study was that "positive outcomes can be expected to be optimised when young people are well prepared for careers events and undertake follow up activities." By definition, regardless of any employer involvement in the careers event itself, such preparation and follow-up takes place outside of the activity itself, typically within the school environment or with the support of a third party. This suggests that the broader school environment can be an important determinant in whether or not employer efforts achieve positive outcomes.

Both Hughes et al. (2016) and Rehill et al. (2017) raise concerns over a shortage of analysis in the literature for assessing the comparative of value of different types of careers events, particularly long-term, impact-centred quantitative analysis. Moreover, there is a shortage of such analysis informing the argument from Rehill et al. (2017) that integrated careers provision may influence the impact of employer contact. The argument is based primarily on a rich set of opinion data, from careers professionals, employee volunteers and school staff. While such opinion data is important to note, it is unable to directly validate the impact on long-term labour market outcomes.

The British Cohort Study is well situated to contribute to this evidence gap. It contains data on externally-supported careers activities, notably careers talks with outside speakers, as well as school-led careers activities. In the longitudinal analysis that follows, adult wage outcomes, with appropriate statistical controls, can be considered in light of individuals' responses at the age of 16 as to whether they took part in a number of different types of careers activities (talks, meetings, informal discussions) with different types of people (outside speakers invited into the school and classroom teachers or careers professionals, typically employed by the school)[1].

Such activities are of particular interest because it is reasonably assumed that they will include many similarities: that they take place within the school context, typically spanning the time of a timetabled lesson, and are designed to share information and insights on career options with a view to helping students ultimately make better choices and achieve better career outcomes. While a modest range of variation in these features should be acknowledged, both in terms of how 16-year-olds recalled activities or interpreted those questions and the nature of the activities themselves, the most significant difference lies in the medium of delivery: an outside speaker, assumed commonly to be a volunteer with personal experience of the outside world of work, whom students would see rarely and would be likely to be meeting for the first time, as opposed to a member of school staff, with whom they are likely to encounter more regularly.

These different types of people with whom students reported various careers-focused engagements can be understood to bring with them very different knowledge content to inform their discussions.

This distinction speaks to the quote that opens this chapter and the argument from Jones et al. (2015) suggesting *that careers activities involving outside speakers can be expected to have more impact on young people than activities which do not.* Whereas career discussions with classroom teachers can be expected to draw on a narrower knowledge-base, the information available to students from a range of external speakers can be expected to be rooted in a broader range of experiences, increasingly the likelihood of potential student interest. A greater effect from an outside speaker can also be expected because of the greater (perceived) authenticity of the discussion. Even if the underlying messages and content are similar between an employer-led and a teacher-led session on a particular career or the nature of working life, the volunteer from the world of work may be more able to convey greater authenticity, ultimately enabling more messages to stick and drive impactful attitudinal or behavioural change. The employer speaker has, after all, successfully navigated the labour market and can share real stories in relation to that, making it easier to convey foundational elements of cultural capital such as an appreciation of workplace norms, an understanding of the keys to success, and the lived reality of routes into the career.

Following Rehill et al. (2017), *careers activities involving outside speakers can be expected to have more impact if they take place in a school that supports the wider provision of career education, information, advice and guidance (CEIAG).* Recent testimony from individual school leaders in London suggest that such practice is known, and consciously delivered, within English secondary schooling: [2]

> We did a lot of speech/trip prep at our school. We'd usually talk within form time about who the speaker was, what the talk was about, how great it was that this person had spent their time to come and speak to them. The kids would then be asked to all write 3-ish questions that they had for the speaker. We'd choose the best and give these back to them to answer. It really helped with their engagement to have an appreciation of the person's background and to have had the opportunity to discuss that beforehand. Knowing that their questions had been checked also gave them confidence when asking them, and a really great feeling of pride in having asked an external speaker an intelligent question in front of everyone. It worked fantastically well and I wouldn't do it any other way.
> (Kate Farrell, Head of Physics, King Solomon Academy, London)

> We regularly give our students the chance to meet with employers and careers advisers to discuss their future options. We find that on those occasions students are developing soft skills like meeting and greeting and questioning – every bit as important as the information they get are the skills that they must employ to get the best out of those opportunities. As

such our students are always advised and prepared – sometimes with role play and practice – to ensure they utilise those opportunities in the best possible way. And we find that we can do this through a comprehensive age-appropriate curriculum that responds to their emerging needs.

(Brian Nelis, Assistant Principal and Head of
Careers Education, Oasis Hadley, London)

Students get the most benefit from talks and career events when the school helps them prepare for the event in advance. Whether this is with a class teacher teaching a particular subject or with their form tutor, the opportunity becomes more meaningful as a result. Before any such event we ask our students to prepare in advance and think about what questions they might ask, what they want to take away from the experience. Only when it evolves into something the students need to invest in and research does it really engender interest and allow students to develop.

(Sabah Ghani, Curriculum Director for Maths,
Crest Academy, London)

On one level, in the case of careers talks with outside speakers, the links are trivially essential: such speakers are only able to operate in schools when invited and supported to do so by school staff. However, the links are also substantive from a quality perspective. For instance, students can be expected to secure more value from talks with outside speakers when they have had the opportunity to prepare in advance, perhaps reflecting on questions they have which the speaker might be able to address or using the fact of the event alone as a catalyst for reflecting on and investigating options. Teachers and other school staff can also help students debrief what they think they learned from the talk, including any assertions the speaker made that they might feel sceptical about, using this as an opportunity for independent research or further discussions to refine their own opinions. It may also be possible to refer to relevant aspects of the talk in future subject lessons or careers sessions, helping to make the link to real-world applications and reinforcing opportunities for learning, creating space in the curriculum for guided preparation and reflection. Where this process feeds into other careers structures within the school, such as discussions with guidance counsellors, prioritised access to certain careers fairs or work experience and so on, any impact can be expected to increase. For these reasons, among others, it is anticipated that talks with outside speakers would be perceived as more beneficial where they take place in schools that also offer a rich array of within-school careers provision.

Methodology

This analysis draws on the British Cohort Study dataset 1970 (BCS70), a study of approximately 17,000 people born in the UK in one particular week in April 1970. Since BCS70 began, there have been seven full data collection exercises, gathering self-reported data from the target individuals as well as other individuals with knowledge of the individual, notably parents and schools. These questionnaires explore a range of topics, including cohort members' health, education, social and economic circumstances. In the current analysis, surveys are drawn on that took place when respondents were aged 5, 10, 16 and 26. There have been significant declines in the response rate, such that only around 6,400 respondents at age 16 also completed at least part of the education questionnaire, with many more suffering missing data for key variables. A declining response rate is common in longitudinal surveys that seek to track people over decades. This declining response rate introduces an element of uncertainty into what it is nonetheless one of the most robust sources of data for evaluating hypotheses in the education sector. This uncertainty is mitigated in the analysis by using a range of control variables, ranging from demography to socioeconomic status and academic background. To the extent that non-response bias or any compensatory weighting schemes might relate to included variables, the analysis will be robust.

The dataset is rare among longitudinal studies in containing several questions on careers guidance aged 16. These answers can be combined with reported earnings aged 26 to analyse the primary relationship of interest for this chapter, supported by a range of control variables as required. In order to explore whether "careers activities involving outside speakers have more impact on young people than activities which do not," this study replicates the methodology used in Kashefpakdel and Percy (2016) to explore the relationship between career talks with outside speakers and wage outcomes among those in full-time employment aged 26 and applies it to three additional variables related to school-led careers activities:

- Number of **careers classes** (reflecting the BSC70 question on "Timeta-bled classes in which careers were discussed": answers ranged from 0 to 72, averaging 11 over all respondents, and were given both for age 14–15 and age 15–16 separately)[3]
- Number of **career chats** ("Any personal contact to discuss your career/job/further education with the following: careers teacher, form teacher/tutor, year head, or other teacher," the results range from 0 to 4, averaging 1 over all respondents, and were given for age 14–15 and age 15–16 combined)
- Number of **careers meetings** ("Any other meetings or classes in which careers/jobs were discussed," answers ranged from 0 to 72, averaging 2 over all respondents and were given both for age 14–15 and age 15–16 separately)

An indication of the distribution of activities at age 14–15 is given in Figure 14.1.

The estimation approach is a linear regression on the natural log of net weekly income, as measured for those in full-time employment aged 26.

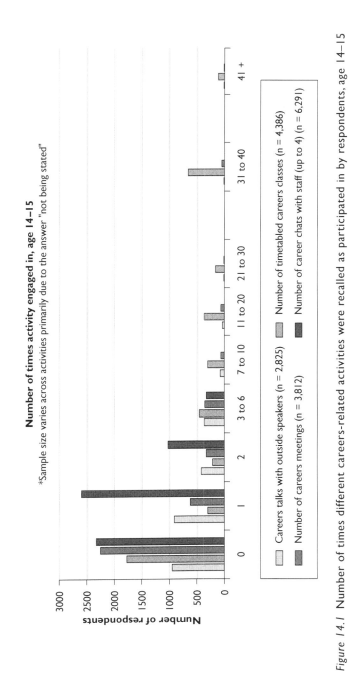

Figure 14.1 Number of times different careers-related activities were recalled as participated in by respondents, age 14–15

Control variables were selected from a horse race regression on wage of 13 variables across demographic, academic ability, home learning environment and socio-economic status, choosing all with a p-value better than 0.10. Six variables passed this test: gender, highest level of qualification aged 26, mother's socio-economic status, number of days watching TV in the evening (Monday to Friday), a cognitive development test at age 5 and "O" level maths score age 16. A control for level of deprivation at local education authority level (employment rate) is added to reduce the impact of endogeneity in our modelling.

These regressions are applied to two samples, one which allowed the sample size to be as large as possible for each regression subject to missing answer constraints and a second which was a strict subset of those used in Kashefpakdel and Percy (2016) to ensure that coefficients can be compared like-for-like across the two analyses. Given that each additional question results in further respondents with missing values, the exact overlapping sample for the 2016 analysis on external speakers was also applied for each of the three internal school activities. For more details on the reduction in sample size through missing values and diagnostic testing, please see the 2016 paper.

Secondly, in order to explore whether careers activities involving outside speakers have more impact if they take place in a school that supports the wider provision of CEIAG, this study contrasts how helpful young people found careers talks with outside speakers with a scale for how rich the CEIAG provision is in the school overall ("the careers-richness score"). The school careers environment scale runs from 0 to 25 points based on the following criteria described in Table 14.1.

Results

Table 14.2 presents the results of an array of identically structured linear regression models to evaluate whether careers activities involving outside speakers have more impact on young people than activities which do not. The only difference between the regressions is which careers education variable is included (number of careers talks with outside speakers vs. the three quantitative metrics for school-led careers activities) and various sample size adjustments to ensure a like-for-like comparison. The first part of the table uses the maximum sample size possible for each regression analysis, given different levels of missing data for different variables. The second part of the table uses the narrower sample sizes that correspond to exact overlaps with the analysis on external speakers, ensuring that any difference between the regressions is not simply the result of missing data and sample inclusion.

Table 14.2 indicates that there is, on average, a higher wage at age 26 (among those in full-time employment) for those who participated in a larger number of careers talks with external speakers while aged 14–15, at around 0.8% per talk, whereas there is no such association for those who participated in internal school activities.[5] There is a statistically significant association for the number

Table 14.1 Scoring system for careers-richness in the internal school environment

For the number of careers meetings in year 10	• 1–3 events reported (or unable to recall how many but confident participated): +1 point • 4–10 events reported: +2 points • 11–20 events reported: +3 points • 21–30 events reported: +4 points • Over 30 events reported: +5 points
For the number of careers meetings in year 11	As above
For the number of careers classes in year 10	As above
For the number of careers classes in year 11	As above
For each separate type of person in school the person described talking to about their future ("careers chats")	+1 point for each (e.g. up to a maximum of four points if they spoke with each of "careers teacher," "form tutor," "year head" or "other teacher")
If the person also reported a careers officer interview	+1 point
Total score	**From 0 to 25 points**

Note: Where individuals cannot recall or decline to answer a particular point-scoring question, they score zero from that question but are still included in the overall rating process.

of careers meetings a respondent recalled, but only on the restricted sample for comparison to the external speakers' regression, and it remains materially weaker than the result for external speakers, at 0.3% per activity rather than 0.7%–0.9%. Moreover, across a broader range of internal school activities, no material or statistically significant association is visible on average across the qualifying respondents. It is important to highlight that the wage premium associated with external speakers remains substantively unaffected by the different sub-samples of respondents corresponding to those who answered the questions detailing the internal school activities.

Figure 14.2 shifts the focus to whether careers activities involving outside speakers have more impact if they take place in a school that supports the wider provision of CEIAG. Figure 14.2 displays the distribution of the careers-richness score according to their view on any external careers talks they experienced from age 14 to age 16, excluding individuals who did not answer the question regarding helpfulness of external careers talks as well as those who failed to answer all constituent questions making up the score.

This distribution splits closest to 50:50 at 0–5 points vs. 6+, so this split is used to summarise Figure 14.2 in Table 14.3 for easier reading.

Figure 14.2 and Table 14.3 support the view that students in schools which organised a large number of internal school-led careers activities for them were more likely to describe as helpful the programme of external careers

Table 14.2 Results of regression on ln wage, incl. controls

Bold rows indicate statistically significant at 5% level or better (in bold), activities in Year 10 (age 14–16) only	1. Sample size	2. R^2	3. Coefficient of careers education variable	4. P-value of coefficient as different from zero
Using the full sample possible given data availability for different variables				
External speakers	**784**	**0.24**	**0.008**	**0.001**
Careers classes	1,292	0.18	–0.001	0.994
Careers meetings	1,138	0.15	0.002	0.217
Career chats	1,804	0.17[4]	0.001	0.979
Restricted samples such that the same respondents are included in both the external speaker sample and the internal careers activity sample it is being compared to				
External speakers (sample for careers classes comparison)	**622**	**0.28**	**0.008**	**0.004**
Careers classes	622	0.27	–0.001	0.358
External speakers (sample for careers meetings comparison)	**571**	**0.23**	**0.007**	**0.021**
Careers meetings	**571**	**0.23**	**0.003**	**0.048**
External speakers (sample for careers chats comparison)	**781**	**0.24**	**0.009**	**0.001**
Career chats	781	0.23	0.000	0.974

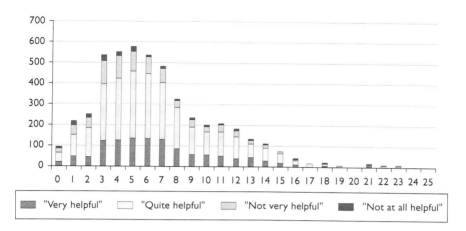

Figure 14.2 Distribution of careers-richness score across how helpful respondents found external speakers on careers

Table 14.3 Summary of respondent perspectives on external speakers by careers-richness score

View on external speakers:	Careers-richness score (split at mid-point of sample size)	
	0–5 points	6+ points
"Very helpful"	42%	58%
"Quite helpful"	45%	55%
"Not Very helpful"	54%	46%
"Not at all helpful"	63%	37%

talks they experienced at school from age 14–16. For instance, 63% of those who described external speakers as "not at all helpful" were in the lower half of provision richness for internal school activities, whereas 58% of those who described them as "very helpful" fall into the upper half of the distribution.

However, it is probable that schools conducting more internal activities were also likely to organise more external speakers and that students simply find external speakers more useful when there are more of them (as demonstrated by Kashefpakdel and Percy, 2016), without any connection to the level of internal school activity occurring around such talks. A further analysis is used to adjust for this scenario, a location-only ordinal regression using a logit link function, which tests how well the careers–richness score can predict the young person's assessment of outside speaker helpfulness, controlling for the number of talks they reported.

212 Christian Percy and Elnaz Kashefpakdel

In the direct regression, without controlling for the number of talks, each extra careers–richness point is associated with a respondent being more likely to find talks helpful (p-value 0.000).[6] Running the same model controlling for the total number of careers talks with external speakers recalled from age 14 to 16 makes no change to the significance and polarity of the careers–richness score (p-value 0.000), reducing the location of the coefficient by only 15% and the odds ratio from 1.040 to 1.034 per point.[7] As expected, each additional careers talk with an outside speaker also makes individuals more likely to report the programme as helpful, but is less impactful on a per talk vs. per point basis (odds ratio of 1.024 per talk vs. 1.034 per point). While this exploration using ordinal regression is not intended to be comprehensive, it is sufficient to demonstrate that the relationship observed by eye in Figure 14.3 is not solely the result of differences in the number of careers talks. Young people who reported a more careers-rich school environment at school were more likely to find outside speakers helpful, regardless of how many such talks they attended.

As a final check, the core analysis from the 2016 paper (wage premium regression with background controls on the number of talks with outside speakers aged 14–15) was run on two subsamples, respondents who described a school experience in the lower half of the careers richness scale and those in the upper half (same definition as Figure 14.3). The results show, again, that the internal schools environment is important. For the upper half of the spectrum (n=455), we derive a 1.0% premium per talk (p-value 0.000), whereas the lower half (n=329) identifies no value (−0.1% per talk, p-value 0.847). We know from previous work that those with a large number of careers talks relative to the average, such as five or more, are those more likely to identify a benefit, and it is possible there are few of these in the lower half of the careers richness spectrum. By homing in exclusively on the internal schools activities reported by students aged 14–15 and splitting the scale such that both upper and lower sets have a similar number of respondents with five or more talks from external speakers, the analysis continues to display a delta in the predicted direction along with an increase in the consistency of the effect, albeit a smaller delta overall. The upper set identified a 0.9% co-efficient (p-value 0.014, n=233) vs. 0.8% in the lower set (p-value 0.025, n=551).

Discussion

This chapter has strengthened the case that outside speakers bring something of particular and additional value to in-school careers provisions. Whereas each talk with outside speakers at age 14–15 can be correlated with a 0.8% increase in wage aged 26, no such effect is found for structurally similar initiatives led by school staff, whether these are timetabled careers classes, careers meetings or one-on-one careers chats. Although these might have similar structure, duration and purpose, there appears to be something about the medium of delivery through an outside speaker that delivers additional value. While this chapter cannot rule out the possibility that this additional value reflects differences in specific content and quality, and while the authors would welcome new research in this area, the more consistent difference between the careers activities is expected to be the authenticity of the speaker with respect to the topic, as set out by Jones et al. (2015).

The weak results for the school-led careers activities bear further examination. Within the 14–15 year cohort, where the authors anticipated greater effects due to avoiding the pressures and distractions of exam year, only one category of school-led careers activities had some identifiable relationship with future wages. Students who recalled more "other meetings or classes in which careers/jobs were discussed" (i.e. other than the more commonplace timetabled careers classes) saw some benefits, to the tune of 0.3% extra income at age 26, for those in full-time employment and comparing like-for-like. While this is statistically significant on a standalone basis at the 5% level, if one were to seek to infer from this that internal school activities in general have an average positive effect, it would fall foul of adjustments such as the Bonferroni correction – that is, if examining multiple variables and treating a success on any of them as approval for the general category, then stricter statistical thresholds for success need to be applied. For the purposes of this chapter, the data suggests that while it is possible some school-led careers activities were effective some of the time in the 1980s, over a large number of initiatives and individuals, the average effect is negligible.

Various explanations present themselves for why school-led careers activities did not correlate more closely with wage outcomes, despite being structurally similar to other activities that were convincingly correlated. We will highlight three possibilities in this discussion: difficulties with tracing cause and effect, subsample effects and variations in quality.

As with many small-scale education interventions examining effects a decade later, there is a significant challenge in tracing the proposed impact from the near-term, visible effects through to long-term outcomes, navigating the many other factors that influence and constrain such complex societally-channelled labour market outcomes. In the case of the BCS70 dataset, we have no surveys in the late teenage years or early 20s where individuals were asked to reflect on the careers guidance they had in various forms, how they were able to use it or not. For instance, given controls for academic attainment, the presented analysis cannot track any correlated benefits that careers activities achieve through improved academic results, such as in choosing more appropriate courses or in being more motivated for exam revision. And as with any analysis on wage alone, there is no visibility of job satisfaction and sector of choice. In other words, even as it closes down one convenient avenue for analysis, the absence of a compelling wage correlation ten years later should not be taken as evidence of no benefit at all; the methodological approach in this chapter is a necessarily blunt tool for unpicking a subtle knot.

The second possibility is that the kinds of internal school activities common in the 1980s could have benefited some groups, but not in a way that escapes through the noise of the majority who gained little from such activities – potentially also counterbalanced by some individuals who were adversely affected, such as through a loss of time in their academic pursuits. Sample size constraints within BCS70 place restrictions on how well small groups can be analysed, but it may be possible to explore this through new research within this dataset. The third possibility reflects the fact that there is no insight in the survey about the exact structure of these activities, how much time staff had to prepare for them, or how much priority the school placed on them overall. If the analysis was able to control for the quality of activities in a more rigorous manner, it is possible that high quality activities would be correlated with labour market outcomes even on average over the sample. If there had only been a small number of such high-quality activities, their impact may have been drowned out in a statistical ocean of their low-quality counterparts.

A more positive picture for the role of school-led careers activities is found in the interaction with externally-supported careers activities. While the effects may not be consistent or strong enough to be visible in direct regressions on later wage outcomes, school-led careers activities can nonetheless be seen to play a role in how helpful students perceived outside speakers and therefore contribute indirectly to earnings at age 26.

Students who were in the upper half of the spectrum for the number of careers classes, meetings or chats that they participated in were more likely to report external careers speakers as being helpful. This effect is robust when including controls for the number of external careers speakers the person reported. Importantly, students who had more careers classes, meetings or chats also had a higher wage premium associated with each outside speakers that they listened to. Taken collectively, this suggests that richer internal school environments enable careers talks with outside speakers to be found more helpful on average and to have more traction on future wage outcomes.

In terms of further work, this chapter has started to push on the limits of what the British Cohort Study can reveal regarding careers activity, such that difficulties in the interpretation of questions and increasingly subtle comparisons between regression results strain the confidence of assessments. Thus, insights can increase or decrease confidence in particular hypotheses, as in this chapter, as well as generating ideas for elements to explore further, but it becomes difficult to demonstrate positions in a conclusive manner. Additional time exploring subgroups and other control variables could build usefully on this work and test its limitations, but is likely to butt up against similar barriers. Nonetheless, there are other related avenues within the dataset that could be explored, such as teenage participation in episodes of work experience, as well as a fascinating series of variables on student attitudes towards school and work and how these have changed over time. As the 1980s recedes further into the institutional past, the authors are increasingly excited by the opportunities posed by new datasets, such as the Longitudinal Educational Outcomes dataset and the maturing Longitudinal Study of Young people in England, as well as datasets outside the English education system, and particularly by the growing appetite within the funding environment to set up quasi-experimental designs and randomised control trials within schools. By building activities specifically to test aspects of the school-to-work journey, this field has the potential to leap ahead in the coming years.

Conclusion

This chapter explores careers talks in schools in light of new assessments of the impacts of careers activities on the economic outcomes of young people (Hughes et al. 2016) and how these activities can be best delivered (Rehill et al. 2017). The analysis uses the longitudinal dataset British Cohort Study 1970, building on earlier work that demonstrated a wage premium associated with external careers talks (Kashefpakdel and Percy. 2016).

The analysis finds quantitative support in wage outcome data for two propositions emerging from research literature: that careers activities involving outside speakers have more impact on young people than activities which do not, and that they have more impact if they take place in a school that supports the wider provision of CEIAG. Classes, meetings and chats with internal school staff had a negligible direct association with later wage outcomes overall, raising important questions about the value of such activities. It is argued that this lack of statistical significance may, in part, reflect some combination of variation across subgroups, variation in quality of talk, as well as the intrinsic difficulty of tracing the impact of small interventions through to wage impact a decade later on declining sample sizes. The finding that school-led careers activity contributes to the helpfulness and labour market impact of externally-supported careers activity argues for taking such school-led activities more seriously, exploring ways both to increase their direct impact on young people and targeting them towards optimising the impact of externally-supported careers activities.

Taken collectively, the results support the principle that the medium of delivery of information can be as important as the content itself. Authenticity is likely to be a driver of why outside speakers were effective. However, no one of good intent comes to a school uninvited. Outside speakers can only be at their most effective if teachers work with them to prepare the classes, brief the speaker and link the content to future in-school activities as appropriate. Just as school staff do not have all the skills to do it themselves, neither do volunteers visit a school in a vacuum – we must all work closely together to prepare young people for the world of work.

Notes

1 In a few cases, professionals employed by the Local Authority, benefits offices or sectoral associations may have also delivered careers activities. The survey questions were not precise enough to explore this specifically and whether or not young people considered these outside speakers or schools staff may vary from case to case depending on the relationship between the professional and the school.

2 Interviews with authors, October 2017.

3 As with previous analysis on this dataset, there is a limitation in the construction of the variable that includes zero activities reported. Individuals were only asked if they

remembered how many activities they did in each year (and zero was not an allowed response, only "not stated" or "not asked"/"no questionnaire") if they had confirmed they did experience such activities in general over the previous two years. If someone reported no activities at all, this is entered unambiguously as a zero for both Year 10 and Year 11. However, if someone reported that activities did take place but only recorded a number for Year 11, that number will be entered for Year 11 and they will be excluded from the Year 10 analyses. This is because it is unclear if they knew they did no activities in Year 10, but the questionnaire was unable to record this explicitly or if they knew they did some in Year 10 but were not comfortable putting a number on how many. This should only affect boundary cases and might result in an under-statement of zero levels of activities relative to others; since there is no a priori problematic correlation between this limitation and the relationships under investigation, the results should be robust to it.

4 Note that the lower R^2 on the unrestricted samples might merit further exploration. It suggests that the other control variables, such as mother's socio-economic status and Maths grades, are materially less correlated with future wage outcomes in the larger sample. The only difference in the selection is that the larger sample includes individuals who declined to answer or who did not know whether they had careers talks with external speakers and how many – but could remember whether they had done various internal schools activities.

5 The analysis was conducted on Year 11 (age 15–16) for the purposes of completeness, but did not explore this Year group in detail as the 2016 paper reported only conditional support for external speakers at this age, potentially due to the pressures and distractions of national examinations. The analysis exploring this conditional support cannot be replicated across the three internal school activities, making it a poor comparison point for testing the hypothesis. As with the 2016 analysis, no significant results were found across the Year 11 activities and are not included here.

6 n=4,442 restricted to match the same sample as the regression with controls, overall fit chi-square of 28.9, p-value of 0.00, pseudo Nagelkerke R^2 of 0.007, 9% of cells with zero frequency.

7 N=4,442, overall fit chi-square of 57.8, p-value of 0.00, pseudo Nagelkerke R^2 of 0.015, 51% of cells with zero frequency. The models fail the parallel lines test at the 5% level. Further specifications are not presented as the analysis is intended only as a directional check. Note that while the performance and exact coefficients vary, the results remain substantively and materially the same without the assumption of unity-scale in the location-only model. Similarly, reducing the large proportion of cells with zero frequency by binning the number of careers talks with external speakers into five categories (reducing the proportion to 25%) has no impact on the findings for the purposes of this chapter.

References

Hughes, D., Mann, A., Barnes, S-A., Baldauf, B. and McKeown, R. (2016). *Careers education: International literature review*. London: Education Endowment Foundation.

Jones, S., Mann, A. and Morris, K. (2015). The 'Employer Engagement Cycle' in secondary education: Analysing the testimonies of young British adults. *Journal of Education and Work* 29(7): 834–856.

Kashefpakdel, E. and Percy, C. (2016). Career education that works: An economic analysis using the British cohort study. *Journal of Education and Work* 30(3): 217–234.

Rehill, J., Kashefpakdel, E.T. and Mann, A. (2017). *What works? The evidence on careers events*. London: The Careers and Enterprise Company.

Chapter 15

Between two worlds
Linking education and employment

Simon Field

This chapter is a reflection, based on many years of experience looking at different systems of education and training around the world. It looks at a curious paradox. Although the world of work is deeply dependent on the skills that arise from learning, employers and other stakeholders from the world of work are often remarkably uninvolved in education in general, and even in vocational education and training systems. Here, I look at the origins of this unfortunate paradox, why it matters, and how it might be resolved.

The issues

Most young people progress from initial education to a working life that will occupy a very large part of their lives, and impact profoundly on their wellbeing. It should be blindingly obvious that education and training therefore need to give the fullest attention, at all levels, to the requirements of the working life which will normally follow. And yet, much that we see, in many countries, is remarkably resistant to the blindingly obvious. Often education tries hard to keep working life at arm's length.

Of course, we sometimes do better. Sometimes, in some places and in some education and training systems, the two worlds come together. The strongest apprenticeships – and some of those are found in the UK – effectively blend mentoring of an apprentice by a practitioner/teacher in the workplace on the one hand, with systematic academic support through classroom teaching on the other. But often, overcoming the barriers and joining up the world of learning and the world of work can feel like an uphill struggle. Why is it so hard to achieve what is so clearly necessary? One reason is that the historical development of education systems has created barriers, and several institutions and incentives now reinforce these barriers. Yet there are opportunities for reform to build a stronger partnership between education and working life.

History: the rise of the education-industrial complex

Just two and a half thousand years ago, in around 387 BC, in a sacred grove of olive trees just outside Athens, Plato established his 'Academy' a place of discussion and learning quite separate from practical education (Cherniss, 1945). It was not purely a Western invention. At around the same time, in China, Confucius was elaborating a philosophy which also gave academic study a privileged place: "By three methods we may learn wisdom: First, by reflection, which is noblest; Second, by imitation, which is easiest; and third by experience, which is the bitterest" (Chambers Dictionary of Quotations, 1997, 279). Back in Athens, the Academy commanded respect. Even the warlike Spartans left the sacred olive grove untouched when they invaded. The Academy, and the sacred grove of olive trees survived until, a few hundred years later, the more pragmatic Roman general Sulla came along and cut down all the olive trees to build siege engines (Appian of Alexandria, undated).

Plato started something important in that olive grove. The education industry – and industry is the right word for an activity that consumes somewhere between 5 and 10 per cent of GDP in developed countries (OECD, 2017) – is one of the most successful of all human innovations, and underpins much of what we value in civilisation. But, and this chapter is about the 'but', that very success has brought with it hubris, overconfidence in the power and status of academic qualifications, the classroom and the lecture hall, an overconfidence that can too easily exclude the world of work. We can paraphrase Eisenhower and speak of the "education–industrial complex" – the supply side lobby that guides policy in the interests of the education industry.

As an example, look what has happened to vocational training. An early form of apprenticeship is visible in the code of Hammurabi from around 1800 BCE, and during the neo-Babylonian period, sophisticated apprenticeship contracts governing the respective responsibilities of employers and apprentices were in place, some hundreds of years before the establishment of Plato's Academy (Kedar, undated). Five hundred years ago, in Britain, and other parts of Europe, much education and training took the form of apprenticeships. One historian estimates that in 1550, 10 per cent of the population of London were apprentices, and fully two thirds of the adult population had served as apprentices (Rappaport, 1989). But apprenticeship in those days was very different from how we now think of the institution. Training was, subject to some legal regulation, the exclusive province of employers. There were no colleges involved because the colleges did not exist. For a large chunk of the population, apprenticeships, run and organised by employers, *were* the education system, while the ancient schools and universities served a tiny elite.

So what has happened in the last 500 years, to shift employers from a previously dominant position into one that is sometimes marginal, although often quite different from country to country? The answer is the rise of modern education. Plato's Academy has risen triumphant, in primary, secondary and tertiary education. The academic culture has acquired an extraordinary independence and power, and while it has achieved many great things, its very triumph has caused some collateral damage. Too often school students, taught by teachers who have spent their entire lives in academic institutions, get to see and hear very little of the world of work which will, later on, consume so much of their lives. Even careers guidance, formally and informally, is delivered by teachers and professors who often have little experience of life in industry and outside the academic world: in their education career they have moved seamlessly from school to university, and then in their working lives back to school or university.

In vocational education, too, we find qualifications created with no involvement of employers, and taught by people at some remove from knowledge of modern industry. While some vocational teachers work part time as teachers and part time as practitioners, others have not worked as practitioners for many years. In these circumstances, it is hardly surprising that we see employers with little interest in the qualifications that emerge. More often, we see a softer version of this disconnect, in which those responsible for vocational qualifications go through the motions of involving employers in their creation, and employers, in their turn, go through the motions of taking those qualifications seriously. Most important of all, the vocational route is never, ever, as prestigious and desirable as the academic route – the royal road that leads through the golden gates of promise, to university and beyond, the triumph of the Academy.

Where are we now? Towards a more comprehensive approach

The challenges faced by vocational education are also a problem, in some ways an even bigger problem, for academic education. It is sometimes said, by way of definition, that a vocational programme, a vocational qualification, is a way of preparing someone for the labour market. The standard international classification defines, at secondary level, 'vocational' as something that prepares for a specific job, while 'academic' prepares for further learning. But further learning cannot go on forever, and so at tertiary level, the distinction between 'professional' and 'academic' is left undefined (UNESCO, 2012). The distinction can be applied pragmatically – many secondary level programmes prepare for specific jobs, and many do not. But stand back for a moment, and the distinction does not make much sense. Virtually all these programmes precede working life.

Education and training systems, unfortunately, are often happier in silos. Vocational programmes and qualifications too often ignore the study and wider skills that can prepare students for further learning. In England, the move to insist on more basic skills of numeracy and literacy in vocational programmes is welcome, but does not go far enough (see, for example, the concerns of Pullen and Dromey, 2016). Upper secondary academic education, in most countries, is far too exclusively fixated on preparation for university – fine for those who make it there, but often leaving a substantial chunk of young people stranded, either because they drop out of the programme or because their grades do not permit entry to the university programme of their choice. Look at A-levels for example – a system that provides a very narrow education for more academic young people relative to what you see in many other countries – and deeply focused on entrance to higher education. Career preparation receives hardly a second thought. This may be fine for the universities that take receipt of the successful, but it does not serve well the substantial numbers of young people who do not make it, and have received very little of the kind of career preparation that might help them survive in a youth labour market increasingly marked by precarious, temporary and part-time work (see for example Pullen and Dromey, 2016 and Huddleston and Ashton, this volume). They too, are collateral damage from the triumph of the Academy.

It is time for a more comprehensive approach. All initial education and training, whether labelled as 'academic' or 'vocational', needs to prepare young people for work, life and further learning, because a full life is going to involve all three of these things, and the life chances of an individual will depend on their ability to perform in all three domains. In an age when working life is evolving rapidly in response to technological change, this breadth of initial preparation is more important than ever. That doesn't mean abolishing the difference between a university philosophy programme and apprenticeship as an electrician. But it does mean that the philosophy programme needs to have an eye on the role that academically trained philosophers might play in the workplace, and that the electrician should acquire the broader education and study skills that will equip them for future learning and career development.

This approach may take both philosophers and electricians out of their comfort zone, a good thing, for it is in precisely that zone of discomfort where learning is often most valuable.

So at all levels, barriers need to be broken down. Historically, employers have been too absent in schools, and therefore working life comes as a great shock to many young people.

Adapting institutions to a comprehensive approach

The institutions that define the two worlds of education and work are powerful influences – sometimes, in some countries, entrenching the barriers between these two worlds. But elsewhere, they can be a force for partnership.

The key institutions of the education industry – universities and schools – build strong walls to defend themselves. But those same walls can also isolate. It is rightly said that education should not be a narrowly utilitarian task, but rather serve the developmental and intellectual needs of young people. This is a good principle – but ask who is to decide on these needs, and the answer, in practice, is that it is very often the educators, the professors and teachers who will decide. Thus universities, in most countries, most of the time, decide what programmes they will teach and the contents of those programmes. (In schools, national curricula make things a little different). All the universities then have to do is to persuade students to fill the lecture halls. Government then often pays the tuition bills, and even in the UK, provides a large subsidy.

In fact, wider society, including the representatives of working life, need to be much more involved in deciding on the contents of higher education and other post-secondary programmes. Employers will want to see the link between these programmes and the skills required in working life. That goes for all the programmes – not just 'vocational' programmes. This is not to narrow education, but, on the contrary, to make education more broadly reflective of diverse social interests and needs. For sure, education should be about the intellectual blossoming of the individual, not just about meeting very specific job requirements, but it is up to all of us to guide what we mean by intellectual blossoming, not just the academics. 'Academic freedom' should not become the dictatorship of the Academy.

Modes of study, as well as their content, need to meet the requirements of the world and not just the Academy. For the last decade or two, not just in the UK, but almost everywhere in the world, there has been a growing crescendo of demands for education programmes to be competence-based, with a strong focus on learning outcomes. The idea is simple – learning comes in different shapes and forms, and works at different paces, and often needs to be adapted to individual needs. What matters at the end of the day is the knowledge and skills that have been acquired. 'Seat-time' should not matter. That compelling logic would seem to make sense for the individual – allowing individuals to learn according to their capacities and their circumstances. For vocational programmes, it looks as if it might work for employers, allowing modes of study and the pace of learning to be organised around working schedules and job requirements.

Some have embraced that philosophy of learning outcomes and made it work. The professional examinations at post-secondary level, found in the German-speaking countries usually have few 'seat-time' requirements, although often working experience in a particular type of job is required. These would include, for example, the 'Meister' examinations which provide higher level qualifications to apprenticeship graduates, offering a blend of deeper technical skills and knowledge, entrepreneurship, and skills in supervising new apprentices. Most examination candidates pursue preparatory courses, adapted to their own needs, to fill in the gaps in their knowledge and skills, but these are rarely mandatory (see for example Fazekas and Field, 2013a, 2013b). In a different way, the French system of recognition of prior learning allows entrants to higher and post-secondary education to have their skills recognised, including those acquired informally through work. The credit obtained can then be used to obtain access, course exemptions and accelerated completion, and even full qualifications (Ulicna, D, Nevala, A-Mand Hawley, J, 2012)).

But the education industry has largely resisted this new-fangled philosophy. In the universities, the standard product – often a three or four-year full-time degree – is marketed very convincingly to the school-leavers embarked on the royal road to university. In the UK as in many countries, seat-time defines the standard programmes of what might be called "half-time/full-time study", where students study for about half the year at the university, but the programmes are called full-time, a study schedule sanctified by centuries if not by logic. Flexible programmes of variable lengths but leading to the same qualifications, tailored to individual needs, are just not how universities want to work, and in this domain, it is the education industry that is in charge.

It is not just that study schedules are too rigid to suit individual needs, it is also that there are so few 'standard' sizes. But for employers, higher level job skills do not come in the standard sizes implied by university education, in most cases requiring three or four years of post-school education, and sometimes more. Common sense tells us that higher level jobs require widely varying amounts of post-secondary preparation – six months, one, two, three or four years, depending on the job. Spending longer than is necessary is wasteful. But looking around the world, there are wide variations visible in the time spent preparing for the same job. In Korea, those who work in coffee shops as Baristas are typically trained in a two-year post-secondary programme in a junior college (Kis and Park, 2012), a world apart from the many countries where a few days training would be required. In Korea, this reflects the sometimes distorting effect of an intense focus on the perceived value of post-secondary qualifications.

Often, the biggest inefficiency is that job skills requiring only one or two years of post-secondary training are tackled at a more leisurely pace in three or four-year programmes. This is better business for higher education, but not for students or government, if government pays. In England, short post-secondary programmes – HNCs, HNDs and the like – are uncommon compared with some countries, and Foundation degrees have not established the mass market that was initially envisaged. There is no evidence that this is because the UK economy has fewer jobs requiring this level of skills development (Musset and Field, 2013). In the United States, vocational 'certificates' typically requiring between six months and two years of full time equivalent training are the fastest growing segment of post-secondary education (Kuczera and Field, 2013).

In England, there is both waste and unfairness in young people running up huge debts to pursue unnecessarily long degree courses. A systematic promotion of shorter post-secondary programmes, such as should emerge from the post-Sainsbury reforms, is very much to be welcomed (Independent Panel on Technical Education, 2016; Departments of Business Industry and Skills and Education, 2016). These shorter programmes do not always have nice, neat names that students, parents and employers can recognise, but they are important (OECD, 2014). Two-year bachelor's degrees directly tackle the problem of the part-time/full-time degree through the revolutionary (in university terms) innovation of students pursuing the schedule of anyone else in working life, studying throughout the calendar year, with weeks of holiday rather than up to six months. This is welcome, although there have been accusations of cartel-like behaviour on the part of universities opposed to this revolution, and the UK universities pursuing these options are not in the Russell group

(www.studyin-uk.com/study-options/two-year-degree/www.bbc.com/
news/education-41125111; Tice, R and Al-Humaidhi, 2017). But why should
a high attaining school-leaver be denied the option of a two-year degree at a
top university? The emergence of online learning, including MOOCs, may also
bear on future developments; although as with the two-year degrees, they do
not look, at least yet, as if they are going to compete with mainstream provision
of three and four-year degree programmes.

On the side of working life, institutions are also important. The world of
work comes together with that of education most effectively through tripar-
tite working between government, employers and trade unions to manage the
vocational education and training system. Handled well, this engenders a sense
of shared ownership of the system, stabilises policy-making and often takes it
out of politics. It is this kind of arrangement – for example, in a country like
Norway – which allows careful consultation on proposed reforms so that they
make sense to all parties and facilitates implementation (Kuczera et al. 2008).
This point has been made many times, but in the UK, it often triggers the
comment that the social partnership arrangements found in continental Europe
work well over there but cannot easily be exported to places without that
culture and history (e. g. Economist, April 26, 2014). That objection is widely
accepted, but in fact, it is only half right. Often the key issue is the political
will to develop such social partnership arrangements. Around 25 years ago in
the state of Washington in the United States, political leaders got together with
officials and, with the support of the German Marshall fund, paid a visit to Germany and some other European countries to explore the way in which social
partnership can support effective vocational training. They liked what they saw,
came back and enacted in state legislation a social partnership model. Today,
the workforce board in Washington state, which runs most of the vocational
system in the state, has one third of the voting members of the board representing employers, one third representing labour unions and one third representing training providers. So the export of continental European models of social
partnership *can* work (www.wtb.wa.gov/WorkforceBoard.asp, WashingtonState
Workforce TrainingandEducationCoordinatingBoard, 2006).

Solutions: using incentives to build partnerships

Labour market regulation has a big potential impact on the willingness of
employers to engage with the education system, including the vocational training system. For example, when employers face a requirement to pay high wages,
either because of collective bargaining or because of a high minimum wage,
and when they face demanding employment protection laws, recruiting skilled
employees becomes a high-risk activity. This is because, in these circumstances,
recruiting the wrong person will be an expensive mistake that is costly to rec-
tify. Employers will therefore look for recruitment tools, like apprenticeship or a
robust vocational qualification, that provide a copper-bottomed guarantee that

their recruit has all the required skills. Several continental European countries approximate this situation.

But where employment protection is weaker, and minimum wages modest – the United States is an extreme example, but the UK is also in this category – recruitment is a less risky affair. It is possible to take on a recruit with few or uncertain qualifications, see how they get on and fire them if they do not perform well. The qualification signal at the point of recruitment is less important. For these reasons, employer engagement in the vocational training system in the United States and the UK tends to be weaker. Emerging trends in the youth labour market, with greater use of temporary workers and self-employed contractors, further allow employers to reduce the level of risk they face in their workforce, and therefore their concern with their qualifications and the education and training system behind them. A degree of employer disengagement from the education and training system is one natural but unintended consequence of weak employment protection.

On the side of the education industry, there are also protectionist incentives. The industry has every incentive to protect its interests from competing models of learning. These would include learning in which the workplace is promoted as a learning environment in competition with the classroom and the lecture hall and recognition of prior learning which fast-tracks qualifications, avoiding costly programmes based on seat-time.

But incentives can be used to encourage education and training systems to enter into partnership with employers and other stakeholders. One simple way to promote partnership is by allowing some flexibility in curricula in response to local economic requirements. Within the framework of national curricula and national qualifications that maintain valued consistency across the country, local curricular flexibility allows schools, colleges and other post-secondary institutions to develop part of every programme in response to local requirements, including local economic requirements. For example, in Germany and Romania some post-secondary vocational qualifications require around 20 per cent of curricula to be developed locally by individual schools (OECD, 2014). This can be backed by a requirement, for example in Romania, for consultation with local employers about this part of the curriculum. This arrangement provides a very powerful vehicle to support local partnerships between schools and colleges on the one hand and employers on the other. Employers might, for example, be granted influence over the curriculum in return for their commitment to offer work placements to students.

Funding of vocational training, and indeed other forms of education, is a key policy lever. Among education and training programmes, apprenticeship has a deservedly privileged position, and, happily, that privileged position is increasingly recognised and celebrated, including in the UK (although most of the recent growth has been in adult apprenticeships). This privilege is because apprenticeship depends on partnership between employers and training providers. Other forms of work-based learning also depend on that partnership.

The status of work-based learning needs to be enhanced, for it is a powerful reminder that not all real learning takes place in the Academy, in the classroom or in a lecture hall, presided over by an academically trained teacher, and leading to an academic examination. Learning in the workplace, guided by teacher-mentor-practitioners, that ancient form of learning going back to a time before Plato's Academy, *is* serious learning. And this is not just something relevant to the trades and crafts. The violinist, the surgeon, the politician, the painter, the orator – they will all report learning their 'trade' primarily through a teacher, who is also a mentor and, critically, a practitioner.

Across many countries, a common funding model takes the form of funding to a training provider for approved training or, less commonly, channelled through the student. But these forms of funding offer no incentive for any engagement of the training programme with an employer. Often, the outcome is school or college-based vocational training programmes in which there is a nominal expectation for a work-based component, but that component is often non-existent, low quality or inadequate in practice. Programmes with these characteristics are found in many countries, and often employers and training providers blame each other for the weakness of the links between them. There is an unhappy history in the UK of previous attempts to establish partnerships between vocational training and industry (see Huddleston and Oh, 2004; Huddleston, 2012).

Alternative funding models can more directly encourage partnership. One approach is to make workplace training a mandatory element of vocational programmes – such training should also be linked to learning objectives, be credit bearing and quality assured – rather than some unmonitored add-on. The OECD has been recommending this approach for some years, and it is good to see it taken up in the Sainsbury review and the follow-up (OECD, 2014; Departments of Business Industry and Skills and Education, 2016). The point of the mandatory work placement is not only that this should be a good learning experience, but also that it builds in powerful incentives for both training providers and employers to work in partnership. The training provider will seek partnership because they know that their funding depends on having good quality work placements for their students. Employers know that unless they provide local work placements in their occupational field, government funding for vocational training will shift to other occupational sectors or other regions. While there will be some real initial challenges in encouraging employers to offer such work placements and a learning curve for all stakeholders, it sets vocational qualifications on the right path.

An alternative approach is to directly fund partnerships between employers and training providers. This approach is adopted, for example, in the Swedish system of higher vocational training where the government funds partnerships between training providers and employers (who provide the work-based element of the training) to deliver two-year postsecondary vocational programmes (Kuczera, 2013). A similar model is being employed in Barbados, in a scheme sponsored by the Inter-American Development Bank (Inter-American Development Bank, 2016).

Conclusion: the practical implications of a comprehensive approach

The irresistible rise of the education-industrial complex has done much to shape the modern world, and, by and large, that has been a very good thing. Now, that success needs to be balanced by some re-appraisal, and an opening up of education systems to wider influences – it is in this vein that this chapter has proposed a more comprehensive approach, in which all initial education and training is developed systematically as a means of preparing for life, work and further learning. While different programmes will naturally emphasise one or other of these goals, every programme needs to give attention to all three.

Under a comprehensive model of education, all young people, in both academic and vocational tracks in school, would receive career preparation in the shape of exposure to employers to prepare them for the world of work. As well as representing better preparation for those concerned, it would also help to break down the barriers between vocational and academic programmes and support bridges allowing young people to transfer from academic to vocational education. England, like many other countries, unquestionably needs post-secondary and university programmes which are more responsive to the world of work, with an expanded and flexible range of options for young people, including a much-enriched offer of programmes less than three years in length. There can be no better way of establishing partnership than by bringing learning into the workplace, in the form of apprenticeships and other education programmes including work-based learning. Partnership between the world of education and work can be encouraged directly, either in the shape of programmes which are required to include some work-based learning as a condition of funding or through the direct funding of partnerships.

References

Appian of Alexandria. (undated). *The mithridatic wars 6*, translated Horace White.

Cherniss, H. (1945). *The riddle of the early academy*. Cambridge, MA: Cambridge University Press.

Departments of Business Industry and Skills and Education. (2016). *Post-16 skills plan*. London: Departments of Business Industry and Skills and Education.

Economist. (2014). *Keeping up with the Schmidts*, April 26th, 2014.

Fazekas, M. and Field, S. (2013a). *A skills beyond school review of Switzerland, OECD reviews of vocational education and training*. Paris: OECD Publishing.

Fazekas, M. and Field, S. (2013b). *A skills beyond school review of Germany*. OECD reviews of vocational education and training. Paris: OECD Publishing.

Huddleston, P. (2012) Engaging and linking with employers, in Huddleston, P. and Stanley, J. (eds.), *Work-related teaching and learning: A guide for teachers and practitioners*. London: Routledge.

Huddleston, P. and Oh, S-A. (2004). 'The magic roundabout': Work-related learning in the 14–19 curriculum'. *Oxford Review of Education* 30(1): 81–100.

Independent Panel on Technical Education. (2016). *Report of the independent panel on technical education* (Sainsbury Review). London: Department for Business, Innovation & Skills and Department for Education.

Inter-American Development Bank. (2016). *Competency-based training in* Barbados: *A silent revolution?* Available from: https://blogs.iadb.org/education/2016/06/03/barbados-training-technical/ [accessed January 10th 2018].

Kedar, S. (undated). *Apprenticeship in the neo-Babylonian period: A study of bargaining power.* Tel Aviv: Tel Aviv University.

Kis, V. and Park, E. (2012). *A skills beyond school review of Korea, OECD reviews of vocational education and training.* Paris: OECD Publishing.

Kuczera, M. (2013). *A skills beyond school commentary on Sweden.* Paris: OECD Publishing.

Kuczera, M., Brunello, G., Field, S. and Hoffman, N. (2008). *Learning for jobs: The OECD review of vocational education and training.* Norway: OECD, Paris. Available from:

Kuczera, M. and Field, S. (2013). *A skills beyond school review of the United States, OECD reviews of vocational education and training.* Paris: OECD Publishing.

Musset, P. and Field, S. (2013). *A skills beyond school review of England, OECD reviews of vocational education and training.* Paris: OECD Publishing, Paris.

OECD. (2014). *Skills beyond school: The synthesis report, OECD reviews of vocational education and training.* Paris: OECD Publishing.

OECD. (2017). *Education at a glance 2017: OECD indicators.* Paris: OECD Publishing.

Pullen, C. and Dromey, J. (2016). *Earning and learning: Making the apprenticeship system work for 16–18-year olds.* London: IPPR.

Rappaport, S. (1989). *Worlds within worlds: Structures of life in sixteenth century.* London, Cambridge, MA: Cambridge University Press.

Tice, R. and Al-Humaidhi, T. (2017). *Timebomb: How the university cartel is failing Britain's students.* London: UK2020.

Ulicna, D., Nevala, A-M. and Hawley, J. (2012). *Youth and skills: Putting education to work recognition of prior learning and experiences as a means to re-integrate early school leavers into education and training.* UNESCO. Available from: http://unesdoc.unesco.org/images/0021/002178/217889E.pdf.

UNESCO. (2012). *International Standard Classification of Education ISCED 2011.* Available from: http://uis.unesco.org/sites/default/files/documents/international-standard-classification-of-education-isced-2011-en.pdf.

Washington State Workforce Training and Education Coordinating Board. (2006). *Washington State workforce training and education coordinating board meeting no. 111,* June 29, 2006. Washington, DC: Washington State Workforce Training and Education Coordinating Board.

Conclusions

Implications for policy, practice and research

Employer engagement: what's there still to talk about?

Prue Huddleston

The fact that this volume has been written in 2017, more than 40 years after the then Prime Minister, James Callaghan's, famous Ruskin College speech urging the education system to align more with the needs of the economy (Esland, 1991), is significant. Not only does it demonstrate that concerns about alleged deficiencies of the education system in terms of turning out young people fit and ready to enter the labour market continue to be reprised, but more fundamentally it highlights the taken for granted assumption that the education and training system holds the key to national prosperity, global competitiveness, social equity and cohesion.

The expectation that employer engagement in education can fulfil a range of purposes – economic, social, political – and that it can provide a 'cure all' for a multiplicity of challenges is a significant demand of something predicated entirely on voluntary commitment and good will (see Huddleston and Laczik, Chapter 1). There is nothing new about employer engagement in education. Exhortations for employers to engage with the education system have featured in government policy documents, White Papers and official Guidance as well as in the myriad publications of those organisations seeking to offer their services to schools in this area for the last five decades. Recent and on-going reforms within the education and training system (DBIS/DfE, 2016) again call upon employers to engage with education in substantial ways and for the education community to embrace opportunities for such engagement. So it is timely to re-visit these issues in light of current research and practice.

This volume of essays, a sequel to *Understanding Employer Engagement in Education: Theories and Evidence* (Mann, Stanley and Archer, 2014) brings together findings drawn from research and practice in the field, both within the U.K. and internationally. It attempts to provide answers to some tough questions about why this interest in employer engagement endures, what confidence we can have in its alleged efficacy and how best we can improve knowledge and understanding of employer engagement for the benefit of learners, teachers, employers and policy makers. It provides insights drawn from practice in schools, colleges and higher education – Hogarth and Gambin (Chapter 10), Hoffman (Chapter 11) and Priest (Chapter 7). New quantitative data are presented to support arguments for the impact of employer engagement activities – Kashefpakdel et al. (Chapter13), Percy et al. (Chapter 14) and Kashefpakdel et al. (Chapter 12), frequently absent from previous debates in the field. However, it is also recognised that education is a social process and that not everything can be explained or resolved by the results of data analysis. Much depends upon the development of partnerships and personal interactions as demonstrated by Lee (Chapter 2) and Hooley (Chapter 9).

Increasing globalisation, the changing nature of jobs and indeed paid employment itself have impacted particularly harshly on young people when making the transition into the labour market (Standing, 2014, Brown, P et al. 2011,Barnett, 2004) as touched upon here by Tomlinson (Chapter 4). In the preface, Schleicher suggests that although young people leave education today better qualified than ever before, making a successful transition to the labour market is particularly challenging. He argues for young people, whilst still in education, to be exposed to the realities of the world beyond the classroom in order to better prepare them for adult life, including employment. However, such engagement is not in and of itself a good thing, as this collection argues. It requires access to experiences that are of high quality, that allow engagement with authentic representations of labour markets – Huddleston and Ashton (Chapter 6) – that provide access to 'trusted accounts' within communities of practice and that are rooted in principles of equity – Moote and Archer (Chapter 3), Jones et al. (Chapter 8).

More than forty years after the *Great Debate* at Ruskin College, this collection of essays proposes that there still remains much to talk about.

What is employer engagement: some necessary ground clearing?

Employer engagement, as described in this and the previous volume (Mann et al. 2014), covers a wide range of activities in which employers participate in the education and training system of young people (p. 248). It extends to include both 'arms-length' involvement – for example contributing to policy development, informing qualification design - and more direct engagement with teachers and pupils – for example providing careers talks and working with teachers to develop teaching materials. Employers provide work experience for pupils and sometimes industry placements for teachers. They also contribute to a wide range of other education engagement activities, for example acting as school governors or donating money for school football kit. Huddleston (2012) identifies 40 activities in which employers engage with education; however, this collection takes as its point of departure specific interventions that focus upon young people's transitions, and how to ameliorate them, rather than the potpourri of activities suggested by some earlier work.

The focus is important since the term 'employer engagement' has come to characterise any and every form of activity in which employers, and information about employment, however fleetingly, brushes with education. Engagement should imply a meaningful, sustained and high quality intervention, not just a wave on the way past. In an environment dominated by 'performativity'(Ball, 2003), it is tempting to 'tick the box' for employer engagement in order to fulfil targets. This is highlighted by Huddleston and Laczik (Chapter 1) in the context of qualification development. Similarly, Huddleston and Ashton (Chapter 6) provide an account of careers advice that was less than useful, but met the criteria of providing a careers interview. Hooley (Chapter 9) acknowledges the importance of sustained relationships within the context of pupil mentoring. The analysis provided by Percy et al. (Chapter 14) and Kashefpakdel et al. (Chapter 13) take us beyond the 'one tick and you're good to go' box-ticking mentality by providing a much-needed longitudinal dimension on the potential impact and effects of employer engagement.

Calls for employer engagement within education and training are predicated on the assumption that employers will happily 'step up to the plate', contributing time, energy and resource voluntarily. This should not be taken for granted; many employers do not engage. Not all workplaces are models of best practice. Two important considerations flow from this. Firstly, if employers are to engage, then it should be made clear exactly on what basis they do so. Secondly, there needs to be an understanding of what benefits might accrue to employers from such engagement to redress the deficit balance in the education-employer relationship (Field, Chapter 15).

This is why some preliminary ground clearing is necessary; particularly at a time when demands on employers continue to increase and when schools and colleges are focused upon the achievement of 'hard targets' in terms of qualifications outcomes. There are clearly opportunity costs to employer engagement.

Compensatory or complementary?

Having cleared the ground, we now turn to the assumed beneficiaries of such engagement – schools, pupils/students, companies and employers and, it is to be supposed, policy makers. The conflation of policy goals – economic, social and educational – presents a number of challenges, some of which may be in conflict. If it is assumed that improved career advice and employer engagement activities will build the skills requirements to service the 21st century economy, then it is to subscribe to the view that "increasing the supply of skills and qualifications as a monocausal prescription for economic success" (Coffield, 2004, 284–5). In the messy reality of schools and colleges decisions about the 'what', 'how', 'where' and 'for whom' of employer engagement are more complex.

Huddleston and Oh (2004) discuss the differential offering and impact of work-related learning activities, including engaging with employers, on pupils. They describe activities which are seen as 'compensatory' in the sense that they ameliorate the disadvantages experienced by pupils without access to constructed social networks of benefit to them in gaining access to employers and, ultimately, employment. In addition, such activities are often presented as an 'alternative' to the formal curriculum and, by association, of less value, particularly since they involve 'taking people out of school'. This fails to recognise that learning occurs in a variety of contexts both within and outside formal education (Kolb, 2014). Examples include extended periods of work experience replacing other curriculum subjects; mentoring for perceived under achieving pupils, or those who lack role models; and 'skills building' activities or clubs.

'Complementary' engagements describe those activities which tend to enhance existing provision, affording opportunities to those who are already well placed to access professional networks and, in the U.K. context, elite Russell Group universities. Visiting speakers, careers events and external site visits "reinforce career development by providing pupils with role models of successful men and women from the professional and business world" (Huddleston et al. 2014: 174). Within the most ubiquitous British manifestation of employer engagement – work experience – access to workplaces is characterised along social class lines.

In this collection of essays, Moote et al. (Chapter 3) and Jones et al. (Chapter 8) provide further evidence in terms of who gets access to careers advice and work experience and the extent to which it is differentiated across class and gender lines. Hoffman (Chapter 11) provides a hopeful and innovative account of how such tendencies might be ameliorated by carefully targeted and structured programmes, 'putting work at the heart of learning', designed to enhance economic mobility and to combat disadvantage in access to employment.

In current education policy, within the English context, the expectation is that all pupils, particularly at post-16, should have opportunities to engage with the world of work. It remains to be seen how far this can be accommodated in all programmes of study. Technical qualifications, for example, are required to demonstrate employer engagement in terms of their design, endorsement and, to some extent, delivery (Huddleston and Laczik, Chapter 1). All students following such programmes are required to undertake a sector-related work placement. Such engagement can be seen as supplementary to the main area of study, but there are clearly capacity issues here and it is yet to be seen how far these expectations can be realised.

For employers, it should be made clear what the purpose of the engagement is – compensatory, complementary or, in the best cases, both – otherwise there is disappointment and the potential for disengagement. Lee (Chapter 2) demonstrates how this may be achieved through a clearer understanding of what employers think they get out of such activities and why they are sometimes disappointed.

Keeping it real

If it is thought desirable for whatever reason, and this volume proposes several, for young people to engage with the world of employment, then it is important that such encounters are realistic, relevant and serve some useful function. They should permit "access to rich and varied learning environments with opportunities to engage in authentic tasks and to encounter, and learn from, experts within communities of practice" (Huddleston, 2011, 43). The data revealed in the work of Kashefpakdel et al. (Chapter13) and Percy et al. (Chapter 14) provide insights into young people's perceptions of the utility of such encounters. Impressions are clearly mixed, but there is the suggestion that the more exposure that young people have to a range of career-focused activities, then the greater the potential impact on outcomes in adult life. However, we have also seen that some of these encounters lack the reality of modern workplaces, or indeed of employment more widely (Priest, Chapter 7; Huddleston and Ashton, Chapter 6).

It is, therefore, important to be clear about purpose: what is it we are talking about? Is it a general introduction to the world of work, picking up some useful generic skills, or whatever nomenclature currently in vogue (for example, 'working in teams', 'problem solving', 'being punctual') along the way, or is it a more focused activity designed to provide a deeper insight into a proposed career? In some cases, particularly within vocational education, it can fulfil both functions (Vaughan et al. 2015). Tomlinson (Chapter 4) provides a helpful frame of analysis in describing this process in terms of the development of 'competencies', 'capacities' and 'capabilities'. Hoffman (Chapter 11) and Hooley (Chapter 9) point to the importance of sustained and targeted approaches rather than the more general exposure. Jones et al. (Chapter 8) discuss the challenges of providing access to realistic, relevant and more focused work experience in the medical profession where competition for such places is intense. This also raises questions of equity as noted above.

A further and often unexplored question is: who engages? The Creative and Cultural sector, as demonstrated in these chapters by way of example, is dynamic and fast growing, contributing substantially to the economy, and yet it is one characterised by freelance working, short-term contracts and self-employment. It is also an area which speaks to young people's interests. But it is challenging and, in light of the current evidence, difficult for the sector to engage, even if it wished to. The sector offers insights into ways of working that are characteristic of modern workplaces and could provide realistic, relevant and authentic experiences for young people. More needs to be understood about who engage –, data on this are limited – and if their offering is truly reflective of modern labour markets and working practices.

So what's new?

This volume reminds us that attempts to link education with life beyond the academy, including the world of work, are longstanding. With increasingly unstable and precarious labour markets, young people, though better educated and more qualified than ever, are struggling to find their way as aspiring craftspeople, artists, technicians, professionals and citizens. Previous, and often rather simplistic, answers suggested that if only the assumed different worlds of educa-tion and employment could come together, then the situation would improve. Supply side interventions – for example qualification reforms, programmes of work experience, careers education, enterprise education and a plethora of other initiatives – have not silenced the cries for education and employers to engage more with each other, nor lessened employers criticisms of school/college/university leavers. It is not sufficiently recognised that this is a 'two way street' and that interventions on the supply side need to be matched with a corresponding response on the demand side: "employers should see themselves as members of the education community, rather than recipients of education's 'outputs'" (Vaughan, 2017, 554).

Employers need to demonstrate that they are willing to engage and that their workplaces provide opportunities in which people can learn and develop, that they afford interesting and stimulating environments in which to work. This should be demonstrated through the ways in which they provide opportunities for those already employed, as well as new entrants, within their organisations. Those entering employment for the first time do not come "*oven ready and self basting*" (author's emphasis) (Atkins, 1999), nor should that be an expec-tation. This volume has provided some further insights, in what has been an under-researched field, about the ways in which more sustained and focused interventions can shed light on what work means in the 21st century and about how young people might make more informed judgements about future employment.

This collection also causes us to reflect upon what can reasonably be expected of employers in terms of their engagement with education. They should not be expected to engage in areas where they have neither the experience nor expertise to make a worthwhile contribution. Since the whole endeavour is predicated on voluntary engagement, it is important to ensure that what is set out in policy exhortations is reasonable, manageable and meaningful.

Workplace learning is a well-established field of research, but we do not yet know sufficient in terms of what those still in full-time education learn from their engagement with workplaces and with employers. This collection seeks to address this deficit in full recognition that it is an area that merits significantly further in-depth research.

References

Atkins, M.J. (1999). Oven ready and self-basting: Taking stock of employability skills. *Teaching in Higher Education* 4(2): 267–280.

Ball, S.J. (2003). The teacher's soul and the terrors of performativity. *Journal of Education Policy* 18(2): 215–228.

Barnett, R. (2004). Learning for an unknown future. *Higher Education Research and Develop-ment* 23(3): 247–260.

Brown, P., Lauder, H. and Ashton, D. (2011). *The global auction the broken promises of education, jobs and incomes*. Oxford: Oxford University Press.

Coffield, F. (2004). Evidence-based policy or policy-based evidence? The struggle over new policy for workforce development in England, in Rainbird, H., Fuller, A. and Munro, A. (eds.), *Workplace learning in context*. London: Routledge: 279–298.

DBIS and DfE. (2016). *Post-16 skills plan*. CM 9280. London: DfE.

Esland, G. (1991).*Education, training and employment volume 2: The educational response*. Open University Press.

Huddleston, P. (2011). *Vocational pedagogy: Bringing it all together? National skills forum / associate parliamentary skills group open to ideas: Essays on education and skills*. London: Policy Connect: 42–49.

Huddleston, P. (2012). Engaging and linking with employers, in Huddleston, P. and Stanley, J. (eds.), *Work-related teaching and learning a guide for teachers and practitioners*. Abingdon: Routledge: 29–45.

Huddleston, P., Mann. and Dawkins, J. (2014). That aroma of where they are likely to go' employer engagement in high performing English independent schools, in Mann, A., Stanley, J. and Archer, L. (eds.), *Understanding employer engagement in education theories and evidence*. Abingdon: Routledge: 163–176.

Huddleston, P. and Oh, S-A. (2004). The magic roundabout: Work-related learning in the 14–19 curriculum. *Oxford Review of Education* 30(1): 81–100.

Kolb, D.A. (2014). *Experiential learning: Experience as the source of learning and development*. Pearson Education.

Mann, A., Stanley, J. and Archer, L. (eds.). (2014). *Understanding employer engagement in education theories and evidence*. Abingdon: Routledge.

Standing, G. (2014).*The precariat: The new dangerous class*. London: Bloomsbury.

Vaughan, K. (2017). The role of apprenticeship in the cultivation of soft skills and dispositions. *Journal of Vocational Education and Training* 69(4): 540–558.

Vaughan, K.L, Bonne, L. and Eyre, J. (2015). *Knowing practice: Vocational thresholds for GPs, carpenters, and engineering technicians*. Wellington: The New Zealand Council for Education Research and Ako Aotearoa.

Index

Page numbers in *italic* indicate a figure and page numbers in **bold** indicate a table on the corresponding page.

222–226; intensive activities of 153–154; need for 220–223; overview of 26–31, 151–153; political motives for 24–25; research study on **27–29**; school to work transition 146–148; variety/benefits of 25–26; work experience and 151–153, *152*; youth labour market 143–146, *144–146*

Education Business Partnerships (EBPs) 148
Education Endowment Foundation (EEF) 172
education-industrial complex, history of 217–219
Education Policy Institute (EPI) 85–86
employability: agency-structure dynamic 62–65; capabilities and 57–59; capitals and 59–62; competences and 55–57; defining 99–100; education policy and 53–55; embedded approach to 107; employment *vs.* 54–55; for freelancers 93–94; research approach 101; research conclusions 111–112; social skills and 166; stakeholder perceptions of 103–111; study of 100–101; unequal access 114–116 (*see also* medical profession); university education and 102–103
employer engagement: compensatory/complementary 230–231; criteria for 229–230; expectations of 232–233; levels of 15; as realistic/relevant 231–232; value of 189–195, **190**, **192**, **194**, 228–229; youth labour market (*see* education-business partnerships); *see also* school-mediated engagement
Employer Engagement in Education: Insights from the International Evidence for Effective Practice and Future Research (Mann, Rehill & Kashefpakdel) 2–3
employer mentoring: description of 129–131; effectiveness of 134–136; impacts of 131–133; overview of 128–129, 136–138; resources for 137; theories regarding 133–134
employers: awarding organisations and 16–19; collaboration with universities 108–110; engagement by (*see* employer engagement); involvement in UTCs 14–16; mentoring by (*see* employer mentoring); partnership with education (*see* education-business partnerships); perceptions of employability 103–106; perceptions of universities' strategies

106–111; qualification development and 8–11; school-mediated engagement 172–174, 186–188; self-employment and 84–86; Tech levels and 12–13; T level programmes and 13–14; unconnected to education 217–219
English Department for Education (DfE) careers strategy 2
Enhancing Student Employability Co-ordination Team (ESECT) 99
EOW *see Ethnographies of Work* (EOW)
EPI (Education Policy Institute) 85–86
equality: career access and 114–116; social capital and 68–81
Eraut, M. 56
Erickson, L.D. 70–71, 72
ethnicity: careers education and 48; cultural capital and 61; educational/occupational choices and 39–40, 43, **44**, 45; research study on 41–43
Ethnographies of Work (EOW): adolescent development and 166–168; course description 158–162; social/cultural capital and 164–166; social skills and 166
European unemployment rates 143–144, *144–145*
Evans, L. 8
external speakers: benefits of 203–205; British Cohort Study and 201–202, 205; current study 205–208, *207*, **209**; discussion of 212–215; past research 202–203; results of study 208–212, **210–211**, *211*

Facebook 93
family connections 118–119
Farrell, K. 204
Field, S. xi–xii, xvi, 5
financial sector, in industry-school partnerships 26–33, **27–29**
fixed mindset 167
formal mentoring 130–131, 134–136
freelancing: careers education and 84–86; creative industries and 86–88; diversity of skills/issues in 88–89; networking and 92–94; overview of 94–95; skills development for 89–93
Free School Meals 190, 195, 199
functional competence 55
functionings 57